The Violoncello
and Its
History

Da Capo Press Music Reprint Series
GENERAL EDITOR
FREDERICK FREEDMAN
VASSAR COLLEGE

The Violoncello

and its

History

By
Wilhelm Joseph von Wasielewski

Translated by Isobella S. E. Stigand

With a new Preface by Robert C. Lawes, Jr.

𝄡 DA CAPO PRESS · NEW YORK · 1968

A Da Capo Press Reprint Edition

This Da Capo Press Edition of
The Violoncello and Its History
is an unabridged republication of the first English edition
published in London and New York in 1894 by
Novello, Ewer and Co.

Library of Congress Catalog Card No. 67-30401

© 1968 by Da Capo Press
A Division of Plenum Publishing Corporation
227 West 17th Street
New York, N.Y. 10011

Printed in the United States

PREFACE

As one reads this book he will be impressed by its informality and charm, and by its presentation of the history of the violoncello through the activities of the men who played upon it. Historical facts, otherwise often dry (and herein often not quite accurate), thus become clothed in human activity, which, after all, is what the art of music is. A book, of course, should not be judged merely by the facts it presents, since the organization of its material in a meaningful way, together with a variety of other features, can add to or subtract from the value of the factual information. An older work such as this one also must be regarded in its historical context, for the importance it held when it first appeared as well as for the significance it now holds.

Das Violoncell und seine Geschichte was first published in 1889. It was the next to last in a series of historical and biographical studies by the author, whose name appears variously as Wilhelm Joseph von Wasielewski, as it does herein, or as Joseph Wilhelm von Wasielewski, apparently an earlier form and the one preferred today. Wasielewski (1822–1896) was a violinist, conductor, and journalist, as well as a pioneer musical historian. It was to music history that he devoted the major portion of his activities during the last forty years of his life. *Das Violoncell und seine Geschichte* proved to be one of his more popular works. It was published not only in the English edition now reprinted, but also in second and third German editions (both edited by the author's son, Waldemar), the last of which appeared in 1925. The English edition has, in addition to a faithful translation of the original, a portrait of Robert Lindley, the famous nineteenth-century English cellist, a few footnotes, some musical examples, a brief appendix, and an expanded and more detailed list of study methods for the instrument.[1] Otherwise the book remains just as the author wrote it.

As a pioneer musicologist, Wasielewski had few reference sources such as those we take more or less for granted today. Such basic research aids as Eitner's *Quellen-Lexikon*,[2] the union lists,[3] and catalogs of the holdings of the world's great libraries, are for the most part products of the early twentieth century. However, a number of reference works were available to Wasielewski, and those from which he drew much of his information include the early Gerber *Lexikons*,[4] the more recent Fétis *Biographie*,[5] and the contemporary history by Vidal[6] (an amateur cellist). Yet, as any pioneer work, Wasielewski's *Violoncello* presents to the modern reader problems of reliability as well as limitation in scope and detail; indeed, the author questioned the accuracy of some of his own sources. Certainly, musicological activity of the past seventy-five years has uncovered substantial new information and corrected many old inaccuracies.

In his *Violoncello*, Wasielewski's principal interest is the period from the second quarter of the eighteenth century to the last quarter of the nineteenth. Concerning the earlier appearance of the violoncello, the author notes that it seems to have been used in Corelli's day, and he is aware that Domenico Gabrieli (1640–1690) was a cellist; but he indicates that he was unable to uncover any detailed information about that period. (It was slightly after the publication of this work that Valdrighi uncovered and reported what are still the earliest compositions known to be for the violoncello, the solo sonatas of Gabrieli.[7]) The most recent coverage of the work is illustrated by a remark which today strikes a rather humorous note: among "other Italian violoncellists at the present time," Wasielewski indicates, is one named Toscanini.[8] As might be expected, the book limits its discussion to European musicians and devotes more space to German performers than to others.

In the end, sheer amount of detail is not as important as a judicious selection of information concerning the teachers, performers, and composers responsible for the main course of the development of violoncello technique and literature. And this Wasielewski provides. For while there is no equivalent modern work to use as a basis of comparison, a check with current studies indicates that Wasielewski provides adequate information and balanced representation within the principal scope of his study, although his Introduction, which deals with the *Viola da gamba* as a precursor of the violoncello, is too brief and too misleading to be of substantial use today.[9] Van der Straeten, a contemporary historian-cellist, said that when he first saw Wasielewski's book he wished to translate it into English; but he did not do so because "although it had the merit of being a pioneer work, yet I already possessed so much additional information . . . and I commenced a more serious study of the subject myself."[10] His study, which was not published until 1915, corrected some minor errors in Wasielewski's work, and is somewhat more extensive (especially with regard to the *viola da gamba*); but it leans heavily on Wasielewski, particularly on his sources, and adds relatively little to the core of the material he had covered.

Here the matter rests. In English, the works of Wasielewski and van der Straeten remain the only ones to present an adequate history of the development of violoncello technique, literature, and performance over an appreciable period of time. Both studies are dated, but they must serve until others are produced.[11] However, as van der Straeten stated, it is Wasielewski's which has the merit of being a pioneer work. Hopefully, its reappearance will spur new efforts toward the goal that its author first tried to attain.

Richmond, Virginia   ROBERT C. LAWES, JR.
August 11, 1967

NOTES

[1] Except for the omission of works which have appeared since its publication, this list is, perhaps, the most extensive thus far compiled. It is more inclusive than, for example, the compilation given in Part IV of Kurt Stephenson's article, "Violoncellospiel," in *Die Musik in Geschichte und Gegenwart* (Kassel: Bärenreiter, 1949–), XIII, col. 1790.

[2] Robert Eitner, *Biographisch-bibliographisches Quellen-Lexikon der Musiker und Musikgelehrten . . . zur Mitte des 19. Jahrhunderts*, 10 vols. (Leipzig: Breitkopf & Härtel, 1900–1904). [Reprint: New York: Musurgia, 1947.]

[3] For example, the National Union Catalog published by the Library of Congress; Edith B. Schnapper's *British Union-Catalogue of Early Music*

Printed Before the Year 1801, 2 vols. (London: Butterworths Scientific Publications, 1957).

4 Ernst Ludwig Gerber, *Historisch-biographisches Lexikon der Tonkünstler* . . ., 2 vols. (Leipzig: Breitkopf, 1790–1792); and *Neues historisch-biographisches Lexikon der Tonkünstler* . . ., 4 vols. (Leipzig: A. Kühnel, 1812–1814).

5 François-Joseph Fétis, *Biographie universelle des musiciens et bibliographie général de la musique*, 8 vols. (Brussels: Meline, Cans & Cie., 1833–1844; 2nd ed., Paris: Firmin Didot Frères, 1866–1870); *Supplément et complément*, ed. Arthur Pougin, 2 vols. (Paris: 1878–1881).

6 Louis Antoine Vidal, *Les Instruments à archet*, 3 vols. (Paris: J. Claye, 1876–1878). [Reprint, London: Holland Press, 1961.]

7 Count Luigi Francesco Valdrighi (1837–1899) published a number of pamphlets called collectively, *Mursurgiana*, concerning the history of musical activities in Modena. In Number IV of the series, he discussed Gabrieli and his *Ricercari e Sonate per Violoncello de Gabrieli Domenico . . . 15 gennaro 1689*. Valdrighi also discovered a group of twelve sonatas by a Modenese contemporary of Gabrieli's, Domenico Galli (cellist, composer, sculptor, painter, and luthier), whose compositions are entitled *Trattenimento Musicale Sopra il Violoncello a Solo. . . .* Both men's works are dedicated to the Duke of Modena, for whom Stradiveri apparently made one of his early violoncellos. Cf. also Gordon Kinney's *The Musical Literature for Unaccompanied Violoncello* (unpublished doctoral dissertation, Florida State University, 1962), which devotes two of its three chapters to the instrument and its literature in the seventeenth century.

8 *Infra*, p. 112; by the same token, the author did not at this time know of Pablo Casals who, however, receives mention in the later German editions of this work.

9 J. S. Bach's six suites for unaccompanied violoncello, perhaps the most famous of the early compositions for the instrument, are discussed in this portion of Wasielewski's work as being compositions written for the *viola pomposa;* and their range is given as extending an octave too high—it should extend only to two-line g, not three-line g. Whether or not one of these compositions actually was intended for that instrument is still under discussion (see the study of Marx, cited below), but most of the suites were certainly written for the violoncello. Apparently Wasielewski was unaware that K. F. Abel played cello as well as *gamba*, or that another cellist, C. B. Linigke, was at Cöthen at the time Bach was there.

10 Edmund S. J. van der Straeten, *History of the Violoncello, the Viol da Gamba, Their Precursors and Collateral Instruments*, 2 vols. (London: Novello, 1915), I, vi.

11 Two other inclusive works, also dated, are not as detailed as either Wasielewski's or van der Straeten's. They are: C. Liégeois & E. Nogué, *Le violoncelle. Son historie, ses virtuoses* (Paris: Costallat & Cie., 1913); and L. Forino, *Il Violoncello, il violoncellista ed i violoncellisti* (Milan: Hoepli, 1905; 2nd. ed., 1930). On the other hand, since Wasielewski's time, there have been a number of more specialized studies, many of which remain unpublished doctoral dissertations. Among the broader of those written in the United States during the past ten years are the following: E. Cowling,

The Italian-Sonata Literature for the Violoncello in the Baroque Era (Northwestern University, 1962); James R. Hladky, *Twelve Etudes in Thumb Position for Solo Violoncello With a Short History of Thumb Technique* (University of Rochester, 1959); Gordon J. Kinney, *The Musical Literature for Unaccompanied Violoncello* (Florida State University, 1962); Joan M. Mack, *The Transition Period in Violoncello Pedagogy As Manifested in Violoncello Methods From 1830 to 1910* (University of Rochester, 1962); Arnalee C. Bacon, *The Evolution of the Cello as a Solo Instrument* (Syracuse University, 1963); and Gertrude J. Shaw, *The Violoncello Sonata Literature in France During the Eighteenth Century* (Catholic University of America, 1963). Finally, the latest published studies of any breadth are J. Bächi's *Von Boccherini bis Casals* (Zürich: Panton, 1961) and Klaus Marx's *Du Entwicklung des Violoncells und seiner Spieltechnik bis J. L. Duport (1520–1820)* (Regensburg: Gustav Bosse, 1963) [*Forschungsbeiträge zur Musikwissenschaft*, XIII]. While the latter is devoted chiefly to performance techniques, it does include considerable discussion of the early history of the violoncello and its music. In all, the reader can see that there is available today a great deal of material awaiting collection, collation, and publication by a modern historian.

The Violoncello

And its History.

The Violoncello
And its History

Wilh. Jos. v. Wasielewski

RENDERED INTO ENGLISH

BY

Isobella S. E. Stigand

WITH ILLUSTRATIONS, MUSICAL EXAMPLES

AND

Portrait of Robert Lindley
(*From the Original Oil Painting*).

LONDON & NEW YORK
NOVELLO, EWER AND CO.

1894.

THIS TRANSLATION IS INSCRIBED TO

Helen Mary,

MY DEAR SISTER.

AUTHOR'S PREFACE.

In the following pages I present to the musical world the History of the Violoncello and Violoncello playing. I have preceded it by the History of the Viola da Gamba, for the reason that this instrument must be considered the precursor of the Violoncello. For my work I have made use of the musical dictionaries extant, especially Gerber's old and new musical Lexicon as well as Fétis's "Biographie Universelle des Musiciens." What has been borrowed from other works will be indicated in the course of the narrative. The great courtesy of Herr Friedrich Grützmacher, the Royal Concert-director of Saxony, in placing at my disposal his extensive collection of old and new Violoncello Literature, has been of especial value to me in my undertaking. By its means I have been enabled to find my way through the historical development of Violoncello composition. I willingly seize this opportunity of expressing my thanks to him for it.

V. WASIELEWSKI.

SONDERSHAUSEN,
December, 1888.

TRANSLATOR'S PREFACE.

It may be that we are not a musical people, but if so the encouragement and appreciation which the sister Art to painting has of late years received in England is not a proof of the truth of the assertion frequently made. Our Concert-rooms are always crowded to overflowing; foreign artists think it worth while to come year by year to England; schools of music are multiplying, and eagerly attended by amateurs as well as professionals; and I think it may now be taken for granted that a musical education may be as thoroughly acquired here as abroad. Every kind of musical instrument is taken up, if not always with a really serious intention; but no instrument has more rapidly or more certainly come into favour amongst all lovers of music, as well with those who study as with those who listen, than the Violoncello. It is therefore somewhat surprising that up to the present time no book has been published in English, either as regarding its History or its Literature. This consideration, as well as the hope that not only those who devote themselves to the Violoncello, either as professors or amateurs, may be interested in its History, but also the general musical public who delight in listening to its deeply pathetic tones as produced by the great masters of it, has induced me to attempt the translation of Mr. Wasielewski's interesting work. We love to know and often take pains to enquire into the history of any favourite picture, to learn something of the artist's life, the circumstances under which he painted it, and often the origin of its conception. I therefore hope that the story of the Violoncello will be acceptable to all who love it and give their lives to the development of its many beauties and capabilities.

The account of the Violoncello's forerunner, the Viola da Gamba, cannot but be especially interesting, this instrument having been formerly cultivated in England to so great an extent. The frequent allusions which Praetorius in his "Syntagma Musicum" makes to English Gamba players, with a decided preference to their manner of playing and tuning their instruments, is a proof of how high their reputation was abroad; and if any further evidence were wanting the dictum of Mersennus that English Gambists excelled all other nations in Gamba playing, is sufficient to show that in the sixteenth and part of the seventeenth centuries they held the first rank. If for a short period we have no violoncellist of extraordinary merit to chronicle, more modern times have produced artists who will bear comparison with any of the greatest players on the Continent. Concerning these and English Gamba players I have ventured to add a few more particulars than Mr. Wasielewski has given, hoping they would prove interesting to English readers. These details have been gathered from Grove's Dictionary, Leslie Stephen's Nat. Biography, and various other works. For the technical portion, Mr. Niecks's Dictionary of Musical Terms has been consulted, as well as Mendel and Dommer. I have supplemented the Violoncello Schools by others collected from Mr. Heron Allen's Bibliography, and various sources, introducing some of the old Instruction books for the Gamba.

I must here thank Mr. Wasielewski for his kind permission to translate his valuable work, as well as Messrs. Breitkopf and Härtel for their courteous assistance. I beg Mr. George Herbert to accept my grateful acknowledgment for his most kind help and encouragement, and Mr. Heron Allen for the interest he has taken in my work. To Mr. Arthur Hill I am indebted for much kind advice, and to Mr. Noseda of the Strand for his courteous permission to reproduce from his oil-painting the portrait of Robert Lindley as a Frontispiece.

THE TRANSLATOR.

CONTENTS.

Introduction.

The Art of Violoncello Playing in the Eighteenth Century.

The Art of Violoncello Playing in the Nineteenth Century.

INTRODUCTION.

Viol da Gamba.

THE history of the Violoncello and Violoncello playing is connected in its early stages up to a certain point with that of the Viola da Gamba and its forerunner, "the Basso di Viola," of the sixteenth century. This last-named instrument formed the bass in the string quartets of that time, to which also belonged, according to the Italian designation, the "Discant-Viola" or "Violetta," as well as the "Viola d'Alta" and "di Tenore." In Germany these instruments were called Diskant, Alto, Tenor, and Bass viols. The terms Viola and Violin,[1] were at that time consequently synonymous. From the foregoing remarks it will be perceived that it is a question not of one kind, but of a whole family of stringed instruments. Descriptions and illustrations of them are found in the following music-authors of the sixteenth century.

SEBASTIAN VIRDUNG : " Musica getutscht," 1511 ; HANS JUDENKÜNIG : " Ain schöne kunstliche Vnderwaisung," u.s.w., 1523 ; MARTIN AGRICOLA : "Musica instrumentalis deutsch," 1528 ; HANS GERLE : " Musica Teusch " (Teutsch), 1532 ; OTTOMAR LUSCINIUS : (Nachtgall), " Musurgia seu praxis Musicæ," 1536 ; and GANASSI DEL FONTEGO : " Regola Rubertina," 1542. Agricola's and Gerle's works appeared in various editions. The work of the former, as well as Luscinius' " Musurgia," are partly reproductions of Virdung's " Musica getutscht."

According to the descriptions of the above-named authors, violas or violins were of two kinds.[2] Some of them had no

---

[1] In the fifteenth and sixteenth centuries the name " Geige " violin, then in ordinary use, must not be confounded with the violin of our time. This term was not applied to the more modern instrument until later.

[2] A more detailed account of the above stringed instruments and their precursors is contained in my work, " The Violin and its Masters," Second Edition (Leipsic : Breitkopf and Härtel), and " History of Instrumental Music in the Sixteenth Century " (Berlin : Brachvogel and Ranft), therefore a repetition of what is there said is unnecessary.

bridge, others, on the contrary, were provided with one. For the object before us the last only claim our consideration, of which, as well as of the bridgeless violins, there were four different examples. The alto and the tenor were the same size, but of different methods of

tuning. The so-called violas (fiddles) were provided with six strings which were called, like the six lute chords, Great Bumhardt (Bombarte), middle ditto (tenor); small ditto (counter-tenor); middle string (great mean); vocal string (small mean); and quint string (treble). The "Great

Bumhardt" was left out in those instruments provided with
five strings only.   In Italy the six strings were called : Basso,
Bordone, Tenore, Mezzanella or Mezzana, Sottanella or
Sotana, and Canto.   In France, according to Mersennus :
Sixiesme, Cinquiesme, Quatriesme, Troisiesme, Seconde, and
Chanterelle.   The same author gives for the violas the names :
" Dessus," " Haut Contre," " Taille," and " Basse Contre."

   In Judenkünig's and Hans Gerle's works are found the
accompanying illustrations of stringed instruments provided
with a bridge.   Their identity is unmistakable, though
they differ from each other in many peculiarities of form.
Both instruments represent the so-called " big fiddle"[1]
or "Basso di Viola."   The tuning was that of the lute, which,
as an older stringed instrument, served in this respect as its
model.   Only in regard to the pitch did any difference exist.
Judenkünig makes it thus :—

Hans Gerle, on the contrary, writes it thus :—

   Here the pitch of the second is a fifth lower than the first.
Judenkünig's pitch represents the tenor and that of Gerle
the bass.   Agricola says in his " Musica instrumentalis,"
regarding the height of pitch for the lute :

> " Zeuch die Quintsait so hoch du magst
> Das sie nicht reist wenn du sie schlagst."
>
> (Draw up the fifth string as high as you may,
> That it may not be broken when on it you play.)

And in Hans Neusiedler's Lute-book (1535) it is said : " He
who wishes to learn how to tune the lute, let him draw up
the Quint string, not too high, and not too low, a medium

---

[1] The " big fiddle " of the sixteenth century must not be confounded with the
stringed instrument of that time, of which the pitch answered to our modern
Contra-basso, and in Italy was already called " Violone," as appears from
Laufranco's " Scintille," 1533.

height, as much as the strings will bear." Similar instructions are to be found in Gerle's "Musica Teutsch."

The capability of tension of the Quint string was consequently
the guide for the pitch in tuning the lute—beyond this there
was as yet no normal pitch—and in stringed instruments it was
in every case so maintained. In playing with wind instruments the stringed instruments had, therefore, to adapt the
pitch to them.

The "great violins" were, in the first half of the sixteenth
century at least, according to all appearance played in two
ways. From the drawing in Judenkünig's treatise, a mode of
handling is seen which requires no further explanation.
That the handling of the "great violin" represented by
Judenkünig without any explanation is treated of as not
exceptional appears also from the accompanying vignette
of another publication of that period.

The bass viol performing with the two lutists represents
the same position and manner of playing as the woodcut in
Judenkünig's treatise, with the sole difference that he is
holding his instrument in the left hand, whereas the peg-box

of the instrument, bent sharply backwards, of Judenkünig's
player rests on his shoulder. It is very evident that in
both cases scarcely more could be executed than the simplest
bass accompaniment. More, however, was eventually to be
produced according to the treatment of the "great violin"
prescribed by Gerle. He says regarding it: "When you have

according to my instructions 'beschriben' (noted),[1] tuned and drawn up the violin, and wish to begin playing, proceed thus : Take the neck of the instrument in the left hand and the bow in the right, sit down and press the viola between the legs, that you may not strike it with the bow, and take care when you play that you draw the bow directly and evenly over the strings neither too far from nor too near the bridge[2] on which the strings lie, and that you do not draw the bow over two strings at once, but only over that which is placed under the figuring in the Tablature, and this must be especially attended to."

It appears, according to Gerle's instructions, that the instrument of which he speaks was a so-called "Knee violin" —in Italian, "Viola da gamba." It seems, however, that in the sixteenth century this description was not in common use. Hans Gerle, a native of Nuremberg, born about 1500, had already received important consideration during the first twenty years of the sixteenth century, not only as a skilful performer, but also as a maker of lutes and viols. Yet the making of these instruments, and especially of viols, had already been carried on at a much earlier period by others. The oldest fiddle or viola maker of whom we have any mention is a certain Kerlino, who, according to Fétis's account, lived and worked in Brescia. It is most probable that he was a German, or at least of German extraction, for the name Kerl, in every kind of variation, both as a common and individual or family name, had been constantly in use among the German races. In the German dictionary[3] of the Brothers Grimm are indicated the various forms of the name "Kerl": Kerle, formerly Kärle; Kerls, Kerles, Kerlis, Kerli, Kerlin, Kerel, Kaerl, Kerdel, and Kirl. They are of German origin, and are derived from middle or low German, whereas the Anglo-Saxon equivalents are "Carl," or "Ceorl."

Originally the word "Kerl" (kerlc), according to Grimm,

---

[1] The word "beschriben" refers to the letters which, for the convenience of the player, it was the custom to mark for the fingers on the fingerboard.

[2] The artist who drew the sketches of the instrument for Gerle's "Musica Teutsch" has left out the bridge in the "great viola." See page 2.

[3] See the article "Kerl."

was synonymous with "Mann" (man), and also with Ehemann (husband). But it was also used as a family or tribal name, as is proved from the names Jacob de Kerle (sixteenth century), Joh. Kaspar von Kerll (also written Kerl, Kherl, Cherle), born 1628, and Vitus Kerle (in the eighteenth century).[1]

Another form of " Kerl," Kerlin, was, according to Grimm, used in the sixteenth and seventeenth centuries. Who can doubt then that the Brescian instrument maker Kerlino was of German origin?[2] He was, evidently, originally called Kerl or Kerlin, to which name was added by the Italians either the diminutive syllable " ino " or the vowel " o." It cannot be of Italian origin, for the Italian has no " k."

Fétis informs us that Kerlino must be considered as the founder of the school of Brescian viola makers which, as the oldest in Italy from the middle of the sixteenth century, attained such a great reputation, through Gaspar da Salò and his reputed pupil, Giov. Paolo Maggini. If what appears so extremely probable has any real foundation, to a German, or, at least, to a man of German extraction, must be justly conceded the merit of having, in a measure, been the originator of the art of Italian stringed instrument making which later on developed to the highest point.

Further, we learn from Fétis that in the year 1804 a Parisian violin maker, named Koliker, was in possession of a violin which had been previously described by the French writer on music, de la Borde, containing the inscription

" JOAN. KERLINO, ANN. 1449,"

and which originally had been a " Viola da braccio." Doubtless this remarkable instrument exists at the present time. Fétis, who saw it himself, describes its quality of tone as "agreeably soft and faintly subdued." Among the composers who wrote for the viola, we must mention Giov. Battista Bonometti, born at Bergamo about the end of the sixteenth century. In 1615 he caused to be published in Vienna a collection of trios for two violas and a bass.

---

[1] Also at the present time it is a family name. We need only mention G. H. Bruno Kerl, Professor of the Royal Berg Academy at Berlin.

[2] Other authorities, however, say he was a Breton—Fétis, Casimir Colomb &c.—(Tr.)

After Kerlino there appeared in North Italy as noted lute and viola makers the monk Pietro Dardelli, in Mantua about 1500; Gaspard Duiffopruggar, in Bologna, 1510; Venturi Linarolli (Linelli), in Venice, 1520; Peregrino Zanetto, in Brescia in 1530; and Morglato Morella, in Venice, 1550. Amongst these G. Duiffopruggar is evidently of German birth,[1] and remarkable as having, as far as we can see, made the first violins.

This artist was in 1515 summoned to France by King Francis I.; he at first lived in Paris and then at Lyons. He made some excellent Bass viols (Gambas), of which two fine specimens are extant in France. A similar bass viol was represented by Raphael in his painting of St. Cecilia. This splendid picture, in the Pinacothek at Bologna, existed in 1515.

After Duiffopruggar, Andreas Amati (1520 to about 1580), the founder of the Cremona school, distinguished himself in the making of violas (as well as violins). His instruments obtained such a great reputation that Charles IX. of France, an enthusiastic amateur of music, had twenty-four violins, six tenors, and eight basses made by him. Amongst the latter there were several bass viols, like the viola da gamba. The instruments made for Charles IX. by Andrea Amati were every one of them destroyed during the French Revolution of 1792.[2]

Contemporaneously with Andreas Amati the manufacture of stringed instruments was vigorously carried on by Gaspard da Salò, in Brescia.

In Germany, from the second half of the sixteenth century, LAUXMIN POSSEN, in 1550, at Schongau, subsequently instrument maker for the Hofkapelle at Munich; JOH. KOHL, who at the same time worked at Munich and in 1599 was appointed Court instrument maker there, and also JOACHIM TIELKE were successively celebrated. The latter lived, as Gerber informs us, at Hamburg from about 1660 to 1730, and even made lutes

---

[1] The name Duiffopruggar doubtless came from the same source as the surname Tieffenbrucker, still existing in South Germany.

[2] Mr. Heron Allen in his " Violin Making, &c.," page 74, says that two were recovered.—(Tr.)

of real ivory and ebony, the necks of which were inlaid with gold and silver and mother-of-pearl, but one especially with nine pegs of the most beautiful tortoiseshell. Tielke, however, made also violins and excellent gambas. One of these, a costly instrument which was formerly in the possession of the Elector Joh. Wilhelm of the Palatinate,[1] was brought from Mannheim to the Duke of Maxburg's Museum at Munich, and thence into the Royal Bavarian National Museum, where it is preserved as a treasure of rare value. The peg-box, the fingerboard, the tail-piece, the sides, and the back are all decorated with designs of flowers, foliage, and tendrils, as well as symbolical and allegorical representations taken from mythology, the subjects representing for the most part love and music. These decorations and designs are inlaid work in tortoiseshell, ivory, ebony, mother-of-pearl and silver.[2]

Another valuable specimen of a gamba made by Tielke in the year 1701, which belonged to the famous cello virtuoso, F. Servais, has been described and represented by A. J. Hipkins, of Edinburgh, in his lately published work, "Musical Instruments: Historic, Rare and Unique."[3]

During the second half of the sixteenth century there must have been a considerable multiplication of the different kinds of violas then in use, and especially of the bass viol, for Michael Prätorius mentions in his " Syntagma

---

[1] The same Prince to whom Corelli dedicated his "Concerti Grossi," published in 1712.

[2] Herr Obernetter, of Munich, has taken two beautiful photographs of this richly decorated instrument, which reproduce with great accuracy all its peculiarities. As far as I know they can still be purchased.

[3] Here may be mentioned also a third magnificent gamba, that of Vincenzo Ruger, said to have been made in Cremona in 1702. It is distinguished not only for its beautiful exterior in every respect, but also by an extraordinarily sonorous and unusually fine quality of tone, which combines the resonant character of the gamba with that of the violoncello. The latter circumstance is attributed to the fact that the back, which is usually flat in the ordinary gamba, is arched in this one. This instrument, which has been lately purchased by the Prussian Government for the Berlin Museum, was formerly in the possession of Herr Paul de Wit, in Leipsic. The account of instrument making published by him contains (Vol. VI., No. 21) a description and illustration of the gamba in question.

musicum," which appeared in 1614—1620, the following examples :

1. Very large Bass Viol with four strings (corresponding to the modern Contrabasso).

2. Great Bass Viol de Gamba in three different tunings, with five and also six strings (also like the Contrabasso).

3. Small Bass Viol de Gamba, five different examples with six, four, and three strings (answering in tone, in some measure, to the modern Violoncello).

4. Tenor and Alto Viol de Gamba, in two different pitches, with six, five, four, and three strings (answering partly to the Violoncello and partly to the modern Tenor).

5. Cant Viol de Gamba (Violetta piccola), four different kinds with six, five, four, and three strings (the tone also partly answering to the Tenor and partly to the Violin).

6. Viol Bastarda, in five different pitches, with six strings (the tone corresponding to that of the Cello).

7. Viola de Braccio, four different examples, with five and four strings (corresponding in tone partly to the Violoncello and partly to that of the Tenor).

Moreover, Prätorius mentions, under the heading " Viole de Braccio Viols," the "Discant Viol " (our modern Violin), the small "Discant Viol " (tuned a fourth higher than our Violin), and two " very small Viols with three strings," of which the lowest string of the first is a ninth and of the second an octave higher than the G String of the Violin.

Of the multitude of these different kinds of Viols then in use, which later on by manifold improvements were gradually reduced to a smaller number, until they resulted in the modern Violin and Tenor, as well as the Violoncello and Contrabasso, we must keep in view, for the object of the present work, the " Viola da Gamba " only, which must be regarded as the precursor of the violoncello. Prätorius gives a sketch (annexed) of the so-named instrument.

A comparison of these gambas with the sketches of viols by Judenkünig and Gerle shows what substantial alterations the stringed instrument in question underwent in the course of the second half of the sixteenth century. The neck had assumed a more modern and more convenient form for the technique of the left hand and the sounding-board had acquired more elegant and attractive outlines. At the same time the sound-holes, corresponding to the curves of the belly, were turned round and placed in a position more agreeable to the eye.

Prätorius expresses himself regarding the Viola da Gamba as follows: "Violas, viols, and violuntzes[1] are of two kinds—1. Viole de gamba; 2. Viole de braccio (or de brazzio)—and the former is so called from having been held between the legs; for gamba is an Italian word and means a leg; le gambe, the legs. And since they have much larger bodies and, on account of the length of the neck, have strings of a much longer tension, they produce a mellower resonance than others, 'di braccio,' which are held on the arm. The two kinds are distinguished by town musicians: the viole de gamba by the name of violas: the viole 'di braccio' (among which Prätorius includes violins) by the name of fiddles or pollish fiddles. . . .

"The Violes de Gamba have six strings and are tuned in fourths and in the middle a third, exactly like the six-stringed lute. Englishmen when they play them alone sometimes tune them a fourth, sometimes a fifth lower, so that the lowest strings are tuned— the bass to D, the tenor and alto to A, and the canto to E. On other occasions each one (reckoning by the chamber-pitch)[2] a fifth lower—as, for example, the bass to G G, the tenor and alto to D, the canto to A; and tuning in this manner produces much more agreeable, grander, and more majestic harmonies than when the instruments are at the usual pitch."

What Prätorius says regarding the mode

---

[1] Violuntzes is synonymous with the old French instrument, violonsse. *Vide* Grimm's Dictionary of the German Language.

[2] The Kammerthon or chamber-pitch, as distinguished from the obsolete "Chorton" or choir-pitch, which formerly prevailed in German churches, was a tone, or even more, higher than the secular pitch.—(*Tr.*)

and way of English viol-tuning is supplemented by Mersennus in his "Harmonie Universelle" (1636-37). This author says: "Il faut remarquer que les Anglois ioüent ordinairement leurs pièces un ton plus bas que les Français, afin d'entendre l'harmonie plus douce et plus charmante, et conséquemment que leur sixiesme chorde à vuide fait le C sol au lieu que la nostre fait le D re sol."

The pitch then in England was a varying one, though the series of intervals borrowed from the lute, to which the gamba like the bass viol was tuned, were those which commonly prevailed.

In other respects, Mersennus gives no more explicit directions for the handling of the Viola da Gamba than Prätorius. He does not use this name for the instrument in question, but calls it "Basse de Viole." The French designation, "Viole de jambe," corresponding to the Italian name, appears consequently to have been in vogue later and to have been generally little used.

Like Gerle's "great fiddle" (Basso di Viola), the Viola da Gamba had also as a rule seven frets on the fingerboard like the lute, for fixing the tones and semitones.

The gamba was played in various ways, and used for a variety of musical purposes, as a solo instrument, as well as in orchestral performances, and as an accompaniment to singing. The way in which it was valued during the first half of the seventeenth century as an obbligato accompaniment to singing, may be seen from the preface to Heinrich Schütz's " Historia of the joyful and victorious resurrection of our only Saviour," and so on, published in 1623. It is there said, after Schütz has named the instruments which are to accompany the parts of the Evangelists: "But when it can be done it is better that the organ and everything else should be left out and instead of these only four Viole di Gamba (which must also be present), should be used to accompany the parts of the Evangelists."

"It will, however, be necessary that the four viols should be thoroughly 'practised' with the part of the Evangelist in the following manner : The Evangelist takes his part to himself, and recites it straight through without any fixed

time, just as it seems correct to him, but not holding
longer on one syllable than is customary in ordinary slow
and distinct speaking. The violas must not mark any
particular time, but only pay attention to the words recited
by the Evangelist, and to their parts written below the
'falso-bordone' and so doing they cannot go wrong. A
viola may also 'passegiren' amongst the others, as is usual
with the falso-bordone,[1] and this gives a good effect."

It appears from the explanation that the gambas were used
to support the harmonies of recitatives. The "passegiren"
suggested by Schütz of one of the accompanying violas was
nothing else than the usual improvised ornamental colorature
or diminuendos used at that time and up to the eighteenth
century.[2]

For solo playing gambas were used not only for the
execution of monotone—viz., compositions of one part only;
but also for several parts, and especially for double-stops
and chords.

The oldest French gambist of whom we have any account
is a certain Granier. Gerber says, concerning him, that he
had been "in the service of Queen Margaret of France," and
died, about 1600, in Paris, and that he was the greatest artist
of his time on the gamba.

Concerning the artistic use of violas, amongst which, as
already said, gambas were included, Mersennus writes as
follows: "Encore que les Violes soient capables de toutes
sortes de musique, et que les exemples que j'ay donné (sic)
pour le concert,[3] des violons leur puissent servir, néantmoins
elles demandent des pièces, plus tristes et plus graves, et dont
la mesure soit plus longue et plus tardiue; de là vient qu'elles
sont plus propres pour accompagner les voix. Or l'on peut
jouer toutes sortes de pièces non seulement à cinq parties,
comme l'on fait ordinairement sur les Violons, mais à six, à
sept, à douze et à tout autant de parties que l'on veut."

At the beginning of the above-quoted passage it is remarked,

---

[1] "Faburden," according to Mr. Niecks.—(Tr.)
[2] Concerning this, see my "History of Instrumental Music" in the Century,
page 107.
[3] By the word concert, Mersennus means concerted piece.

that violas were used for every kind of music, but the use
of these instruments for solo playing is not expressly
mentioned. In another passage of his work Mersennus says,
however, with regard to gamba playing and the French
performers of his time :—

" Personne en France n'égale Maugars et Hottman,
hommes très habiles dans cet art : ils excellent dans les
diminutions et par leurs traits d'archet incomparables de
delicatesse et de suaveté. Il n'y a rien dans l'harmonie qu'ils
ne savent exprimer avec perfection, surtout lorsqu'une autre
personne les accompagne sur le clavicorde. Mais le premier
exécute seul et à la fois deux, trois ou plusieurs parties sur la
basse de viole avec tant d'ornements et un prestesse de doigts
dont il parait si peu se préoccuper, qu'on n'avait rien
entendu de pareil auparavant par ceux qui jouaient de la viole
ou même de tout autre instrument. . . . . "

It is here clearly expressed that solo playing on the gamba,
and notably in several parts, was much cultivated and highly
appreciated.

The Maugars[1] here mentioned by Mersennus expresses
himself regarding his own performances as a gamba player in
his " Réponse fait à un curieux sur le sentiment de la
Musique d'Italie écrite à Rome le premier Octobre, 1639,"
which was published either at the end of 1639 or the beginning
of 1640. After having spoken of his intercourse with the
artistic family Baroni during his residence in Rome, he
relates : —

" In this worthy house, at the solicitation of these gifted
people, I was induced for the first time to exhibit in Rome the

---

[1] Maugars is called in the " Historiettes de Tellemant des Réaux," as Fétis
informs us, the " greatest fool that had ever lived." His " Réponse faite à un
curieux " (completely unprejudiced, although somewhat conceited) in no way
agrees with this. It is easy to discover that Maugars was not liked by his
countrymen, because he openly declared that French music was far behind the
Italian. On that account he had incurred the displeasure of French artists.
The Parisian musician, Corrette, in the eighteenth century, was guilty of the same
offence. He had been candid enough to say to the French that the standard of
French violin playing of the eighteenth century was, compared to the Italian, in
a disorganised condition. In retaliation they called his pupils scornfully
" les anachorètes " (" les ânes à Corette ").

talent with which God had endowed me. It happened in the presence of ten or twelve of the most experienced people of Italy, who, after they had listened to me attentively, bestowed on me some eulogiums ; not, however, quite ungrudgingly.

"In order to test me further the Signora Leonora (Baroni) induced me to leave my viola at her house, and begged me to return the following day. This I did, and as it was reported to me by a friend that it was said I played studied things very well, on the second occasion I gave them so many kinds of preludes and fantasias that they really granted me more appreciation than the first time. The respect, however, of these worthy people did not succeed in winning over the experts, who were somewhat over-refined and reticent to concede applause to a foreigner. It was told me they acknowledged that I played very well alone, and that they had never heard such harmonised viola playing, but they doubted if I were capable of extemporising a theme and playing variations on it. You know, sir, that in this I am not a little successful. The same words had been told me on the eve of St. Louis' day in the French church, while I was listening to the fine music then being performed there. This determined me on the next day; excited thereto by the name of Saint Louis, as well as for the honour of the nation and the thirty-three cardinals who were present and taking part in the Mass, to ascend into the gallery. When I had been greeted with applause, I was given fifteen to twenty notes, in order to make myself heard after the third Kyrie with the accompaniment of a small organ. This subject I treated with such infinite variety that great satisfaction was shown, and the cardinals caused me to be invited to play again after the Agnus Dei.

"I considered myself very fortunate that I had been able to afford this little pleasure to so distinguished a company. I was given another somewhat more cheerful theme than the first, which I treated with so many variations and such a diversity of movements that they were extremely astonished, and immediately came to me in order to requite me with eulogiums. On account of the friendship which you cherish for me, my dear sir, I am convinced you will not accuse me of vanity in this digression. I have only made it in order that you may know that if a Frenchman desires to gain a reputation in Rome he must be well armed; and so much the more because it is thought here that we are not capable of improvising on a given theme. In fact, whoever plays an instrument deserves no extraordinary consideration, unless he shows himself equal to such a demand, especially for the viola—to play on which, by reason of its few strings and the consequent difficulty of playing in parts, is always a thankless task—it is necessary to possess some individual talent in order to be inspired by a subject and expand into beautiful inventions as well as agreeable variations. The capacity to do this requires two real and innate qualifications—viz., a lively and strong imagination and skilful execution, in order promptly to carry out one's ideas."[1]

The unlimited tribute of praise which Mersennus pays to the performances of Maugars, renders credible the remarkable account given by himself. Maugars' gamba playing excited in Rome the greatest consideration, because at that time neither there nor anywhere else in Italy was there any prominent artist for that instrument. "As regards viola playing, Maugars declares there is no one in Italy who is distinguished for it, and in Rome it is very little cultivated. This has greatly astonished me, as formerly they had a certain Horace of Parma who performed wonderfully on this instrument, and left behind him some excellent compositions, which some of our musicians cleverly made use of for other instruments besides those for which they were composed. The father of the great Italian, Ferabosco, was the first to make them known to the English, who from that time have excelled all other nations."

From the last words it is to be inferred that gamba playing in England was much in vogue at the time of Maugars. The Ferabosco (Ferrabosco)—with the christian name of Alfonso—mentioned by him, who first made the English acquainted with this art, can be no other than the composer of that name

---

[1] I give this and the following quotations from Maugars' writings, according to my translations in the monthly parts of the "History of Music," published in the year 1878.

referred to by Fétis as born in Italy about 1515. He settled
in London about 1540, and about the year 1587 appears to
have been in the service, as "gentilumo," of the Duke of
Savoy.[1]

Amongst English gambists of distinction must be named
Thomas Robinson, Tobias Hume, William Brade, and John
Jenkins. Probably they were all pupils of the elder Ferabosco.

Concerning THOMAS ROBINSON, who was born in the second
half of the sixteenth century, and lived and worked in the
beginning of the seventeenth in London, nothing further
is known than that he published a curious work under the
title, "The Schoole of Musicke: the perfect method of true
fingering the Lute, Pandora, Orpharion, and Viol da gamba.
London, 1603."

His contemporary, TOBIAS HUME, was an officer in the
English army, and spent much of his time in Sweden.
He was reputed one of the cleverest gambists of that
period; he caused to be published, in 1605, a work with
the following title: "The first part of Ayres, French, Pollish,
and others together, some in Tabliture and some in Pricke
song. With Pauines, Galliards, and Almaines for the Viole di
gamba, and other Musicall Conceites for two Basse-viols,
expressing five partes, with pleasant Reportes one from the
other; and also for two Leero-Viols, and also for the Leero-
Viole with two Treble Viols, or two with one Treble. Lastly,
for the Leero-Viole to play alone; and some Songes to bee
sung to the Viole with the Lute, or better with the Viole alone.
Also an Invention for two to play upon one Viole. Composed
by Tobias Hume, gentleman. Printed by John Windet Loud,
dwelling at the sign of the Cross Keyes, at Powles Wharfe,
1605." It is evident that the composition of arrangements for
two instruments, which might also be played on one only,

---

[1] The English writers on music affirm that the well-known composer,
Ferabosco, who was born at Greenwich in the second half of the sixteenth
century, and who was also called Alfonso, was the son of the above Ferabosco,
with which the remarks of Maugars agree. Fétis doubts the truth of the
assertion made by the English writers on music. The younger Ferabosco
appears also to have been a gamba player, for he published, in the year 1609, in
London, "Lessons for one, two, and three viols." He died in 1665.

was no invention of the Salzburg violinist, Joh. Hein. Biber.[1] In 1607 he published another work, under the title "Captain Hume's Poeticall Musicke, principally made for two basse viols yet so contrived that it may be plaied eight severall waies upon sundry instruments with much facilitie. London." This work, of which the British Museum possesses a copy, was dedicated to Anne of Denmark. He was received into the Charterhouse as a poor brother in 1629, and known as " Captain Hume." His mind seems to have given way, and he died there on April 16, 1645.

WILLIAM BRADE flourished about 1615, and spent much of his life out of England. He was appointed violist to the Duke of Holstein-Gottorp and of the city of Hamburg at the beginning of the seventeenth century. In 1619 he seems to have been Capellmeister to the Margrave of Brandenburg and went subsequently to Berlin. He was esteemed a good performer on the gamba, and published in 1609, 1614, and 1621 a number of Paduans or Pavans, Gaillards, Canzonets, Volts, Courantes, in five and six parts (Berlin, 1621). A great confusion exists regarding the bibliography of his works, authorities differ as to their titles. They are of unusual interest, as containing many English airs, some of which are mentioned by Shakespeare. He is said to have died at Frankfort in 1647.

JOHN JENKINS, born at Maidstone in 1592, was one of the most celebrated composers of music for viols. In early life he made choice of music as a profession, and was appointed musician in ordinary to Charles I. He lived in the family of Sir Hamon l'Estrange and instructed his sons in music. In 1660 he gave lessons to the sons of Lord North at a salary of £1 a quarter! Roger North in his autobiography calls him, " that eminent master of his time, Mr. Jenkins, not conceited nor morose, but much a gentleman." He was appointed musician to Charles II., and spent the last years of his life with Sir Philip Wodehouse, at Kimberley, in Norfolk, where he died on October 27, 1678. He had for his time extraordinary capacity on the lute, viol, and several bowed

---

[1] See my work " The Violin and its Masters," Part ii., p. 203.

instruments, and wrote a great number of compositions for viols, which were not printed; but in 1660 he published " Twelve Sonatas for two violins and a bass, with a thorough-bass for the organ or theorbo " (London, 1660), the first of the kind produced by an Englishman. Indeed he is credited with having been the earliest English composer of instrumental music. Most of his compositions he called Rants or Fancies. He also wrote music for " Theophila, or Love's Sacrifice; a Divine Poem, by Edward Benlowes, Esq., several parts thereof set to fit Aires by Mr. Jenkins " (London, 1652). Many of his MSS. exist at Christchurch, Oxford. Hawkins reports that it was said of him, " he was a little man, but had a great soul."

THOMAS SIMPSON is another Englishman who stands out conspicuously as a violist and gamba player; in 1615 he was appointed violist in the service of the Prince of Holstein-Schaumberg. He published : Opusculum, Neuer Pavanen, Gaillards, Couranten und Volts (Frankfurt, 1610); besides Pavanen, Volts und Gaillards (Frankfurt, 1611), and a " Tafel-Consort," containing all kinds of cheerful songes for four Instruments and a Thorough-Bass (Hamburg, 1621).

JOHN COOPER, born about 1570, was a most distinguished performer on, and good composer for the Viol da Gamba. In his youth he travelled in Italy, and returned with the Italianised name of Coperario. He was master to the children of James I., who was himself not only very musical, but had an excellent judgment on music. He is said to have played eight different instruments, amongst them especially well the harp. Two of Cooper's pupils were the celebrated musicians, William and Henry Lawes. The elder, William, besides his other numerous compositions, wrote his " Great Consort," consisting of six Suites for two treble viols, two theorbos, and two bass-viols. Charles I. was also Cooper's pupil and played the gamba well, since he was able to perform the organ fantasias of his master on that instrument. Cooper published a great number of compositions, and among them were many for the Gamba. He died during the Protectorate.

By far the most eminent English gamba player was

CHRISTOPHER SYMPSON[1] (or Simpson), who was born at the beginning of the seventeenth century, and died in London between 1667 and 1670. He was a follower of Charles I., and served as a soldier in the army commanded by the Duke of Newcastle against the Parliament. After the defeat of the Royalists, Sir Rob. Bolles, an important adherent of this party, granted him a refuge in his house and entrusted to him the education of his son, John Bolles, who was noted as a very clever musical dilettante and player on the gamba; he died in Rome, 1676, where his mortal remains were laid in the Pantheon. Christopher Sympson is the author of several noteworthy instruction books on music, of which we shall mention only those relating to the viol da gamba. The first of them has the title, "The Division-violist, or the Introduction to the playing upon a ground. Divided in two parts—the first, directing the hands, with other preparative instructions; the second, laying open the manner and method of playing, or composing division to a ground. London: John Playford. 1659."[2] The title of the second of Sympson's works referred to for the gamba is "A brief Introduction to the Skill of Music. In two books. The first contains the grounds and rules of music. The second, instructions for the viol and also for the treble violin.[3] The third edition enlarged. To which is added a third book, entituled ' The Art of Descant or Composing Music in Parts,' by Dr. Thom. Campion,[4] with annotations thereon by Mr. Ch. Simpson. London, 1660."

THOMAS BREWER was also a celebrated performer on the gamba, who was born in 1611. He was admitted to Christ's Hospital at three years of age, and learnt the viol from his music master. He composed various fantasias for his favourite

---

[1] His name was usually written Sympson, but he sometimes himself spelled it Simpson.—(*Tr.*)

[2] This seems to have been the title of the first edition, a copy of which is in the possession of Messrs. Hill, of New Bond Street.—(*Tr.*)

[3] This work contains, besides the viola tutor, an introduction to violin playing. It is the first attempt at a violin school.

[4] Thomas Campion was a physician, poet, and musician in the reign of Queen Elizabeth, and an authority on music. He published two books of Ayres, and various other pieces, besides the above.—(*Tr.*)

instrument, besides airs, catches, rounds, as well as Pavins, Courantes, &c., for which kind of composition he seems to have been noted.

The English gambists of the first half of the seventeenth century must then have had some considerable reputation abroad, for the Frenchman, André Maugars, already mentioned, went about 1620 to London, lived there for nearly four years, and perfected himself after the models of the best gamba players. He does not seem to have had pupils. But his compatriot and rival Hottmann[1] (or Hotteman) not only taught, but distinguished himself especially by some charming compositions. One of his most noted pupils was Marais (Marin), born in Paris on the 31st of March, 1656. At first a choirboy in the Sainte Chapelle, he educated himself further under the direction of Hotteman, and then under Sainte-Colombe, another excellent Parisian gamba player at that time. Lully gave him instructions in composition. In 1685 Marais became solo gambist at the Court Chamber Music Concerts, which position he held until 1725. He died August 15, 1728.

Besides Sainte-Colombe there were at that time two able French gamba players—namely, Desmarets and Baisson. Marais, however, excelled them in artistic execution. He added to the six strings of the instrument tuned in the accepted manner—

also a seventh, the A of the "contra octave."[2] This enabled him to surpass in harmonised playing all his predecessors and contemporaries. He was the first who caused the lowest strings of the gamba to be cased in metal wire so as to give them greater tension and resonance, a step in advance which was soon adopted for the two lower strings of the violoncello. Besides some operas, Marais was the

---

[1] He has already been mentioned, p. 13.

[2] Michael Corrette ascribes this to Sainte-Colombe in his violoncello school, which appeared in 1741, concerning which we shall speak farther on.

author of a considerable number of gamba compositions which appeared in five parts. The fifth of them, for one and two gambas with a bass, was printed in 1705.

Out of his nineteen children, three sons and a daughter devoted themselves to the study of the gamba. Amongst them the most distinguished for his performances was

ROLAND MARAIS. In the year 1725 he succeeded his father as solo gambist at the Royal Chamber Music Concerts, the prospect of which had been assured to him some years previously. Quantz, who heard him in 1726, reported him as a very skilful player. He published, in 1711, a " Nouvelle méthode de musique," and in the years 1735 and 1738 two volumes of gamba pieces with figured bass.

The Sainte-Colombe mentioned above had, besides Marais, two noteworthy pupils, ROUSSEAU and HERVELOIS. Jean Rousseau perfected himself as a distinguished gamba player, and was actively engaged in Paris during the second half of the seventeenth century. He also made himself more widely known by the production of two " livres de pièces de viole," as well as a gamba school, " Traité de la viole." The latter work appeared in Paris in 1687.

CAIX DE HERVELOIS, born about 1670, became, under the direction of Sainte-Colombe, an excellent player, and after further study entered the service of the Duke of Orleans. In Amsterdam he had two books of his compositions published : " Pièces pour la basse viole avec la basse continue."

Another French gambist of distinction in the seventeenth century was Antoine Forqueray. He was born in 1671 in Paris, and was one of the performers at the chamber music Concerts of Louis XIV. Forqueray received instruction from his father. At the age of five years he already excited the astonishment of the king by his performances, who called him " his little wonder." In the year 1745, on June 28, he died at Nantes, whither he had retired upon his pension.

His son, Jean Baptiste Antoine, born on April 3, 1700, in Paris, was esteemed as the most able French gamba player of his time. He also at five years of age was heard with such favourable result before Louis XIV. that he later on became a member of the royal music society. He again had a son, whose christian name was Jean Baptiste, born about 1728, who was also a gambist and published several books of compositions for his instrument. He does not seem, however, to have made himself conspicuous as a performer.

Gerber mentions in his musical Lexicon a Parisian gambist of the eighteenth century of the name of Forcroix, or Forcroy, "whose delightful playing Quantz, who was in Paris in 1726, admired." Possibly this artist may be identified as the A. Forqueray mentioned above.

The art of gamba playing was pursued in Germany with as great or perhaps greater zeal than in England and France. While the pursuit of music by the English and French was confined chiefly to London and Paris, there were in Germany many courts who admired and cherished with fostering care the art of music; and the result was, especially after the tumult of the thirty years' war had subsided, a widely-spread musical life throughout the whole of the German nation.

Amongst the first German players to be mentioned is DAVID FUNK, born about 1630, in the Saxon town of Reichenbach. Gerber says of him, he was "an excellent musician and master of the violin, the viola da gamba, the angelica,[1] the clavier, and guitar"; and then goes on: "Funk was in every way a genius. His chief study, which he carried to no small degree of perfection, was that of the law. He was, besides, a wit and a poet, and was reckoned among the good German poets of that time. As a musician he was not only a virtuoso on all the above-named instruments, but he was also a composer, and won the applause of the public in a variety of styles, for the church as well as for the chamber. . . . How and where he had gained all these distinctions there is no account. He was first known as a composer in the year 1670, by the publication of his work on the gamba." This enthusiastic account emanated, according to Gerber's report, from

---

[1] Concerning this instrument, Mattheson says: "The Angelique, somewhat resembling the lute, must have been far easier to play, and has more cords or strings, which one can accurately touch by reason of their arrangement without moving the left hand much. There is nothing specially besides to remember." It was, therefore, an instrument of the lute kind.

the precentor Joh. Martin Steindorf, of Zwickau, who was personally acquainted with Funk.

In the year 1682 Funk gave up his appointment in Reichenbach and accompanied the "East Friesland Princess" into Italy as secretary, where he remained with his mistress seven years. After her death there in 1689 he returned to his native land, and, driven by the necessity of beginning again to earn his livelihood, he had no other choice but to accept, at "Wohnsiedel (Wunsiedel?), the miserable post of organist and girls' schoolmaster." Funk's dissolute character led him to misuse his office as teacher to immoral purposes with the girls entrusted to his care, so that he was compelled "by night and fog to fly in order to escape the rage of the parents."

From that time Funk led a vagabond life. He next betook himself to Schleitz, and remained three months at the Court there. Thence he was obliged to decamp as he was rigorously pursued by the police of Wohnsiedel. He made his way to Arnstadt, but did not reach that place. He was found one day lying dead underneath a hedge.

At the same time as Funk, the virtuoso August Kühnel was at work—born August 5, 1645, in the little town of Delmenhorst, in Oldenburg. From 1695 to 1700 he lived at Cassel, holding a position at the Court. During this time he published "Sonatas or Parts for one or two Viole da gamba, together with a bass, 1698." According to Gerber, several of his works should be in the Museum at Cassel. In composition, Kühnel was a pupil of Agostino Steffani during his residence in Hanover. His successor in office appears to have been a certain Tielke,[1] for he was from 1700 to 1720 gambist in the Cassel chapel.

Another gambist of the name of Kühnel (Johann Michael) lived in the second half of the seventeenth century, and was engaged at the Berlin Court. From here he went, in 1717, to Weimar, and later on to Dresden, in the service of Field-marshal Flemming. He seems to have ended his life in Hamburg. Of his compositions there appeared at Rogers's in Amsterdam, "Sonates à 1 et 2 Violes de gamba."

---

[1] He was perhaps a brother or relation of the instrument maker Tielke mentioned pp. 7 and 8 of this work.

One of the most important gamba players of Germany at the end of the seventeenth and beginning of the eighteenth century was Johann Schenk. As he appears to have had his second work, "Konst œffeningen," printed at Amsterdam in 1688, consisting of fifteen sonatas for the gamba and bass, it may be concluded that he was born about the middle of the seventeenth century. Towards the end of it he was chamber musician in the Elector Palatine's service, which post however he must have given up at the beginning of the eighteenth century, for he is said to have settled in Amsterdam about that time. Whether he remained there to the end of his life is doubtful, for on the title-page of his sixth work, "Scherzi musicali, per la viola di gamba con basso continuo ad libitum," he calls himself "Chamber Commissary and Chamberlain of the Elector Palatine." On the other hand, Mattheson informs us that he (Schenk) was named inspector of the fish market, because he had played the gamba so well! On the whole, he published eight works, chiefly pieces and sonatas for the gamba, as well as for the violin with a bass; a copy of the one, of which the title is mentioned above, is preserved in the Royal Library at Sondershausen. This comprehensive collection, consisting of 101 musical pieces, is dedicated to the Elector Palatine Prince William, consequently to the same art-devoted Prince to whom Corelli, in the year 1712, dedicated his "Concerti Grossi."[1]

The title-page of the "Scherzi musicali" bears no date, but it may be assumed that they appeared between 1692 and 1693, for Schenk published his Op. 3 in the first and his Op. 7 in the latter year, and the collection in question, as already observed, bears 6 as the number of the work. The compositions which it contains are grouped after the manner of "Chamber Sonatas" or "Suite." It is true that the author has made use of neither of these terms, but the keys chosen by him leave no manner of doubt as to the description of instrumental compositions to which these "Scherzi musicali" belong. We know that it was usual for all the subjects of a suite at that period to be in the same key.

---

[1] Compare p. 8.

Looking from this point of view at Schenk's work for the gamba, it is apparent that it contains twelve suites or chamber sonatas, of which some indeed are unusually long. For example, the second suite (F major) and the fourth (A minor) consist of fourteen pieces. Dances, such as Allemandes, Courantes, Sarabandes, Gigues, Gavottes, and Minuets, make up by far the greater portion of the volume. There are also a couple of Bourrées ; but then the composer gives also Chaconnes and Passacailles with variations, which in some cases are of great length, as well as Rondos and "Arias." The fourth sonata contains moreover a Canzone and an "Allabreve"; the ninth, a Fugue ; the eleventh, the same[1] and an Overture. The greater number of the suites begin with a Prelude, though, on the contrary, the second begins with a Fantasia, the fourth with a " Sonata con Basso obligato," and the eighth with an " Overture," the ninth with a " Capriccio," and the twelfth with a "Caprice." The mode of writing alternates from one to several parts, and the chords, by frequently doubling the intervals, are extended to five notes struck simultaneously. For the notation Schenk required four different keys—viz., bass, alto, discant, and treble, by which

means the compass extends from 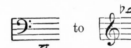 to

We conclude from this that Schenk, like the French gambist Marais, used a gamba with seven strings, and, indeed, the highest of them must have been tuned up to the one-lined G. Schenk must have gone considerably above the seventh fret of the fingerboard in order to reach the twice-lined B flat. With regard to the artistically musical quality of Schenk's compositions for the gamba, they are mediocre ; they bear no comparison with the violin compositions of Corelli of the same

---

[1] It is worthy of observation that this second fugue (D minor) has the theme

which Mozart, nearly 100 years later, made use of for the second *Finale* of the " Magic Flute." There is no doubt this was purely accidental, as Mozart could hardly have seen Schenk's work.

period. He succeeded best in the dances, compared with which the more elaborate productions appear poor and are in some measure incorrect. Especially is this true of the two so-called fugues, which do not rise above feeble attempts at fugues. It is, however, interesting to know what position Schenk took as one of the best reputed gamba virtuosos at that time with regard to composition, for his productions give an average idea of the executive capabilities of his contemporaries. At the same time, Schenk's works prove very surely what double-stoppings, chords, and figures were possible on the gamba, and in this respect reveal a remarkable richness in various styles of playing.

Opposed to this by its simplicity in a technical point of view is a " Sonata a Cembalo Obligato col Viol da Gamba," by Handel. Double-stops and chords are altogether omitted. It is true that he has quite another object in view, for Handel treated the gamba not like Schenk, as a solo instrument, but as subsidiary only to carry out a musical idea, thus placing it on a level with the clavier. He chiefly uses also the middle positions of the gamba in the alto key throughout. Otherwise this Sonata,[1] though solid in form, is of small importance, and gives the impression of a composition quickly thrown off for some special occasion.

Handel's great contemporary, Joh. Seb. Bach, treated this instrument, in his three sonatas composed for it and the clavier, in quite another manner. It is true that with rare exceptions he makes no use of the scored and harmonised technique for the gamba; but the artistic and complete mode of working out by which all his instrumental works are more or less distinguished is also peculiar to the gamba sonatas just mentioned, of which the most important are the first in G major and the third in G minor.

Charmingly and with characteristic effect did Bach employ the' gamba in his Passion Music from the Gospel of St. Matthew and St. John, as well as in some of his Cantatas. One has only to recall the splendid, deeply touching alto aria "It is finished," in the Passion Music of St. John. Now at

---

[1] A MS. copy exists in the Royal Library at Berlin.

the performance of this sublime work the gamba part in the aria referred to is played by the violoncello, which does not quite express the deeply melancholy, pathetic tone that Bach's music was designed to express. But there is no more appropriate substitute in the modern orchestra for the gamba than the violoncello.

One peculiarity of Joh. Seb. Bach is that, with a rare knowledge of art, he made use for his purpose of all the instruments current in his time which adapted themselves in any way to the representation of a special effect. But he further conceived the idea of enriching the choir of instruments by an invention of his own. During his work at Köthen he constructed the "Viola Pomposa," a stringed instrument of the cello kind, though, like the violin, for the hand, which had five strings tuned to C, G, d, a, ē—

Gerber remarks concerning it: "The limited way in which the violoncello in Bach's time was handled compelled him, for the quick basses in his works, to the invention of the so-called viola pomposa, which, rather longer and higher than a tenor, had a fifth string, e, in addition to the four lower strings of the violoncello, and was placed on the arm. This convenient instrument enabled the player to execute more easily the high and rapid passages which occurred."

It may be seen from Bach's Suites for Violoncello Solo, which were originally written for the viola pomposa, the compass of this instrument extended from the great octave C

the "Viola pomposa" did not attain to general use. It scarcely survived its inventor, and disappeared, as it seems, even before the gamba, out of the musical sphere.

Bach's eldest son, Philipp Emmanuel, also wrote for the gamba. Amongst other things a sonata in three movements, with the clavier, in G minor,[1] which was apparently composed about 1759. The three-part movement in this is solid, though somewhat meagre and dry.

Amongst the gamba compositions of the previous century, which have lasted up to our time, there is also to be noted an unpublished Concerto by Joseph Tartini, the famous founder of the old Paduan violin school, with accompaniment for four stringed instruments and two horns.[2] Possibly Tartini wrote it during his three years' residence in Prague (1723—1726) for a German gambist, as about that time the gamba was still cultivated in Germany with great enthusiasm, though it had been, in Italy, thrust into the background of music by the violoncello. The Concerto bears all the marks of the author's manner of expression, but it is in the main quite as antiquated as all his violin concertos. The introduction and *Finale* are in G; the "Grave" between the two movements is in D minor. The single part theme of the solo, with the exception of a few double-stoppings and chords, is throughout written in tenor and bass clef. It is worthy of remark that all the pieces are provided before the full close with cadences, written at full length, for the solo instrument, after Tartini's usual manner in all his violin concertos.

As a contemporary of Schenk, the War Minister of Hesse-Darmstadt, ERNST CHRISTIAN HESSE, who was born on the 14th April, 1676, in the Thuringian town of Grossengottern, distinguished himself. Gerber says of him, that he was the first and most famous gambist of his time in Germany. Having spent his school years at Langensalza and Eisenach, he entered the Darmstadt chancery service as supernumerary and followed the Court of his new master in 1694 to Giessen. At the Academy there he continued his work and also his legal studies. In 1698 he had permission from the Court to go to Paris in order to perfect himself there on the viol da gamba, which he had already begun to study in early life. He remained there three years and had instruction at the same

---

[1] The MS. is preserved in the Royal Library at Berlin.
[2] It is to be found in the autograph collection of Count Wimpfen at his estate near Gratz.

time from the two famous masters, Marais and Forqueray.
As privately they were at enmity with each other he was
compelled to give his name to one as Hesse and to the other as
Sachs. Both were delighted with his skill and progress, and
severally boasted of the excellent pupil whom he had taught.
At last they challenged each other to put to the test, in a
concert arranged for that object, the proficiency of their
pupil. But what was their astonishment on Herr Hesse's
appearance to find he was the pupil of both! He did his
two masters, each in his own manner, special credit, but
immediately after the occurrence left Paris.

After his return to the Darmstadt Court, in the year 1702,
Hesse was named Secretary of the War Department and
Foreign Office. In the following year he married.

In the year 1705 Hesse travelled through Holland and
England, and two years later he betook himself to Italy, in
order to increase his knowledge in the art of composition.
Everywhere his gamba playing excited the greatest admiration.
On his return journey from Italy he visited Vienna and was
heard at Court, together with Hebenstreit, famous in his time
as the inventor of a dulcimer-like instrument, called Pantaleon.
The Emperor was so charmed with his playing that he presented
him with a gold chain and his portrait. In the year 1713 he
lost his wife. About the same period the vacant post of Kapellmeister at the Darmstadt Court was given to him *ad interim*.
He then married his second wife, the famous singer,
Johanna Eliz. Doebbrecht (Döbricht), and in 1715 he was
promoted to the post of War Commissary and eleven
years later to the dignity of Minister of War. "In 1719,"
says Gerber, "Hesse made another musical tour with his
wife to Dresden, to the famous festivals held in honour of the
Elector's marriage and where several operas by Lotti and
Heinichen were represented. They both gained extraordinary
honour and abundant appreciation. From this time he
devoted himself quietly to the Court until his eighty-sixth
year, and died May 16, 1762, after he had participated in
every kind of good fortune. Besides the airs which he
arranged for the church during the time that he filled the
Kapellmeister's vacancy, he left behind him many Sonatas

and Suites for the Viola da gamba, which fully bring out all the
possibilities of this instrument.

Hesse had twenty children, only eight of whom, however,
survived him.   His eldest son, Louis Christian, became,
under his father's tuition, a clever gambist, and entered as
such into the service of the Prince of Prussia in 1768.

Besides his son, Hesse formed the excellent gamba player,
Joh. Christ. Hextel, born 1699, in the Swabian town of
Oettingen.   His father, who was Kapellmeister to the
Prince of Oettingen, and then worked in the same capacity at
the Ducal Court of Merseburg, wished that the boy should
study, and entered him, in 1716, at the University of Halle.
Here he occupied himself by preference with music, and when
he returned home he gained his father's permission to devote
himself exclusively to the art.   The Duke of Merseburg
announced his willingness to grant him the means of pursuing
his studies either in Paris, under Marais and Forqueray, or
at Darmstadt, under Hesse's direction.   The young Hextel
himself decided for Hesse, who took him as a pupil under exceptional conditions.   After two years' study he left Darmstadt,
performed at concerts at the Courts of Eisenach, Merseburg,
Weissenfels, Zerbst, and Köthen, and accepted a post in the
Eisenach Kapelle.   During the years 1723-27 he was travelling
in Germany and Holland ; played in 1732 before Frederick
the Great at Ruppin, while he was still Crown Prince ; and
then undertook the post of Concert Director at Eisenach.
When, after the death of its prince (1742), the Eisenach
band was dissolved, through the recommendation of Franz
Benda he was appointed Concert Director at the Court of
Strelitz.   He filled this place until 1753, and died a year after.
Of his numberless compositions only six sonatas for violin
" solo e continuo," 1727, were published at Amsterdam.

As noteworthy German gambists belonging to the first half
of the eighteenth century must be mentioned—

Emmerling, Hard, and Bellerman.   The former of these,
born at Eisleben, was in the year 1730 Chamber Musician and
Viola da Gambist to the Margrave Louis of Brandenburg, and
also, as Gerber says, instrumental composer.

Joh. Daniel Hard, born May 8, 1696, in Frankfurt on the

Main, remained at the outset of his musical career for five years in the service of King Stanislaus during his residence at Zweibrücken, and then was Chamber Musician to the Bishop of Würzburg and the Duke of Franken, Joh. Phil. Franz von Schönborn. After four years he gave up this service and took a post as Chamber Musician at the Wurtemburg Court. Later on he again became Concertmeister and finally Capellmeister to the Duke Carl Eugene. He still filled this office at Stuttgard in 1757. Further accounts of him are wanting.

CONSTANTINE BELLERMAN, "Imperial Crowned Poet" (poet laureate), as Gerber calls him, studied as amateur gamba player. He was born in 1696 at Erfurt, there studied law, and also pursued music theoretically and practically, playing the lute, gamba, violin, and flute. He was called to Münden as Cantor, and then, in 1741, as Rector of the School there.

Of his many unpublished compositions, there are amongst them Church pieces, Cantatas, an Opera, Suites for the lute, Concertos for the Oboe d'Amour and the Flute, Clavier Concertos with violin, and Overtures; here only six Sonatas for Flute, Gamba, and Clavier will be noticed. The year of his death is unknown.

Amongst the German gambists of the first half of the eighteenth century a lady held a prominent position, DOROTHEA V. RIED, one of the five daughters of the Austrian musician, Fortunatus Ried. Johann Frauenlob says of them, according to Gerber, in his Essay on Learned Women: "That although two of them were still very young—one was scarcely eight years old—their father had brought them on so well in music that with their two brothers they had given at Vienna, Prague, Leipsic, Wittenberg, and other places such evident proofs of their talent as to have excited universal admiration, for people thought they heard heavenly rather than earthly music."

Here also must be mentioned a royal personage—namely, the Elector MAXIMILIAN JOSEPH, born March 28, 1728; died December 30, 1777. He played the violin and the cello, but was especially an excellent gambist. Burney, who heard him in 1772, says that he needed not to be a great prince in order to discover that his skill, his rendering of adagio, and his accuracy in time were perfect. Maximilian also composed. His teacher for composition was Bernasconi.

Finally, CARL FRIEDRICH ABEL must also be mentioned as a gambist of the first rank. He was born at Köthen, 1725, where his father held the appointment of gamba player in the Hofkapelle. " The young Abel," says Gerber, " seems to have had instruction, as Thomas' scholar, at Leipsic, from the great Seb. Bach ; then came in 1748 to the Hofkapelle at Dresden, where, during the more flourishing period of Hasse's life, and for nearly ten years, he found time enough to form his taste.[1] His small salary and a split with the director Hasse caused him to leave that Court, according to Burney, in 1758, with three thalers in his purse. In order to increase this capital, he went on foot to Leipsic, laden with the MS. of six symphonies, where, through the generosity of the publisher of these symphonies, he became six ducats richer. He now went from one German court to another, and, by repeated good receptions and applause, he regained not a little confidence. Finally he turned to London, in 1759, where he found a great patron in the lately deceased Duke of York, who supported him until the formation of the Queen's Band, to which he was appointed in the capacity of chamber musician, receiving an annual payment of £300.

" This salary was considerably increased by the music dealers giving him a stipulated sum of £150 for six symphonies. His duty at the Queen's Concerts was generally to play the tenor on his gamba, and now and then, in the absence of Bach,[2] to accompany on the piano. For some years he lived in Paris during the summer, where he found in the house of a fermier-général not only a friendly reception, but also what he liked better than all, the best of wine. On his first appearance in London, his discretion, his taste, and his pathetic manner of expression in the rendering of his adagios so captivated the young virtuosi that they very soon followed his

---

[1] According to Fürstenau, Abel was engaged as violoncellist at Dresden. See his " History of Music and of the Theatre at the Elector of Saxony's Court," Vol. II., p. 240.

[2] Sebastian Bach's youngest son, Joh. Christian, was born in 1735, in Leipsic, and died in London in 1782, whither he had gone in 1759 as Band Conductor.

school, with less expenditure of notes and with more successful result. His taste and knowledge especially made him the umpire on all contested points, so that he was looked upon in all difficult cases as an infallible oracle. With his dexterity on the gamba he also possessed the talent, like many other older virtuosi, of exciting the astonishment and admiration of his hearers by free fantasias and learned modulations. And although he had considerably less power on the harpsichord, yet he knew how to modulate in arpeggio with consummate skill and in endless changes."

"Abel remained in London until 1782, in which year the desire of once more seeing his brother and his country induced him to return to Germany. It was on this journey that he displayed, both at Berlin and Ludwigslust, the greatness of his talent, his wonderful power of expression, the richness of his tones, and his stirring execution on the gamba. The present king, then Crown Prince of Prussia, before whom he performed in Berlin, presented him with a costly casket and 100 louis d'or. A few years later he stayed some time in Paris on account of the disordered condition of his finances. But he returned again to London and died there on June 22, 1787, after a three days' lethargy, without the least suffering. Shortly before his death he played a recently finished solo which astonished his warmest admirers. His cadences especially were excellent."

It is remarkable that, amongst Abel's numberless published works, which consist partly of concertos and orchestral pieces and partly of chamber music, there are no compositions for the gamba. This must be explained by the fact that the zenith of gamba-playing had been reached, and the art was on its decline, at the beginning of the second half of the eighteenth century. It went out of fashion, and with it also gamba music, and in its place only violoncello compositions were in request. In many ways this change was as much lamented as was the case at the banishment of the lute to cabinets of curiosities or the lumber room.

After Abel there were no German gambists of conspicuous importance to mention. From the middle of the last century the gamba was more and more neglected, in consequence of

the violoncello being brought forward, and the younger
geniuses devoted themselves by preference to this instrument,
which approached more nearly to the violin, then at the
summit of all instrumental music.

Amongst stringed instruments, which had shared the same
fate as the gamba, belong the Viola bastarda and the Viola
di Bordone (English, Barytone). The first instrument was in
shape somewhat thicker than the gamba and was provided
with six or seven strings.[1] In order to increase the resonance,
as many steel strings were introduced under the fingerboard
and bridge, which were tuned to the same pitch as those
above, like the Viola d'amore. Another variety of the gamba
was the barytone, which was cultivated in the last century.

In Leopold Mozart's violin tutor is found the following
description of it: " This instrument has from six to seven
strings like the gamba. The neck is very broad and the back
part hollow and open, down which nine or ten brass or steel
strings are run beneath, which are touched and pinched by
the thumb; so that, at the same time as the principal part is
played with the bow on the upper cat-gut strings, the thumb
by striking the strings stretched under the neck of the
instrument can play the bass; and therefore the music
must be arranged specially for it. Moreover, it is a most
agreeable instrument." From this description it is evident
that the barytone was a bass instrument resembling the
Viola d'amore. The barytone in its time was much liked in
Austria. Several Austrian composers, as Cybler, Weigl, and
Pichl, and at their head Joseph Haydn, composed for this
instrument. The latter was incited to it by his benefactor,
the Prince Esterhazy, who looked with particular favour on
the barytone. Haydn wrote no less than 175 pieces for it.[2]
The tuning of the strings on the fingerboard of the barytone
was on the same principle as that of the gamba.

The Viennese, ANTON LIDL, who was born about 1740, was
much esteemed as a most distinguished barytone virtuoso.

---

[1] According to Pohl, the number of these metal strings was raised to twenty-
seven. (S. C. F. Pohl: " Haydn," I., 250.) Information regarding the barytone
and barytone compositions are to be found there.

[2] Pohl: " Haydn," I., 257.

Gerber says of him, "that he rendered still more perfect his instrument, which had been invented about the year 1700. It is in shape like the Viola da gamba, except that it has brass strings at the back, which are played at the same time with the thumb. These lower strings he increased to twenty-seven and the semitones were played with them." He must have been an extraordinary artist on this instrument. The author of the *Almanack* of 1782 says: "His performance united the most charming sweetness to German vigour, the most surprising syncopations with the most harmonious melody." According to Burney, Lidl was no longer living in 1789. Up to 1783 he had published, in Amsterdam and Paris, Duets, Quartets, and Quintets— altogether seven works. His compositions for the gamba were not published.

The barytone disappeared with the gamba, in the course of the second half of the last century, from musical practice.

The same change took place in Italy about the same time or somewhat earlier, when a lively interest in the violoncello was aroused there by Franciscello, of whom we shall speak farther on. It appears, indeed, that in the land of the arts, as the quotations already given from Maugars' papers inform us, no predilection had prevailed for the higher study of the gamba, either for the reason that among stringed instruments the cultivation of the violin—which from the seventeenth century had decidedly usurped the first place in the study of music— was chiefly pursued, or that the Italian composers did not specially concern themselves with the gamba. As a matter of fact, so far as can be perceived, with the exception of Tartini, no noteworthy Italian composer considered it worth his while to bring it into the field of creative activity. Besides Ferabosco, of whom mention has already been made, there are amongst famous Italian bass violin players and gambists to be named: Allessandro Romano with the cognomen " della Viola," and Teobaldi Gatti. ROMANO was born about 1530 at Rome, and in 1560 was a singer in the Papal (Sixtine) Chapel. He later became a monk of the monastery of Mount Olivet, under the name of Giulio Cesare. But he did not find his sojourn there agreeable, for he was at strife and contention with one or other of the monks of his order through incompatibility of temper. His compositions, published between the years 1572-1579, consist of " Canzone alla Napolitana " for five voices and a book of Motets in five parts.

TEOBALDI GATTI, born at Florence about 1650, not only distinguished himself as a gamba player, but also made himself known in his time as an operatic composer. In the latter respect he was influenced by Lully, whose first opera-overtures so impressed him that he resolved to go to Paris in order to do homage to his illustrious country-man. Lully, who was flattered, showed his gratitude for this attention by making Gatti a member of the Parisian Opera orchestra, which post he filled for nearly fifty years uninterruptedly.[1] He died in 1727, in Paris. There were published in 1696 twelve " Airs Italiens " by him, two of which are duets.

As skilful Italian gambists are conspicuous also MARCO FRATICELLI and CARLO AMBROSIO LUNATI,[2] of Milan, with the cognomen " Il gobbo della Regina." The latter came to England during the reign of James II. Nothing further is known concerning either of these instrumentalists. It is worthy of remark in this place that the famous Italian singer, Lenora Baroni, born about 1610, was, according to Maugars' testimony, a clever theorbo and gamba player. As such she was in the habit of accompanying herself in singing.

It has already been pointed out that the viola da gamba, which for nearly three hundred years (for the "Basso di viola," or Gerle's "great violin," was, in fact, a gamba, although as yet of a somewhat primitive form) had played an important part both as an orchestral and solo instrument, was replaced by the violoncello in the course of the eighteenth century. Subsequently when the violin as a leading instrument in melody

---

[1] Gerber mentions him as a violoncellist, which must be a mistake, since in the Parisian Opera orchestra, up to 1727, as far as is known, only gambists were employed. He may, however, have played both instruments.

[2] See " The History of the Violin," by W. Sandys and Simon Andrew Forster. London, 1864.

usurped the place of the cornet (Zinken), and the discant viola (French par dessus de viole), it became necessary to provide an equivalent for the bass part of string quartets, as the tone of the gamba in *ensemble* playing proved too weak and thin in proportion to the violin.

Mattheson says of it, in his " Neu eröffneten Orchestre," which appeared in 1713 : " The plaintive Viola da gamba (Fr., Basse de Viole, properly so called) is a beautiful delicate instrument, and he who wishes to signalise himself on it must not keep his hands long in his pockets. . . . Its chief use in concerts is only for the strengthening of the basses, and some indeed pretend to execute a ' Thorough Bass ' on it, of which, up to now, I have never seen a good attempt."

In opposition to this last somewhat sarcastic remark of Mattheson is what Gerber states a hundred years later (Vol. I., p. 6, of his " New " Musicians' Lexicon) concerning the gamba. He there says : " It is remarkable in the history of music that his (Abel's) instrument was buried with him in the year 1787 in total oblivion : the indispensable gamba, without which for a hundred years neither church nor chamber music could be arranged, which in all public and private concerts had the exclusive right to be heard before all other instruments from the beginning to the end, and which there-fore, like caskets, must not only be exquisitely finished in every size, large and small, but was also ordered, bought, and paid for adorned with the most costly artistic carving—ivory, tortoiseshell, gold, and silver—then available. In the course of time there will be no vestige left in the whole of Europe of this instrument, once so universal and admired ; henceforth it will have to be sought for amongst the old wood-cuts in Prätorius, or specimens of it, stringless and worm-eaten, in a royal music chamber. Another sad proof how greatly Apollo is overruled by the goddess Fashion. The taste of our forefathers for these soft, modest, humming viola tones is also remarkable ; they were a quiet, contented, peace-loving people ! In the present time the instruments for our musicians cannot be chosen sufficiently high and shrill."[1]

---

[1] What would Gerber have said had he lived to see the present demand for instruments required to make up an orchestra ?

It is plain that although Gerber himself played the cello, this instrument was also known to him, and he had not only remarked the disproportion between the tone of the violins and those of the gambas in the orchestra with regard to strength, but also the circumstance that, by the creative faculty of Haydn and Mozart in the region of higher instrumental music, the gamba had become wholly superfluous. The superior qualities of the violoncello to the gamba as a solo instrument had escaped him, although the conspicuous success of cello players in the second half of the last century could not have remained unknown to him. It seems, therefore, as if Gerber had a special predilection for the gamba—a taste which only a few of his contemporaries shared with him.

Gerber's[1] confident assertion that the French priest, Tardieu, of Tarascon, had invented the violoncello " in the year 1708," is simply to be relegated to the region of fable, for the instrument had already existed long before in Italy.[2]

Fétis remarks (p. 47) in his article "Antoine Stradivari" (Paris, 1856) : The violoncello had already been mentioned by Prätorius in his " Syntagma Mus." (1614-1620), which is a mistake, for the work referred to contains neither the name nor the illustration of this instrument.[3] But the violoncello must already have been in use about this time in Italy, for (according to Rob. Eitner)[4] it is mentioned in a publication of

---

[1] Gerber's "Old Musical Lexicon," p. 617, and Note, p. 86.

[2] In the preface to the violoncello tutor already mentioned, by Corrette, the untenable assertion is made that the violoncello was discovered by Bonocin (Buononcini), "présentement Maître de Chapelle du Roi de Portugal." A Bononcini, with the Christian name of Domenico, actually lived in 1737 at the Lisbon Court. At that period, according to Fétis, he must have been eighty-five years old. He must therefore have been born in 1652. He could not have invented the violoncello (if one could call it an invention), as it evidently existed before his birth. It is not even certain that Domenico Bononcini was a cellist. Possibly Corrette confounded him with Giov. Battista Bononcini mentioned later.

[3] Another inaccuracy in Fétis's "Stradivari," p. 46, is that the name of violino "had already appeared in Lanfranco's work ' Scintille' of 1533." This announcement has caused some confusion. Before Lanfranco's work was accessible to me, I also in bonâ fide had made the same assertion in my "History of Instrumental Music of the Sixteenth Century" (p. 73), and I now correct it. The word "Violino" is not mentioned by Lanfranco, but in every case only the termination "Violone," which is bass viol.

[4] See monthly Magazine for the History of Music, Year XVI., No. 3.

the year 1641, and then in a work of Freschi's, which appeared in 1660 as "Violoncino." In Arresti's Sonatas in two and three parts, of the year 1665, it is called "Violoncello." It was of great importance for the Italian instrument makers to produce a bass instrument of the violin type which had already been in use from the middle of the sixteenth century, and this certainly happened towards the end of that period. This is proved by the Brescian Gaspard da Salò[1] (1550-1612). Whether Andreas Amati, the founder of the famous Cremona school (born 1520, died 1580), constructed similar instruments appears doubtful. Apparently the gamba as well as the violin served as guides for the proportions in the construction of the violoncello. From the violin were borrowed the outlines of the soundbox, the arched back, which the more ancient gambas, whose backs were flat, did not have; also the F holes and the fingerboard without frets. From the gamba were taken the large proportions of the violoncello. It was at first constructed like the gamba, in smaller and larger dimensions, until Stradivarius established a standard size. Whether the most famous German violin maker, Jacob Stainer (born 1621, died 1683), made violoncellos is much doubted by experts. It is, however, certain that he made gambas, which were often converted into violoncellos.

According to Eitner's previously mentioned assertion, it appears that the last-named instrument was at first called "Violoncino," and a little while after "Violoncello." The Italian affixes "ino" and "ello" have a diminutive meaning, and therefore both names have an identical signification. As violino is the diminutive of viola, violoncino and violoncello are the diminutives of "violone." The tenor of our day, which also at that time sprang from the alto or tenor viola, after the pattern of the violin, received the name of Viola da braccio, which means "arm viola." Besides the Viola da braccio there was also a "Viola da Spalla," which was not placed beneath the chin, but rested on the left shoulder. Concerning this bass

---

[1] The well-known violin maker, Aug. Riechers, in Berlin, possesses a violoncello by Gaspard da Salò (small size).

instrument Mattheson remarks : " The Viola da spalla, or shoulder-viola, has a particularly grand effect in accompaniment from its penetrating and pure tone. A bass can never be more distinctly and clearly brought out than by this instrument. It is fastened by a ribbon to the chest and thrown over the right shoulder, but has nothing which can stop or prevent in the smallest degree its resonance."

To return to the violoncello. It offered the player two very important advantages over the gamba. First, the finger technique was wholly unlimited because the fingerboard had no frets, which, in regard to runs and cadences, as well as change of positions, opposed a substantial hindrance to the gamba player. Then the player on the violoncello could obtain more tone than on the gamba, by drawing the bow more forcibly over a single string. The upper edge of the bridge of the gamba, over which the strings passed, was so flatly cut for harmonised or part-playing that it was necessary to avoid a strong tone, lest the neighbouring strings should be thereby sympathetically affected. But the bridge of the cello, on the contrary, was of a more convex form, whereby playing in parts was indeed precluded. As is known, on the cello as on the violin, only double stops and chords are possible, and the last only broken up. In this manner the violoncello was used formerly at the performances of operas and oratorios as solo accompaniment of recitatives, for which of course it was requisite that the player should have a thorough knowledge of music theoretically, as he had to execute at sight figured basses.

Corrette gives already in his violoncello tutor (1741) instructions for accompanying recitative. These directions are, however, by no means exhaustive ; such are first found in the cello tutor compiled for the Paris Conservatoire by De Baillot, Levasseur, Catel, and Baudiot, which appeared in print in 1804. Therein it is said :

" In order to accompany well a recitative, a complete knowledge of harmony and of the violoncello is necessary ; one must be intimate with figured basses, and know how to execute them readily. He who can do this has reached the summit of art ; for it presupposes a great deal of necessary information, and still more the power of judging how to turn it to account.

"If the bass player is not certain of the resolutions of discords, if he is unable positively to indicate to the singer when he is to make a complete or a broken cadence, if in his concords he does not know how to avoid forbidden fifths and octaves—he is in danger of confusing the singer, and in any case he will produce a most disagreeable effect.

"As in good compositions, a recitative always follows a well-defined progression and adapts itself to the character of the part, to the situation portrayed, and to the voice of the singer : in the accompaniment—1. The strength of the tone must be regulated according to the effect to be produced, for the accompaniment must sustain and embellish the singing and not spoil and drown it. 2. The chord must not be repeated, except when the harmony changes. 3. The accompaniment must be quite simple, without flourishes or runs. Good accompanying always has in view the best rendering of the subject, and when the player allows himself to fill up certain gaps with a short interlude, this must only consist of the notes of the chord. 4. The chord must be played without Arpeggio, ordinarily in the following manner "—

Notation.   Played.

Baudiot in his violoncello tutor, which appeared later than the above, makes the following remark concerning the accompaniment of recitative : "It sometimes happens that the actors linger on the scene without reciting (speaking), be it that they have forgotten the text of what they have to recite, or that for some other reason they are silent. At times their appearance on the boards is delayed. In such cases, the accompanist (*i.e.*, the cellist) can perform short preludes and embellishments at his pleasure. But he must

---

[1] The French call this kind of recitative accompaniment "le recitatif italien."

be modest about it, and employ his ornaments at the right moment, and always with taste."[1]

To the art of violoncello making the same applies as to the violin. The productions of the Italian makers surpass those of all other nations. Amongst them, those manufactured by Nicholas Amati, Stradivari, and Gius. Guarneri del Gesù are most to be preferred and justly so.[2]

Stradivari and Amati made their cellos of two different sizes; the larger one was formerly called " il Basso," while the smaller was distinguished as the Violoncello proper. The latter is the more preferable as being more manageable; in these days it is used as a valuable model.

As to the violoncello bow, which had the following form in the first half of the eighteenth century,[3] its progress went

hand in hand with that of the violin bow. The improvements which were successively made on the latter were effected on the former. The greatest perfection reached by the bow was the work of a Frenchman, François Tourte. To this day he has never been excelled in this department. (See Appendix A.)

The fabrication, however, of good violin and cello bows has latterly become very general; and especially in Markneukirchen the manufacture of bows as well as instruments has received a great impulse.[4]

---

[1] Accompanying the recitative with the cello was customary far into our century. I heard it in Italy at the representation of the old operas up to the year 1873. I am unable to say if the practice is continued. It has been abolished in Germany for the last ten years.

[2] The widespread opinion that Gius. Guarneri of the Gesù did not make violoncellos is unfounded. Aug. Riecher informs me that Major H——r, in Berlin, is in possession of a cello which is undoubtedly genuine. Yet it seems as if this member of the Guarneri family had only made a limited number.

[3] The above sketch is taken from Corrette's Violoncello Tutor, which was published in 1741.

[4] In my paper " The Violin and its Masters," second edition (Breitkopf and Härtel), I have given a more detailed account of it as well as of the productions of the Italian, German, and French masters, which it is unnecessary to repeat here. See also the fabrication of musical instruments in Saxon Voigtland, by Fürstenau and Berthold, 1876.

THE

ART OF VIOLONCELLO PLAYING

IN THE EIGHTEENTH CENTURY.

Violoncello.

In the seventeenth century the violoncello still occupied a very subordinate and modest position; during the period mentioned, with very few exceptions, it was employed only as a bass instrument in the orchestra. At the beginning of the eighteenth century, however, there was already a great change; for Mattheson says in his "Neu eröffneten Orchestre," which appeared in 1713 :—

"The PROMINENT Violoncello, the Bass Viol, and the Viola da Spalla are small bass fiddles (viols) similar to the larger ones, with five or six strings, on which can be played all kinds of quick things, variations and movements much more easily than on the larger machines" (Mattheson means the contra-basso).[1]

It is, therefore, quite conceivable that some time was necessary, before the players, who were unaccustomed to the undivided fingerboard of the cello, were sufficiently confident of a finger technique differing so completely from that of the gamba. They were at first limited to the lower part of the fingerboard, as was the case primarily with the violin.[2] The position of the thumb, by means of which the higher and highest positions on the fingerboard could alone be fixed and maintained with certainty, could hardly have been known before the beginning of the eighteenth century. The violoncello at this time, as appears from Mattheson's account just mentioned, had sometimes a set of five or even six strings like

---

[1] Mattheson expresses himself about this in his original manner as follows: "The growling Violone (French, Basse de Violon; German, Grosse Bass Geige) is quite twice the size of the former, sometimes even more, consequently the strings, in thickness and length, are in proportion. They are of sixteen-feet tone, and most useful on the stage as a solid foundation for polyphonous pieces, such as choruses and similar things, as well as for airs and recitatives; its deep humming tone penetrates farther than the clavier and other bass instruments. It must, however, be heavy work if one has to practise this monster for three or four hours unceasingly."

[2] Concerning this, I refer to my work "The Violin and its Masters," second edition, 1883. (Breitkopf and Härtel, Leipsic.)

the gamba.   On the five-stringed instruments the tuning
was :—

The Abbé Tardieu already referred to, who played the violoncello, according to Gerber, had the same tuning on his
instrument.   About the third decade of the last century,
those who used five-stringed instruments gave up the highest
string—(the D). From that time the four-stringed instrument
with the tuning C, G, D, A came very generally into use.
The latter was not altogether a novelty.   Prätorius mentions
it in his "Syntagma Mus." as the "Bass Viol de Braccio."[1]

In Germany the use of the violoncello as an orchestral
instrument ensued later than in Italy, though much sooner than
in France.   For although it had been introduced into the
Parisian Opera in 1727, by the cellist Batistin, to be mentioned
later on, it had been already in use since 1680 in the
Vienna Hofkapelle.   The Saxon Hofkapelle at Dresden
next followed by the installation of four violoncellists.   Their
names are Daniel Hennig, Agostino Antonio de Rossi, Jean
Baptiste José du Houbondel, and Jean Prach de Tilloy.[2]   As
two of these players have French names, it is to be assumed
that the violoncello had already found representatives in
France at the beginning of the eighteenth century.

The example set by Vienna and Dresden was soon imitated
also by other German Courts.   The band of Duke Charles
Ulrich of Holstein-Gottorp affords a case in point.   As this
prince, the future son-in-law of Peter the Great, found
himself obliged, in 1720, to reside at the Russian Imperial
Court, his private musicians followed him thither, amongst
whom there was a cellist.[3]

As the gamba enjoyed a great amount of favour[4] in

---

[1] Michael Corrette in the preface to his Violoncello Tutor refers to a stringed
instrument in general use before the introduction of the violoncello into France
with the tuning B, F, C, G, which he calls Basse de Violon. The instrument
must be identical with the one described by Mattheson as Basse de Violon.

[2] Fürstenau : " On the History of Music and the Theatre at the Court of the
Princes of Saxony."

[3] Hiller, *Weekly News* of May 21, 1770.

[4] Mattheson says, in his " Neu eröffneten Orchestre," that this instrument
(Basse de Viole) was singularly prized and cultivated.

Germany, the introduction of the violoncello was not effected without difficulty, to which indeed the gambists, who thought their pretended rights were thereby infringed, not a little contributed. For in a paper which appeared in 1757 in the French language, "Observations sur la Musique," &c., it is said : " La seule basse de viole a déclaré la guerre au violoncelle qui a remporté la victoire et elle a été si complète que l'on craint maintenant que la fameuse viole, l'incomparable sicilienne ne soit vendue à quelque inventaire à un prix médiocre et que quelque luthier profane ne s'avise d'en faire une enseigne."[1]

It was not quite so bad as the last words of the announcement lead one to suppose. Even if the violoncello caused the gamba to be quite superfluous in the orchestra, the latter was cultivated as a solo instrument for some time longer, and many of the good old gambas were in course of time metamorphosed into violoncellos, and made available for further use; while the more insignificant specimens were destroyed, if they were not required for completing instrumental collections and so preserved from destruction.

The art of violoncello playing in the first stages of its development was, as regards the method of treatment, not so much favoured as violin playing. To the latter a definite direction for imitation was early given, as soon indeed as the end of the seventeenth century, by the Roman school founded by Arcangelo Corelli, which was soon followed by the foundation of the Paduan and Piedmontese schools. Violoncello playing lacked such classical parent schools. When a few prominent artists of this instrument had brought it into greater consideration, centres were formed by distinguished masters for the study of the cello, which supplied the want of proper schools, about which we shall have more to say farther on.

It is easy to understand how it followed that the violoncello was first valued in the land of its birth—that is, in Italy, not only as an orchestral instrument but also for solo playing. How this important branch of art was there developed we shall see in the next section.

---

[1] H. Leblanc published a " Défense de la Basse de Viole contre les entreprises du Violon et les prétentions du Violoncel." Amsterdam, 1740.—(*Tr.*)

I.—ITALY.

ITALY has the claim of priority in violoncello as well as violin playing. It was the birthplace of the violin and of the cello, and from thence emanated the artistic executive development of both instruments. The first famous Italian cellist of whom we have any notice is—

DOMENICO GABRIELI, with the surname of MENGHINO DEL VIOLONCELLO, born about 1640 at Bologna, died in 1690. This artist found a sphere of work in the church of San Petronio in his native town. Then he entered the service of Cardinal Pamfili in Rome. Gabrieli was also a composer of some repute. Fétis mentions eight of his operas which were written partly for Bologna and partly for Venice. His other works consist of a " Cantata a voce sola," in a collection of Motets, entitled " Vexillum pacis," for alto solo and instrumental accompaniments, as well as " Baletti, gighe, correnti, e sarabande a due violini e violoncello, con basso continuo " (Op. 1). These three works, of which the last is a reprint, appeared successively in 1691, 1695, and 1703, consequently after Gabrieli's death. He appears to have composed nothing specially for the cello.

More remarkable as a cellist must have been ATTILIO ARIOSTI, the Dominican monk, born at Bologna in 1660. Gerber at least says of him that he was one of the most excellent violoncellists of his time. But he was also a distinguished performer on the Viola d'amore. He occupied himself chiefly, however, with opera compositions, for which the Pope granted him a dispensation from the rule of his order, as without it, being a Dominican, he was forbidden to meddle with anything connected with the theatre. In 1698 Ariosti was sent for to Berlin as Kapellmeister to the Elector of Brandenberg. Thence he went in 1716 to London, where, in the proximity of Handel, he could make no way, and therefore at last returned to his fatherland. He chose Bologna as his place of residence. Like Gabrieli, he appears to have produced no independent[1] violoncello compositions.

---

[1] Some pieces composed for the viola d'amore by Ariosti, consisting of Cantabile, Vivace, Adagio, and Minuet, have been arranged by Alfred Piatti for the violoncello, and brought out lately in London.

His fellow-country man, GIOVANNI BATTISTA BONONCINI (Buononcini),[1] famous as an able cellist, also devoted his talent by preference to the operatic stage. He was the eldest son of the choirmaster, Giov. Maria Bononcini, at the church S. Giovanni, in Monte, at Modena, and was born in 1672, or, according to Fétis, in 1667 or 1668. At first instructed in music by his father, and then perfected by Colonna at Bologna, he betook himself, at twenty-two or twenty-three years of age, to Vienna, where he found a post as cellist in the Imperial Kapelle. Here he turned to opera, which at that time was a favourite means of entertainment for the seeing and listening public, and promised more reputation and gain than all other kinds of composition.

Fétis mentions twenty operas by Bononcini, but he doubtless wrote more. Even in his eightieth year he was occupied for the theatre in Venice. Besides, he wrote an Oratorio, " Joshua," several orchestral pieces, masses, chamber duets, " Trattenimenti da Camera," &c., some of which were composed before his entrance into the Vienna Hofkapelle. He also wrote "Sinfonie" for violin and violoncello as well as cello solos. Of the latter there appeared at J. Simpson's (London) a sonata for two violoncellos in a collection of sonatas by Pasqualini, San Martino, Caporale, Spourni, and Porta. As Caporale was born in 1750 and Porta in 1758, the publication of this collection must have taken place late in the second half of the eighteenth century. The Bononcini sonata contained in it does not give a very favourable impression of this composer's talent. The development is dry and in places very formal, even here and there somewhat incorrect. To the two figured parts are given accompanying basses, partly simple and partly contrapuntal. The interest which attaches to this composition, consisting of an *Allegro*, with introductory *Andante*, a movement marked " *Grazioso*," and a "*Minuet*," after which the " *Grazioso* " is to be repeated, rests chiefly on the light which it throws upon the technical condition of cello playing at the beginning of the eighteenth century (for doubtless the composition belongs to that period).

---

[1] Concerning the diverse vicissitudes of Bononcini's and Ariosti's lives, which can find no particular mention here, see " Musical Lexicons," extant.

In reference to this is to be remarked : the principal part is confined chiefly to the middle tones ; the lower ones are only occasionally touched, and the compass of the higher notes reaches· to the one-lined A ; the thumb position does not come into use. Figure is little developed, and only modest attempts are made at playing double stoppings and chords ; the notation is in tenor and bass clefs.

It is reported that during Bononcini's residence in Paris, between 1735—1748, he composed a Motet with cello obbligato accompaniment, for the royal band there, which last he himself played at the performance of his work in the presence of the king.

Alessandro Scarlatti,[1] the founder of the Neapolitan opera school, had given an example of this use of the violoncello about twenty-five years before in one of his cantatas. Geminiani, Corelli's pupil, related that this cello part was performed during Scarlatti's presence in Rome, and with his assistance on the clavier, by the famous violoncellist, Franciscello (Franchischello) ; his playing was so beautiful that Scarlatti described it as heavenly.

This event must have occurred in the year 1713, when Scarlatti was in Rome the last time. Consequently, Franciscello's birth must be placed with all probability in the year 1692. He would have been twenty-one years of age when he played with the Neapolitan master.

Gerber says that Franciscello went from Rome to Naples in 1725. That he was actually there in the year mentioned is affirmed by Quantz, who himself heard him play. Through Franciscello's extraordinary performances the violoncello was soon so generally accepted in Italy, that the gamba had, in 1730, almost entirely disappeared from the Italian orchestras.

In the year 1730, Franciscello was summoned to Vienna as Imperial chamber musician, a proof that his name had already penetrated beyond his country. Franz Benda, afterwards celebrated as a violinist, and founder of the Berlin violin

---

[1] Born in 1649, at Trapani, in Sicily ; died on October 24, 1725, at Naples. In Grove's Dictionary, 1859 is given as the date of his birth—other authorities as above.—(*Tr.*)

school, heard him in the Austrian capital. Franciscello's manner of playing so impressed him that he took him from that time as his model.

Franciscello remained, it appears, ten years in Vienna. If a notice in the " Musical Almanack for Germany, of the year 1782," is to be credited, he had already been a member of the Imperial Court and Chamber Music Society in 1766, which is by no means beyond the bounds of possibility, though not very probable. We hold then to the assumption that he was born in 1692 so that, in 1766, he would be already seventy-four years old. It is not known where Franciscello closed his life. Tradition only says that at an advanced age he resided in Genoa, to which the supposition was attached that that city had been his birthplace. It is stated that the elder Duport, the cello virtuoso, who was born in 1741, went from Paris to visit him there.

During his long period of work at Vienna, Franciscello doubtless instructed pupils in cello playing ; who they were is however, as little known as the question if or what he composed for his instrument. On both points we are no better off than concerning his somewhat older compatriot

CERVETTO, called JACOPO BASSEVI, who was born in 1682. Until his forty-sixth year he remained in his fatherland. Then, like so many other Italian musicians of this time, he was seized with a desire to travel, and betook himself to London. There he trafficked at first in instruments which he had brought with him from Italy ; this, however, was so little remunerative that he very soon gave it up, and joined the orchestra of Drury Lane Theatre. According to Burney's judgment, Cervetto was, for his time, a very clever violoncellist, who knew how to manipulate the fingerboard with much dexterity ; but his tone must have been rough and harsh. Of his eccentricity the following anecdote is an illustration : Once when the famous Garrick was representing a drunkard and sank down senseless upon a seat, Cervetto broke upon the sudden stillness with an unseemly loud and long-drawn yawn. Garrick immediately got up, severely censuring such behaviour, upon which Cervetto pacifying him answered : " I beg your pardon, I always yawn when I am

very pleased." A few years later Cervetto became Director
of Drury Lane Theatre, and thus he laid the foundation of
his fortune.

Cervetto must have had a very strong constitution, for
he lived to the unusual age of 101 years. His death took
place on January 14, 1783. He left a fortune of £20,000
sterling, which he bequeathed to his son James, who was
also a cellist; but soon after inheriting from his father he
retired into private life. He, also, reached a respectable age,
for as he came into the world (in London) in 1747, and died
February 5, 1837, he was ninety years old. In 1783 he was
performing at the Court concerts of the Queen, as well as
taking part in the musical *réunions* in the house of Lord
Abington as one of the best reputed cellists in London, Of
cello compositions he published : 1. Twelve " Solos for a
Violoncello, with a Thorough Bass for the Harpsichord "; this
work, dedicated to the Elector Palatine of Bavaria and Jülich-
Eleve-Berg, appeared at the author's own expense, without
date. 2. "Six Solos for a Violoncello, with a Thorough Bass for
the Harpsichord, Opera Terza." London. 3. " Twelve
Sonatinas for a Violoncello and a Bass, Op. 4ta." London.
Fétis adds, besides, " Six solos pour la flûte " and " Six trios
pour deux violons, et violoncelle," which must have been in
existence not long before the end of the last century. We
shall have occasion to refer again farther on to Cervetto's
violoncello compositions.

Taking up again the chronological thread, after Cervetto the
elder, the cellist Batistin, whose real name was JOH. BAPTIST
STRUCK, must be mentioned. He was of German origin and
was born in Florence in the second half of the seventeenth
century, from thence he went to Paris at the beginning of the
eighteenth century. He there entered the band of the Duke
of Orleans and the opera orchestra, in which he, conjointly
with the brothers Abbé (properly Philippe Pierre and Pierre
de Saint-Sévin), played the cello parts. He must have
performed well, since Louis XIV., in order to retain him in
the French capital, gave him a liberal allowance and, in
addition, a sum of 500 francs for certain theatrical compositions to be supplied by him. Besides this he wrote a
long list of ballets and operas specially for Court festivities.

There appeared in print, by him, during the years 1706 and 1714, in Paris, four books of "Cantatas" and a collection of airs. He does not appear to have composed for the violoncello. He died on December 9, 1755, at the scene of his work. Among the masters of the Neapolitan school, LEONARDO LEO, at that time the famous opera composer, distinguished himself as a violoncellist, who was born, 1694, at S. Vito degli Schiavi, in the province of Lecco, and died at Naples in 1746. He also composed six cello concertos with quartet accompaniments, which belong to the years 1737 and 1738. The MSS. of these are in the Library of the Royal Conservatoire at Naples. It is supposed that these are the oldest of existing cello concertos.

Another Italian cellist of that time was DOMENICO DELLA BELLA, of whom nothing further is known than that, in 1704, he published, in Venice, Twelve Sonatas "a due violini e violoncello."

The information is equally meagre regarding the cellist PARASISI, of whom Gerber says he was an extraordinary artist on his instrument and was with the Italian Opera orchestra at Breslau in 1727.

Concerning the Italian violoncellists JACCHINI, AMADIO, VANDINI, ABACO, DALL 'OGLIO, and LANZETTI, born in the second half of the seventeenth and the beginning of the eighteenth century, we know very little.

JACCHINI, whose Christian name was Giuseppe, noted by Gerber as one of the first cellists of his time, was appointed to the church of S. Petronio in Bologna at the beginning of the eighteenth century. That he had distinguished himself as an artist is proved by his nomination as a member of the Bologna Philharmonic Society, a distinction which is only conferred on men of great musical reputation. Of his compositions there is a work entitled " Concerti per Camera a 3 e 4 stromenti, con violoncello obligato (Op. 4). Bologna, 1701," to be mentioned.

PIPPO AMADIO, who flourished about the year 1720, was, according to Gerber's account, a violoncellist, "whose art surpassed all, that up to his time had been produced on his instrument."

ANTONIO VANDINI, first violoncellist at the church of S.

Antonio, Padua, seems to have been no less remarkable. The Italians called his manner of playing and his expression "parlare"—he understood how to make his instrument speak. He was on terms of such close friendship with Tartini, who as is known was engaged at the same church at Padua as solo violinist, that he accompanied him in 1723 to Prague, and remained with him for three years in the service of Count Kinski. Vandini was still living in Padua in 1770. The year of his death is unknown.

ABACO, born at Verona, according to information contained in the second year of the "Leipsic Musical Paper" (p. 345), was a prominent violoncellist, who lived in the first half of the eighteenth century. Gerber possessed a cello solo of his composition, of which he says that it appeared to have been written in the year 1748.

GIUSEPPE DALL 'OGLIO, the younger brother of the famous violin player, Domenico dall 'Oglio, was born about 1700 at Padua,[1] and went to St. Petersburg in 1735. There he remained in the Russian imperial service twenty-nine years, after which he returned to his native land. On his journey thither he stopped at Warsaw, on which occasion King August of Poland nominated him his agent for the Venetian Republic.

SALVATORE LANZETTI, born at the beginning of the eighteenth century in Naples, was pupil of the Conservatorio there, Santa Maria di Loreto, and was during the greater part of his life in the service of the King of Sardinia. He died in Turin in 1780. In the year 1736 two volumes of violoncello sonatas appeared by him, and later also a book of instruction, the title of which Fétis gives as : "Principes du doigter pour le Violoncelle dans tous les tons." It is somewhat differently named by Gerber : "Principes ou l'applicatur de Violoncel par tous les tons." Lanzetti must have carried out with great skill the staccato touch both up and down the instrument.

We are somewhat better informed regarding the violoncellist CAPORALE. Neither the place of his home nor the year of his

---

[1] Gerber gives Venice as his birthplace ; but in the *Weekly News* of the year 1770, Padua is mentioned, which is probably correct.

birth nor that of his death are, indeed, known to us, but of his life
and work in England we possess some information. In 1735
he came to London and worked under Handel, who wrote for
him a cello solo in the third act of his opera " Deidamia "
composed in 1739.

His musical education could not have been very thorough,
but he must have had certain qualifications which induced
Handel to connect himself with him. Simpson's Collection
(see p. 49), published in London, contains a Cello Sonata by
Caporale, which does not speak much for his talent in
composition. It consists of *Adagio*, *Allegro*, and a *Theme*
with three variations after the manner of studies. As a player
Caporale was remarkable for his tone, but as regards finish he
could not rival either the elder CERVETTO or PASQUALINI.

This last-named artist, by whom a sonata, scarcely rising
above the level of Caporale, was contained in the volume
already mentioned as appearing at Simpson's, was performing
in London, in 1745, as a concertist of great repute. Further
information regarding him does not exist.

Greater consideration must be yielded to CARLO FERRARI,
brother of the violinist Domenico Ferrari, so often referred to
in the previous century. On account of an injured foot he
was called " the lame." Born at Piacenza about 1730 he
betook himself to Paris in 1758 and appeared with great success
in the " Concert spirituel." In 1765 he accepted an engagement
offered to him by the Count of Parma.[1] He remained in this
position until his death, which took place in 1789. It is
reported of Ferrari that he was the first Italian cellist who
made use of the thumb position. If this be true, France
must have been beforehand in the difficult matter of the art
of fingering ; for the thumb position was already known in
Paris, as we have seen, before 1740, consequently at a time
when Ferrari was only ten or twelve years old. But if it be
acknowledged that violoncello playing was cultivated much
earlier in Italy than in France, and had already advanced
beyond the elemental stage before it had found representatives

---

[1] In Jahn's biography of Mozart is found the notice that Ferrari had been
appointed to the Court of the Archbishop of Salzburg ; at what period is not
mentioned.

among the French, we must be inclined to concede to the Italians the discovery of the thumb position, and indeed to the predecessors of Ferrari. It is highly probable that Franciscello and Batistin already availed themselves of its assistance for the use of the upper parts of the fingerboard. The trick must have been brought into France by the last-named artist who, as we know, settled in Paris at the beginning of the eighteenth century.

The proof that the thumb position was known in Paris before 1740 is established by the violoncello method of Michel Corrette in the year 1741, and which, as far as one can see, was the first work of instruction for the instrument in question. Considering the scarcity at that time of cello compositions this instruction book is the more important, as from it is to be determined with certainty the average standard to which violoncello playing had attained towards the middle of the previous century. This circumstance seems to justify our entering somewhat more fully into Corrette's school.

The title is: " Méthode, théoretique et pratique, pour apprendre en peu de temps, le violoncelle . . . dans sa perfection composée par Michel Corette. XXIV⁰ Ouvrage à Paris, chez l'auteur, Mᵉ Boivin et le Sʳ le Clerc ; à Lyon chez M. de Bretonne. Avec Privilège du Roy. MDCCXL1."[1]

After some introductory paragraphs regarding the use of the F and C clef, in notation for violoncello music, concerning the value of notes and pauses, the formation of sharps, flats, and naturals, as well as regarding the usual marks, the various measures and syncopes, Corrette treats:

1. Of the manner of holding the violoncello ; 2. Of the holding and action of the bow ; 3. Of its use in the up and down strokes ; 4. Of the tuning of the violoncello ; 5. Of the division of the fingerboard into diatonic as well as chromatic tones ; 6. Of the fingering in the lower (first) and following positions ; 7. Of the way and manner of returning from the higher positions to the first ; 8. Of trills and appogiaturas ;

---

[1] Fétis says in his "Biographie universelle des Musiciens" (Vol. II., 365): "The first edition of Corrette's music tutor appeared in 1761." On the title page, however, is plainly printed MDCCXL1. Fétis has inadvertently put the number L before the X instead of after.

9. Of the various kinds of bow action ; 10. Of double-stops and arpeggios ; 11. And also of the thumb position. He also gives instruction for those who wish to go from the gamba to the violoncello, and then in conclusion gives hints for the accompaniment of singing and for instrumental solos.

It is evident that the directions of Corrette have chiefly a mere historical importance, as the technique of the violoncello, after the appearance of his method, underwent substantial changes. His explanation concerning the finger positions of that period and the thumb position which in the higher parts of the fingerboard takes the place of a moveable nut, concerning the manipulation of the bow, and the considerations to be observed in exchanging the gamba for the violoncello have a special interest for us.

With regard to the first of these four points, we remark that the finger position adopted by Corrette for the diatonic scale on all the strings was, in the first two positions, 1, 2, and 4 ; in the "third position," 1, 2, 3, 4 ; and in the "fourth," 1, 2, and 3 ; after the latter position the fourth finger was as a rule no longer needed, for which Corrette adduces as a reason that it is too short to be made use of in the higher positions of the fingerboard ; in case however it should be necessary to use it, the use of the left arm would be impeded. In exceptional cases, says Corrette in another part of his school, the fourth finger could be used in the " fourth position," without altering the thumb position, for the B flat and B on the A string, for the E flat on the D string, for the A flat on the G string, and for the D flat on the C string. The finger positions were then, in the first half and about the middle of the last century, somewhat different in the diatonic scale of the violoncello than they were later on. It is especially to be remarked that the E and the B were touched with the second finger upon the two lower strings, though the notes marked were far more convenient for the third finger, which very shortly took the place of the second.

As to the exclusion of the fourth finger, when playing with the thumb position, no proof is needed to show the reason was that it gave an awkward manner of holding the left hand. The finger positions for the chromatic scale still more widely differed from the fingering employed later, as the following scale shows—

It very nearly happened, that as early as the seventeenth century when a stringed instrument was so much desired as a standard one for the violoncello, that the violin mode of fingering was adopted for the former, which according to the foregoing remarks really was the case, with the exception of the use of the third finger. It had however been overlooked that the cello, on account of its much larger dimensions, demanded an entirely different method of fingering. The regulation of this important point, which offered peculiar difficulties, occupied cellists up to the beginning of our century In some measure the fingering which Corrette teaches for descending intervals of a second from the higher to the lower tones is unavoidable. He gives the two following examples—

He gave the preference to the second example.

The almost total exclusion of the fourth finger caused a very great restriction in playing with the thumb position. But when Corrette wrote his work this limitation would hardly have been felt, as the higher parts of the fingerboard were little, and, only in exceptional cases, used by cello players and composers. Corrette mentions, as the highest tone, the one-lined B. Caporale and Pasqualini do not go beyond this note in their sonatas, already mentioned, excepting in one instance,

when Caporale casually uses the two-lined C. It appears
that, with many cellists, in place of the thumb the
first finger was made use of in the higher positions as a
support, for Corrette remarks concerning his method : " If the
first finger is used instead of the thumb the fourth finger must
necessarily be made use of ; it is, however, on account of its
shortness, really useless in the upper ' positions.' "   To
beginners Corrette recommended the attempt then in vogue—
but a little later combated by Leopold Mozart in his violin
school[1]—to introduce marks on the fingerboard indicating
the intervals in order to learn to play clearly in tune.
For gamba players who, following the spirit of the time, gave
up their instrument and turned to the violoncello, which was
rapidly coming into use, this means of assistance had a
certain value, accustomed as they were to the frets of the
gamba fingerboard, for the finger positions of both instruments differ considerably from one another, as appears from
the comparison given below by Corrette.

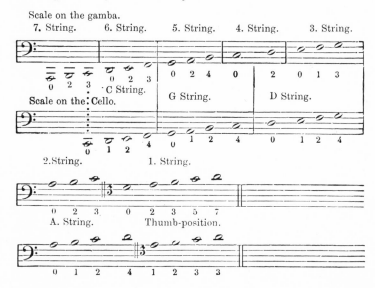

The figures placed under the gamba scale relate to the frets

---

[1] The first edition of this appeared under the title : " Versuch einer Gründ-
lichen Violinschule."

which are to be attended to by the player, while those of the cello scale are the finger positions to be used.

The lower C, which the string itself forms on the cello, had on the gamba to be touched at the third fret ; the succeeding D on the gamba was the open string, while on the cello it was to be touched with the first finger, and so on.

The four highest tones, *e*, *f*, *g*, *a*, fell in the gamba on the 2nd, 3rd, 5th, and 7th frets, whereas, according to Corrette's account, those in the cello required the use of the thumb position. It is plain that the gamba players who took up the violoncello had to adopt an entirely different system of fingering.

To a certain extent the handling of the bow presented difficulties to those who exchanged the gamba for the violoncello. The former instrument, on account of the flatness of the bridge, did not allow of an energetic use of the bow. From the violoncello, on the contrary, a powerful tone must be brought out, which had to be learnt by gamba players. Besides, they had also to accustom themselves to other strokes of the bow for the cello. What was played by the latter instrument with a down stroke, was played by an upward one on the gamba, and the reverse.

The holding of the bow was again rather different from the present manner. Corrette gives three ways for this. According to Corrette's testimony, the most usual way in Italy consisted in placing the 2nd, 3rd, 4th, and 5th fingers upon the rod and the thumb beneath it, so that the bow was held not exactly at the nut, but about a hand's breadth from it, as formerly and even at the beginning of our century was done by many players. The second way of holding the bow was, the other four fingers being placed as above, to lay the thumb upon the hair. Finally, the bow was also held, so that the 2nd, 3rd, 4th, and 5th fingers were laid upon that part of the rod to which the nut is attached, while the thumb had its place beneath the nut.

Corrette does not give the preference to either of these ways of holding the bow, which in the course of the second half of the last century became more and more obsolete. He was of opinion that they were all good, but left it to each one to choose the manner in which the most power could be attained.

It seems, however, noteworthy that Corrette laid it down as a rule that the middle of the bow should be used in playing, whereby its use was limited to a third of its length.

In the preface to his method Corrette speaks of several systems amongst violoncellists, but adds, the best and most generally followed was that of Bononcini, of which also the most skilful masters in Europe made use. From this remark it follows, that in the composition of his school, he took Bononcini's manner of playing, which he was able to study, soon after the latter's arrival in Paris, as his guide. In surveying the above principles, detailed by Corrette, regarding the technique of violoncello playing, it must be admitted that, needing improvement in almost every respect about the middle of the last century, it had not progressed, with few exceptions, beyond the elementary stages. The chamber sonatas and suites of Joh. Seb. Bach for violoncello solo, the last of which were originally composed for the Viola pomposa, cannot be cited as proofs to the contrary. In them Bach forestalled the technical capacity of his time by a decade. Although they are composed for that part of the fingerboard on which there is no question of the thumb position, yet they contain difficulties of an extraordinary kind which Bach's contemporaries had not been able to master.[1] And even in the second half of the last century there could have been no cellist who would have been fully capable of playing them. Therefore it must be considered either, that these compositions, so remarkable of their kind, were not absolutely composed for the cello ; or that the violoncello technique took another direction, which was called out by these suites of Bach.

The violoncello, like the violin, is primarily an instrument for the voice. As such it was chiefly used by the Italians, who, up to the second half of the last century, gave the impulse to stringed instrument playing. This is to be gathered from the cello pieces by Italian composers belonging to this period. As instances, next to the sonatas already mentioned, two musical pieces of the same kind may

---

[1] These cello pieces by Bach existed in all probability during this master's directorship at Kothen (1717—1723). Spitta : " Joh. Seb. Bach," I., 678 and 707.

be cited, by San Martini (Giov. Battista Sammartini)[1] and Bernardo Porta.[2] Neither of these composers were violoncellists. Their sonatas are, however, adapted to the nature of the instrument for which they were composed. As compositions they are indeed of little importance, and as regards the technique, they do not rise above the measure of the modest demands which were then required.

With regard to cello technique the younger Cervetto, whose compositions have already been mentioned, p. 52, goes really farther. In them there is a greater variety in the manner of playing, in the use of double-stops and different passages derived from the scale and the chord. Such ways of playing could naturally only at first be found out and perfected in a proper manner by those who were already experienced practised players on an instrument of extreme difficulty on account of its extensions.

The cello pieces of Cervetto formed after the manner of Tartini's violin sonatas are, as to their contents, quite antiquated, and are only interesting in a purely technical point of view. Like the compositions already considered, they occupy mostly the parts of tenor and bass. Only twice in the first *Allegro* of the tenth Sonata of his Op. 4 does Cervetto venture to the twice-lined E, and at the conclusion of the same piece to the twice-lined A. In both cases he has to use the treble clef, which does not appear elsewhere.

Besides Cervetto the younger, amongst Italians who cultivated cello playing must be mentioned Gasparini, Moria, Joannini di Violoncello, Zappa, Cirri, Aliprandi, Graziani, Piarelli, Spotorni I. and II., Barni, Bertoja I. and II., Lolli, Sandonati, and Shevioni. We give below the meagre information which exists regarding them.

QUIRINO GASPARINI, a distinguished cellist, was in 1749 Kapellmeister at the Court of Turin. He remained there until 1770. As a composer, he was chiefly occupied with church music, no cello pieces are known by him.

---

[1] Born towards the end of the seventeenth or the beginning of the eighteenth century, in Milan ; died after 1770, in which year Burney found him still living.

[2] Born, in 1758, in Rome; died, 1832, in Paris. The two sonatas by San Martini and Porta have already been mentioned, p. 49.

Of Moria, the fact only is known that, in 1755, he was heard at the "Concert Spirtuel" in Paris.

Joannini di Violoncello, from the year 1759 Kapellmeister at St. Petersburg, had a great reputation in his own country as a player.

Zappa, called Francesco, according to Gerber was making a concert tour in 1781, and "enchanted his hearers in Dantsic by his soft and delightful execution."

Giambattista Cirri, born in the first half of the eighteenth century, at Forli, lived and worked for a long time in England. On the title page of his first work, published at Verona in 1763, he called himself a "Professore di Violoncello." Of his compositions there appeared in print seventeen different works in London, Paris, and Florence.

As a clever violoncellist, Bernardo Aliprandi, son of the opera composer, Aliprandi, born in Tuscany, was distinguished. His father was composer and Court band-conductor in Munich during the first half of the previous century ; but he himself became a member of the orchestra there, where he still was in 1786. His cello pieces, of which several were published, are as obsolete as those of Cirri.

Gerber, in his dictionary, says of Graziani, that after the death of the gamba player, Louis Christian Hesse,[1] he was summoned to Potsdam to take his place as tutor to the Crown Prince of Prussia. When the French violoncellist, Duport (the elder), came to Berlin, in 1773, Graziani lost his post at Court. He died at Potsdam in 1787. The six violoncello solos, Op. 1 (printed in Berlin about the year 1780), as well as the six cello pieces brought out in Paris (Op.2), mentioned by Gerber in his old Musical Dictionary under the name of Graziani, must have appeared in the latter years of the author's life.

In the second half of the last century there was a violoncello virtuoso, by name Piarelli, who, about 1784, had printed in Paris six violoncello solos. This is all that is known about him.

Of the brothers Spotorni, Gerber only says that, in 1770, in Italy, "their native land, they were esteemed as violoncellists."

---

[1] P. 29.

A very skilful player was Camillo Barni, born on January 18, 1762, at Como. He received his first instructions in cello playing at the age of fourteen years from his grandfather, David Ronchetti. Later on, Giuseppe Gadgi, Canon of the Cathedral at Como, taught him for a few months. At the age of twenty Barni joined the opera orchestra of Milan, of which he became first violoncellist in 1791. In the year 1802 he went to reside permanently in Paris, where he appeared as solo player, and then, for several years, was an active member in the orchestra of the Italian Opera. Between 1804 and 1809 he published several duets for his own instrument and the violin. He also wrote a cello concerto.

Concerning the brothers Bertoja, Gerber only says that both were employed in Venice about 1800, as virtuosi on the violoncello, and were reputed in Italy the first masters of their instrument.

Filippo Lolli, son of the violin virtuoso, Antonio Lolli, was born at Stuttgard, in 1773; practised the cello from early youth, and at eighteen years of age made a concert tour, which led him to Berlin. Here he was heard by the King, who was so pleased with his performance that he recognised it by an honorarium of 100 louis d'or. Lolli then went to Copenhagen, and in the year 1804 played at concerts in Vienna. There is no more information about him extant.

Of Sandonati, Gerber says that he lived in Verona in 1800, and was one of the most renowned violoncellists of those times. Gerber announces the same of the Mantuan, Shevioni, who worked about the same time apparently in Verona.

While all these men were endeavouring to make an advance in violoncello playing, and especially in violoncello compositions, the Italian nation possessed in Boccherini an artist who surpassed in every direction his countrymen.

Luigi Boccherini, the son of a contra-basso player, was born on February 19, 1743, at Lucca. He there received his first musical instruction from the archbishop's choirmaster, Vanucci. Besides the cultivation of theory, he devoted himself with peculiar zeal to cello playing, of which he was to prove a master. The very promising progress which he made decided his father to send him to Rome for the further prosecution of his studies, and where his talents attained their full development.

When Boccherini, after the course of a few years, returned to his native town, he found there Tartini's pupil, Filippo Manfredini, his countryman, who was an excellent violinist. He soon formed an intimate friendship with him, which led to an arrangement for making a concert tour. The two artists went to Spain, afterwards to Piedmont, to Lombardy, and the South of France. The favourable reception which the friends experienced encouraged them about 1768 to proceed to Paris. In the French capital they had a splendid success. The compositions of Boccherini gained such great applause that the Parisian music publishers, La Chevardière and Venier, declared themselves ready to undertake the expense of printing all the works already heard. Notwithstanding, he received very little for his compositions, and later on he was not more fortunate.

At the persuasion of the Spanish ambassador in Paris the artists proceeded, at the end of 1768, or the beginning of the next year, to Madrid. Here Boccherini roused the special interest of the Infanta Don Luis, who named him his "Compositore e virtuoso di camera." When this prince died, on August 7, 1785, Boccherini became Court Kapellmeister of King Charles III. of Spain, a post which he also filled under the succeeding king, Charles IV. He received a still further recognition from the King Frederick William II. of Prussia, who designated him his chamber-composer, when he, in the year 1787, dedicated a work to this art-loving monarch, who conferred on him a considerable honorarium. From that time Boccherini dedicated to him everything that he composed. We may conclude that he was adequately remunerated, for when the king died in November, 1797, and the allowance ceased, Boccherini fell into difficulties, his compositions being badly paid by the publishers. At the same time he seems to have lost his place as Kapellmeister to the King of Spain. However it was, he spent the last years of his life with his family in great need, from which death only released him on May 28, 1805.

Having in view the great quantity of his compositions, Boccherini must be distinguished as an extremely prolific

composer. There are in existence 400 instrumental works by
him. They consist of 20 symphonies, 125 string quartets—
amongst them are 113 for two cellos, of which the first cello
is more or less an obbligato—91 string quartets, and numberless
trios, septets, quintets with flute or oboe, violin sonatas, as
well as several vocal compositions for the church, &c.
Very little has proved capable of surviving, and this little only
awakens a limited interest. The cause of it seems to be in
a certain simplicity which underlies all Boccherini's music.
With great cleverness of form, added to an apt and easy
flow, it is certainly not wanting in originality, which has
even a humorous tendency ; but the manner of expression is
characterised by a certain formality which gives to Boccherini's
music an antiquated air. His ideas are wanting in power of
thought and depth of feeling; they rarely rise above the
pleasing and agreeable.

At the beginning of the century the chamber compositions
of Boccherini had an extraordinary popularity, especially
amongst the *dilettanti*. From that time, however, they
have been little played, at least in Germany. The interest
in them was maintained much longer in France, where they
were unusually prized, according to Fétis's " Biographie
Universelle des Musiciens." There also they have been
for some time laid on one side.

Boccherini composed six concerti specially for the violoncello. There are also extant several cello sonatas with bass
by him. It is surprising that there is no mention made of
them in the list of Boccherini compositions by Fétis. Six of
these sonatas have been republished on the one hand by
Fredrich Grützmacher, and, on the other, by Alfred Piatti, with
piano accompaniment. The violoncello concerti of Boccherini,
on the contrary, have fallen almost entirely into oblivion.
They are only so far interesting in that by them is shown to
what degree of technique cello playing was developed by this
master. We must here observe that he was one of
the first of the Italian school who gave decided expression to
the solo and virtuoso side of his instrument. He not only
made possible for cello music the higher and highest parts of
the thumb position, with the exception of the complicated
harmonics first discovered and made available after his time,

but he also considerably extended beyond his predecessors the playing of double stops as well as the execution of passages.[1]

If in form they were somewhat superficially elaborate and worked out after the manner of studies, yet instructive material for practice of an extent and variety hitherto unknown was provided for cellists. For Italy it was a sensible loss that Boccherini spent the greater part of his life abroad, his native land was in consequence deprived of the advantage which the personal influence and example of his strikingly artistic proficiency might have gained. If he had remained there he would, doubtless, have been to his countrymen as regards cello playing what Corelli and Tartini were to Italian violin playing. But under the prevailing conditions Italy lacked a recognised musician who might have been the means of further successfully developing that branch of art. Moreover, the decided preference of the Italians for opera from the end of the last century, which prevailed to the cost of all other musical efforts, checked for a time further impulse to or demand for the cultivation of stringed instrument playing, which until then had been so successfully pursued on the Apennine Peninsula. What, however, Italy's sons attained in the art of violoncello playing was not lost, but was further perfected by German and French masters, concerning which the following sections will give the necessary explanation.

II.—GERMANY.

The Violoncello had already found its place as an orchestral instrument about the year 1680 at Vienna, and in 1709, in the Dresden Royal orchestra, as we saw. Towards 1720 it had penetrated also into Northern Germany, since the band of the Duke of Holstein Gottorp evidently possessed one. At the same period this stringed instrument must have been extensively used in other parts of Germany—otherwise Joh. Seb. Bach would scarcely have conceived the idea of composing for it his solo sonatas, which were already extant between the

---

[1] "That which renders Boccherini's compositions unlike all others of the kind is that he commonly assigns the principal part to the first violoncello."—(Tr.)

years 1717—1724. There were even at that time two German violoncellists who appeared to Gerber of sufficient importance for him to give them a place in his Dictionary of Music. Their names are : Triemer and Riedel.

JOHANN SEBALD TRIEMER was born at the end of the seventeenth or the beginning of the eighteenth century, in Weimar, where he was instructed in instrumental playing by the Ducal Chamberlain and Musician, Eylenstein, and in the theory of music by Ehrbach, an old musician of Weimar. As soon as Triemer had made progress sufficient to figure as a soloist, he undertook a concert tour which led him to Hamburg, for, in 1725, he was a member of the theatre orchestra there. Two years after he went to Paris, and remained until 1729. During this time he pursued the study of composition under the direction of Boismortier.[1] He then went to the Dutch city of Alkmaar, and, later on, to Amsterdam, where he died in 1762. At Amsterdam he had six " Sonate a Violoncello solo e continuo " published.

The Silesian, RIEDEL, was not only a cellist, but also chief of the Fencing School at Liegnitz. He must have been a very good player for his time. About 1727 he went to St. Petersburg, and was there the instructor of the EMPEROR PETER II. (who, as is known, only reigned three years—1727-1730), both in cello playing and in fencing.

Riedel was also member of the Russian Court band, where he still was in 1740.

The number of German violoncello players very soon increased. Amongst them, Werner must next be mentioned, born at the beginning of the eighteenth century in Bohemia, and died in Prague, 1768. He must have been a most excellent player, since, as Gerber says, in his time no foreign cellist ventured to play in Prague. Werner was for some time established at the Crusaders' Church, in Prague. Of his numberless concertos and solos for violoncello, none seem to have been printed.

The violoncellist, CASPAR CRISTELLI, born in Vienna at the beginning of the eighteenth century, was, in 1757, chief

---

[1] Fétis mentions him as a mediocre composer. He was born at Perpignan in 1691, and died in Paris in 1765.

composer in the service of the Archbishop of Salzburg. He specially distinguished himself as an accompanist, a talent at that time highly prized, for the cellists who accompanied the vocal recitatives played an important part. Cristelli also wrote several compositions for his instrument.

JOHANN BAPTIST BAUMGÄRTNER, born 1723, in Augsburg, died May 18, 1782, at Eichstädt, as chamber virtuoso of the Prince Bishop, was educated in Munich, and then made a concert tour through Germany, England, Holland, and Scandinavia. Besides some violoncello concertos he wrote: "Instruction de musique théoretique et pratique à l'usage de violoncelle." This instruction book appeared in 1774 or 1777, at the Hague.

WENZEL HIMMELBAUER, born 1725, in Bohemia, was in Prague in 1764; went, however, to Vienna, and had a good reputation as cellist. His playing was chiefly famed for firmness of the bow stroke and quickness at sight reading. C. F. Daniel Schubart remarks of him in his "Ideen zu einer Aesthetik der Tonkunst": "He was a sincere and a most agreeable violoncellist, without any artistic pride; a man of the most upright and amiable heart"; and he further remarks: "No one uses his bow so quietly and easily as this master. He executes the most difficult passages with the most extraordinary ease, and especially pours out his heart in the *Cantabile*. His sweet expression, his delightful phrasing, and, moreover, his great power in the middle tints are the wonder of all connoisseurs and hearers." He composed little for his instrument, but this little has all the more intrinsic value.

Of Himmelbauer's compositions there appeared at Lyons, 1776, as Op. 1, duets for flute or violin and violoncello. A few duets for two violoncellos remained unpublished. The MS. was, in 1795, in the possession of the Bohemian cellist, Emeric Patrzik, and later fell into the hands of the author of "The Art Lexicon for Bohemia," G. J. Dlabacz.

PHILIPP SCHINDLÖKER must be mentioned as a noteworthy pupil of Himmelbauer's. Born on October 25, 1753, at Mons, in Hennegau, he went very young to Vienna, whither his parents betook themselves. There he began the study of the violoncello. In 1795 he was appointed solo violoncellist at the Royal Opera House, Vienna, and three years later to the orchestra of the Cathedral, S. Stephan. In the year 1806 he received the title of Imperial Chamber Virtuoso. He died April 16, 1827. Sixteen years previously he had already retired into private life. Of his compositions only a serenade for the Violoncello and Guitar was published. The rest, consisting of a Concerto, Sonatas with bass accompaniment, and a Rondo also with bass accompaniment, remained unpublished.

His nephew, WOLFGANG SCHINDLÖKER, born in 1789 at Vienna, was educated by him as a clever cellist. After he had been heard at fourteen years of age at a concert, he went in 1807 as chamber musician into the service of the Court at Würzburg. His compositions consisted of a "Grand duo" and three Duets, which were published.

FRANZ JOSEPH WEIGL belonged to the best German cellists of the last century ; he was the father of the opera composer, Joseph Weigl, formerly in much repute. He was born on March 19, 1740, in a Bavarian village, and through the special recommendation of Joseph Haydn was received on June 1, 1761, into the orchestra of Count Esterhazy. In 1769 he left and joined the orchestra of the Italian opera in Vienna. After three years of active work there he was appointed to the Imperial band, and made Court and Chamber musician ; his death took place on January 25, 1820. Weigl composed, but if for his own instrument is unknown.

ANTON FILTZ, a member of the Electoral Chapel at Mannheim, was a gifted cellist and composer. He died in 1768 in early manhood, before his talent had fully developed. He left in MS. several duets and solos, as well as Concertos for the Violoncello.

JOH. GEORG SCHETKY, born 1740, at Darmstadt, deserves special mention as a pupil of Filtz, whose instruction he enjoyed for one month, after his father, who was Secretary to the Grand Duke of Darmstadt and tenor singer at the Cathedral, had given him his first musical education. He seems to have taken up cello playing by himself at first, but his theoretical education was carried on by the Concertmaster Enderle. In the year 1761 Schetky went for six months with his father and two sisters to Hamburg. There he had the opportunity of hearing great artists, which incited him to zealous study on his instrument. On his return to Darmstadt he found a post in the orchestra there. Now and then he performed at concerts in the neighbouring towns. After the death of his parents he finally quitted Darmstadt in 1768. He visited Hamburg and then London, where the patronage of Joh. Christoph Bach was of service to him. Schetky did not however remain long in the English capital, as he received a proposal to go to Edinburgh, which he accepted. He very soon, in consequence of his marriage with a rich widow, retired into private life, being known to fame only through his compositions. These, taking no account of an important collection of various orchestral and chamber music works, consist of numberless Violoncello Concertos, Duets for Violin and Violoncello, Sonatas for Violoncello and Bass, and "Twelve Duets for two Violoncellos, with some Observations and Rules for playing that Instrument" (Op. 7). In these duets, as the title says : " Schetky had a scholastic aim in view." Yet they can scarcely be called a violoncello school.

One of the last of Schetky's published works is his Op. 13, which contains six Sonatas for Violoncello with unfigured bass. The compositions therein contained give a distinct idea of his fluent though superficially mechanical manner of writing. It can readily be discerned that Schetky had for the time in which he lived a remarkable technique in playing. He must have been able with ease to play at sight the first violin part in Quartets, a talent which proves at once his skill and readiness. His power and agility in bowing as well as his staccato playing in up and down strokes were famous.

According to Gerber's account, Schetky died in Edinburgh in 1773. In Forster's "History of the Violin" it is said, on the contrary, that his death took place only in 1824.[1]

As a " clever and solid concert player and composer for his

---

[1] The sketch of Schetky contained in Forster's "History of the Violin," deviates substantially from Gerber's information, which I have followed. Forster says that this artist studied jurisprudence at Jena and, under Frederick the Great, followed as a volunteer the forces commanded by Blucher in the seven years' war. Then he also mentions his being a pupil of Philip Em. Bach. Whether this statement have any real foundation, and to what extent, must remain undetermined.

instrument," MARKUS HEINRICH GRAUL, who was born in the first half of the last century, is mentioned by Gerber. In the year 1766 he belonged to the Royal orchestra at Berlin. He also composed pieces for the cello, but did not publish them.

His pupil, JOH. HEINRICH VIKTOR ROSE, born on December 7, 1743, at Quedlinburg, was early instructed to play on various instruments by his father, who was town musician in the above-named place. The Princess Amalie, who then filled the office of Abbess in the Quedlinburg Convent, became interested in him, and took him with her to Berlin in 1756, where he studied cello playing for some years under Graul and Mara. In 1763 he entered the service of the Prince of Anhalt-Bernberg. Four years later he relinquished that in order to travel, and accepted a place in the band of the Duke of Dessau. He did not long remain there, for in the year 1772 he accepted an offer to be organist at the place of his birth. According to Gerber's account he possessed not only an extraordinary readiness on the violoncello, but also a most expressive, graceful rendering. Of his compositions, there were three solos with bass accompaniment published as Op. 1.

His best pupil was FRIEDRICH SHRÖDEL, born on February 4, 1754, in Baruth; died January 10, 1800, at Ballenstedt. Gerber calls him one of the greatest masters on the violoncello of that period, and adds that many were of opinion that he surpassed the famous Mara in precision and delicacy.

JOHANN JÄGER must be noticed with special distinction as belonging to the German cellists of the last century. Schubart, who must have known him personally, says in his eccentric manner : " Jäger is quite original; his bowing new, unconstrained, and impetuously fiery. All masters apply the thumb to the D string, and so bring out the high passages; but Jäger departs entirely from this method—a proof that his genius has more than one way of attaining his aim. He goes with lightning dexterity up to the D and A strings in the highest parts and brings out the most delicate phrases with the greatest tenderness and sweetness. . . . Jäger is also a great reader, *prima vista*—that is, he can play from the music at sight the most difficult pieces with wonderful art."

In regard to the Jäger Violoncello compositions, which altogether remained unpublished, Schubart remarks : " He follows no rules in composition, but is guided solely by his ear. His Concertos and Sonatas consist chiefly of original themes, which are grand, noble, adapted to the instrument, and full of difficulties. Jäger caused his pieces to be revised by good musicians, whereby they were put into correct form. At the same time it must be confessed that the superfluous boughs, the offspring often of an unbridled fancy, have not all been pruned off."

As Jäger's compositions are not extant there is no possibility of putting to the proof the justice of Schubart's judgment.

We can only gather that Jäger was self-taught. He appears to have been so even as a player. There is nowhere any intimation that he had any regular instruction on the violoncello. Gerber makes only the remark that Jäger became, under the influence of the Kapellmeister at Würtemburg, " the great man " whom the world admired.

As Fétis informs us, Jäger was born on August 17, 1748, in the little town of Schlitz.[1] He was originally oboe player in the service of Holland. He cultivated at first as his favourite instrument the French horn. After he had been actively engaged at the Court of Stuttgard, the post of chamber virtuoso in the Anspach Bayreuth orchestra fell to his lot. The position left him a great deal of spare time, so that he was able to practise diligently the violoncello, and also to undertake concert tours, which led him to London in 1781.

Jäger had two sons who were educated as violoncellists under his direction. The elder, JOHANN ZACHARIAS LEONHARD, born 1777, at Anspach, showed an early development and was able, even at nine years of age, to execute solos with rapidity, certainty, and accuracy. In 1787 he played at the Prussian Court, and on that occasion so greatly excited the admiration of the Queen that she wished to acquire him for the Royal band in Berlin, to which, however, the father of the boy would not yield on account of his youth. The Queen, therefore, proved her interest in him by granting him a life-long pension of 100 thalers. On his return home the Margrave of Anspach appointed him his chamber musician.

---

[1] Gerber gives 1745 as the year of Jäger's birth, and Lauterbach in Upper Hesse as the place.

He did not, however, remain long in this position, and went with his father to Breslaw. There Jäger's younger son was born, whose christian name was Ernst. He possessed even more talent than his brother, for it was not long before he overtook him in cello playing, to which the instructions he received from Bernhard Romberg greatly contributed. Until the year 1825 he lived at Breslaw, after having travelled through a great part of Germany and Hungary. Then he responded to a summons from the Bavarian Court to go as solo cellist to Munich.

Besides his two sons, Johann Jäger educated also ALEXANDER UBER, born at Breslaw, 1783, as a capable violoncellist. His father, by profession a solicitor, was an enthusiastic lover of music, occupied his leisure hours with the composition of chamber music, and instituted weekly two concerts in his house. At one of them symphonies were produced, at the other quartets and quintets. At the beginning of our century, Carl Maria v. Weber, who began his career at the Breslaw Theatre, took part in these musical entertainments, as did also the Director of music in the University at Berne and the piano player Klingohr. The intercourse with these men was not of less importance for the musical development of young Uber than his musical life in his father's house. At first he enjoyed the violin instruction of Jannizeck, while Schnabel conducted his theoretical studies. But he very soon took up the violoncello, for which Jäger was his teacher. In the year 1804 he undertook his first tour, but returned soon to Breslaw. In the course of time Uber filled many positions as Kapellmeister, until about 1820 he settled at Basle, where he was married. In 1823 he undertook the post of Conductor with the Count of Schönaich and Prince von Karolath, but, in the following year, death carried him off. Of his compositions for the violoncello, Uber published a Concerto (Op. 12), Variations with Quartet accompaniment (Op. 14), Six Caprices (Op. 10), and Sixteen Variations upon a German air.

During the second half of the last century the art of violoncello playing had already very extensively spread throughout Germany and had many more noteworthy representatives than in Italy and France. In the latter country the higher pursuit of music was confined chiefly to Paris, and in Italy, as we have already remarked in a previous paragraph, the opera was most decidedly in the foreground, while there was no great demand for instrumental music. On the contrary, Germany called out more instrumental vigour in order to satisfy the need of good musicians for the numberless Courts. According to Gottlieb Friedrich Krebel's European genealogical handbook of the year 1770, there were, including the Romaic-German Emperor and the King of Prussia, over two hundred secular and spiritual princes and sovereign counts, the greater number of whom supported Kapelle (bands) or at least chamber music. These persons considered it of utmost importance to have about them not only good violin and wind instrument players, but also capable violoncellists, and consequently more talented young men devoted themselves in Germany to instrumental music, and especially to violoncello playing, than elsewhere.

We have already seen that the introduction of the Violoncello from Italy to Germany was by way of Vienna. At least, up to the present time, there are no proofs that the appreciation of this instrument and its reception into the orchestra had taken place sooner in other German places than in the Austrian capital. There was an eager demand for music from the reign of Maximilian I., to which the musical inclinations of the Imperial family contributed. Maximilian II., Ferdinand III., Leopold I., Charles VI., Francis I., and Joseph II., each in his own way, presented to the inhabitants of Vienna a good example as regarded the encouragement of music. Already several decades before the birth of the last-mentioned prince, who himself played the violoncello, this instrument had been naturalised in Vienna as an orchestral instrument. Under his reign, after the advent of Franciscello, whose performances gave an impulse to emulation, Vienna was already in possession of some remarkable solo cellists. To them belong the two SCHINDLÖXERS and JOSEPH WEIGL, who have already been mentioned, as well as JOHANN HOFFMANN, member of the Court band, MARTEAU, HAUER, and KÜFFEL;[1] somewhat

---

[1] Ed. Hanslick : " History of Concert Life in Vienna," p. 115.

later followed the cellists CAJETAN, GOTTLIEB, SCHEIDL, and HAUSCHKA.

Nothing is known concerning Scheidl. We have more information regarding VINCENZ HAUSCHKA, who was born on January 21, 1766, at Mies, in Bohemia, and died in Vienna, 1840. He received his first musical education as choirboy in the Prague Cathedral. After six years' study he devoted himself to violoncello playing, in which the Bohemian, Christ, instructed him for a short time. He eventually studied independently. At sixteen he had made such progress that he found a place in the Kapelle of Count Thun. Two years later he was released from this engagement by the death of his benefactor. Hauschka then undertook a tour in Germany. In 1792 he appeared in Vienna, where he gained everywhere applause by his performances. Later, a situation was offered to him in the Imperial State service. From that time he made no professional use of his art. But he did not quite abandon it, as he took part in the foundation of the " Society of the Friends of Music," or " Gesellschaft der Musikfreunde," as well as the " Concert Spirituel," and was occupied also in both these musical institutions which were of such importance to musical life in Vienna.

The Dresden Kofkapelle possessed, in the second half of the last century, two noteworthy cellists, HEINRICH MEGELIN and CALMUS. The first, according to Gerber's testimony, was counted amongst the cleverest players of his instrument. Calmus belonged, in 1797, to the orchestra of the Altona " National Orchestra," and was then a highly reputed member of the Kofkapelle at Dresden, where he died January, 1809.

In Berlin the violoncello first came to be appreciated at its due value through Frederick William II. It is true it had been already well represented under Frederick the Great, in the Court band, by GRAUL[1] and the two cellists MARA (father and son), to be mentioned elsewhere; but that great monarch, whose favourite instrument was the flute, does not appear to have thought much of the violon-

---

[1] See p. 72.

cello, which he feigned to allude to as the "nasal instrument," an expression which might have been bestowed formerly on the gamba.

His nephew, Frederick William II., liked the violoncello, and well understood how to handle it. He appears to have played the gamba in his younger days, for it is reported that the gambist Hesse[1] first taught him, though this instruction might also have referred to the violoncello, which many gambists took up at the same time. Later on the cellist GRAZIANI was master to the Prussian heir to the throne. But when DUPORT THE ELDER came to Berlin, in 1773, GRAZIANI was dismissed in favour of him. The future king, Frederick William II., must have played with taste and readiness. It is well known that Beethoven dedicated to him his two Cello Sonatas (Op. 5).

Amongst the cellists who belonged to the Berlin Chapel towards the end of the last century must be mentioned—

JOHANN GEORGE FLEISCHMANN, a skilful player, who was at first in the service of the Duke of Courland, but afterwards went to Berlin. In 1792 he followed the king, on his expedition against the French, as his accompanist.

A second cellist, who worked at the same time in the Berlin Kapelle, was S. L. FRIEDEL.

As a pupil of Duport the younger, HEINRICH GROSSE, born at Berlin, is distinguished. In 1798 he joined the Royal band.

The elder Duport[2] educated the cellist O. F. G. HANSMANN, who was born at Potsdam on May 30, 1769, and was engaged at fifteen years of age in the Berlin Kapelle. In 1790 he undertook the post of Choir-director at the opera. He appears to have quite given up his work as Kapellmeister when, in 1809, the place of Organist at the Church of St. Peter, at Berlin, was given to him. He continued in the service of the church until the year 1833, when he was appointed Royal Accountant. Three years later, on May 4, 1836, death called him away.

Finally, the Berlin Kapelle possessed, in HERBIG, a pupil of the younger Mara.

---

[1] See p. 28.
[2] Concerning the brothers Duport, see the following section.

At the Court of Mecklenberg, in 1785, FRANZ XAVER HUBER, born in the little Bavarian town of Öttingen, was working as a much esteemed violoncellist.

In the Brunswick Kapelle was A. W. F. MATERN, after the middle of the last century a player of some repute, who brought up his two sons as cellists.

Hanover was represented by the brothers FRIEDRICH ERNST and PHILIPP FRIEDRICH BENEKE. Both belonged to the Elector's Court and Chamber Music Society.

The Hofkapelle at Dessau possessed, in JOH. CHRISTOPH BISCHOFF, born in 1748 at Erfurt, a very fair violoncellist.

As one of the most creditable cellists of the second half of the last century, JOH. CONRAD SCHLICK must be mentioned. He is said to have been born at Münster in 1759, and died at Gotha in 1825, where he was established for more than forty years with the title of Concertmaster of the Ducal band, after he had, about 1776, belonged to the Episcopal Chapel at Münster. In the year 1785 he married the very celebrated violin virtuoso, Regina Strinasacchi, with whom he was engaged, in the winter of 1799-1800, as solo player at the Leipsic Gewandhaus.

Schlick had a gifted pupil in J. G. HEMMERLEIN, born at Bamberg, who held the post of Concertmaster to the Elector Bishop of Fulda at the end of last century.

At the same time with Schlick, JOHANN DAVID SCHEIDLER, born in 1748, died on October 20, 1802, was employed as a much-liked violoncellist in the Gotha Kapelle.

The Ducal band of Meiningen also possessed a good violoncellist. It was J. J. KRIEGCK, originally violinist and member of the Flemish Opera at Amsterdam. During his residence in Paris he took up the violoncello, and received there instruction from the younger Duport. After he had studied for awhile under this artist he was engaged by Prince Laval Montmorency, in whose service he remained four years, when he was summoned to Meiningen. There he worked and was still living in the year 1810. Kriegck was born on June 25, 1750, at Bibra, in the neighbourhood of Eckertsberga, in the district of Merseberg. His cello compositions, consisting of three Concertos and some Sonatas with bass, are among the best of that period.

The violoncellist HIZELBERGER was, in 1786, in the service of the Bishop of Würzburg as chamber musician.

At the Court of Wallenstein, about 1790, PAUL WINNEBERGER was engaged as Director of the Royal Hunt and Table Music. In the year 1800 he exchanged this post for that of cellist and composer to the French Theatre at Hamburg.

In the Thurn-and-Taxis Kapelle at Regensburg were two cellists, GRETSCH and KARAUSCHEK. The first was there until his death, which occurred in 1784. Karauschek, on the contrary, who was famous as an excellent cellist, only belonged to it from 1750-1760. Religious fanaticism caused him later to go into a Carmelite cloister. He died in 1789.

To the Munich Court music, in the second half of the last century, belonged VIRGILI.[1] He is remarkable as having given his first instruction to the violoncellist MORALT. This last artist, who was born in the Bavarian capital in 1780, and died in 1829, finished his training under the violoncellist ANTON SCHWARZ, of Mannheim, and, having completed his studies, went into the Hofkapelle of his native city.

Another pupil of Anton Schwarz whose name is well known was MAX BOHRER, born at Munich in 1785. He made such progress, that already as a boy of fourteen years of age he entered the Hofkapelle there. Soon after he undertook a concert tour with his brother Anton, who was an able violinist, and this led him to Vienna. There he heard Bernhard Romberg, who henceforth became his model. Towards 1830, after he had for a time been a member of the Royal band at Berlin, he went to Paris, where his fine tone and his ease in surmounting the most difficult passages excited admiration. Then he travelled through Germany, in 1832 was appointed first cellist to the King of Wurtemburg with the title of Concertmeister, went in 1838 (for the second time) to St. Petersburg, and then proceeded to Italy. The years 1842-1843 he spent in America giving concerts. He took his last journey, which led him to the countries of

---

[1] According to Fétis. Gerber says in his "Dictionary of Musicians" that, about the year 1755, a cellist, by name VIRGIL MICHEL, belonged to the orchestra at Munich. Apparently he is identical with the one mentioned by Fétis.

Northern Europe, in 1847, but he was not able to obtain the same amount of approbation, for he had lost a great deal of his power of execution. He died in 1867. He edited three Concertos, several " Airs variés," a " Fantasia " on a Russian Volkslied, a Rondoletto with a quartet accompaniment, and some Duets with violin.

Contemporary with the above-named Moralt in the Bavarian Court Kapelle, " PETER THE GREAT," so-called, according to Gerber, "on account of his talent," born at Zweibrucken, in 1778, was actively engaged, and in 1792 was promoted to be member of the Bavarian Hofkapelle.

For Stuttgard the violoncellists Zumpsteeg and Kaufmann deserve consideration.

JOH. RUDOLPH ZUMPSTEEG was the more important. He was born on January 10, 1760, at Sachsenflur, in the Odenwald, and died on January 27, 1802, at Stuttgard. The royal Kapellmeister Poli (at Wurtemburg) was his teacher. Under his direction Zumpsteeg became not only an excellent performer, but also a creditable composer of music. He received a learned education at the Karlschule, where he entered into friendly relations with Schiller, and set to music many of his poems. He made himself particularly known through ballad compositions, which were first attempted by him.

After he had quitted the Karlschule, Zumpsteeg devoted himself entirely and actively to art. Up to the year 1792 he was simply member of the Stuttgard Court band, of which he became the head after the decease of his master, Poli. Zumpsteeg played the violoncello with " deep feeling, rare precision, and decisive power," as Gerber remarks. He wrote for it a Concerto, Sonatas, a Duet, and a Trio.

JOHANN KAUFMANN, born in 1760, was likewise a pupil at the Karlschule, whence also came—

ERNST HÄUSLER, born in 1761, in Stuttgard. He led a somewhat variable life. In the year 1788 he went on an artistic tour, during which he played especially in Vienna and Berlin. Soon after he took an engagement in the band of the Prince of Donaueschingen. But in 1791 he relinquished this position in order to obey a summons to Zurich. Thence, six years later, he returned to his native town, and in 1801 went to Augsburg, and, in 1802, to Vienna, to hold concerts.

Finally he assumed the office of choir director at the Evangelical Church at Augsburg, in which place he died on February 28, 1837.

The Electoral Kapelle at Mannheim possessed in CARL LOCHNER, born about 1760, died 1795, as well as in PETER RITTER, remarkable cellists. Ritter, born at Mannheim in 1760, must have had higher claims to distinction on account of his musical education than Lochner, for he was promoted to the direction of the opera at the theatre of his birthplace. With the exception of a journey to Berlin, undertaken in the year 1785, where he played before the Court, he seems to have pursued uninterruptedly his official duties.

To the Mannheim orchestra belonged the violoncellists, JOHANN FÜRST, LUDWIG SIMON, and ANTON SCHWARZ, already mentioned.

As an offspring of Mannheim, FRANZ DANZI must also be mentioned, the son of the first violoncellist in the orchestra there, Innocenz Danzi. His father gave him instruction on the cello, and Abt Vogler in composition. He soon made such rapid progress in playing that already, in 1778, he was received into the Electoral Kapelle, which, as is known, was transferred to Munich about this time in consequence of the union of Bavaria with the Palatinate. He immediately began his work as a composer for the opera. Meantime, in the year 1790, he was united in matrimony to the exquisite singer, Margaretha Marchand, daughter of the Opera Director in Munich. The following year the.young couple went to Leipsic and Prague, where Danzi conducted the opera of Guardassoni's Italian Opera Company, while his wife took part as a singer. In 1794-1795 he travelled with his wife in Italy, and in 1797 they both returned to Munich on account of the failing condition of the latter's health. Danzi was immediately appointed Vice-Kapellmeister, and displayed most praiseworthy activity. He was, however, so overcome by the death, in 1799, of the partner of his life, that for many years he seemed unable to perform the duties of his vocation, and as it was repugnant to his feelings to take up work again in the place where his family happiness had been wrecked, he obeyed a summons to Stuttgard as Court Kapellmeister. He there remained a year, at the end of which he assumed the direction of the opera at Carlsruhe. Danzi was born May 15, 1763, and died April 13, 1826.

In the chapel at Mainz, in the year 1783 to 1784, there were the clever cellist and lutist, Joh. Christian Gottlieb Schindler, the brothers Joseph and Andreas Schwachhofer, and at the Court of Treves was also at that time Carl Caspar Eder, born 1751 in Bavaria, who made himself known as a cello player in several tours.

To the Electoral Kapelle at Bonn belonged Joseph Reicha and Maximilian Willman.

Reicha, uncle of the gifted composer, Anton Reicha, was born at Prague in 1746 ; found at first a position with Count Wallenstein, and a few years later received the appointment of Concert leader at Bonn. He was working there with some reputation until his death in 1795.

Willman, born in 1768, at Forchtenberg, a village between Würzburg and Mergentheim, was member of the Bonn Hof-kapelle in the last decade of the past century, after he had been resident for a few years in Vienna. Later on he returned to Vienna and found a post there as solo player at the theatre. Willman, who died in 1812, had two daughters, the elder of whom was a pupil of Mozart for the pianoforte, and the younger an excellent singer. Louis von Beethoven solicited the hand of the latter, but in vain.

Besides Reicha and Willman, the celebrated violoncellist, Bernhard Romberg, belonged to the Kapelle at Bonn from 1790-1793. With regard to this artist the necessary informa-tion will be given in the next section on Germany, for the distinctive influence of his work belongs to the nineteenth century. To the above-mentioned German violoncellists are to be added Immler, Schönebeck, Rauppe, Bauersachs, Alexander, and Arnold.

Immler, born in 1750, at Weitramsdorf, near Coburg, found a sphere for work in Göttingen. His playing was distinguished especially for its fine tone and agreeable manner of rendering. He was also a good violinist.

Karl Siegmund Schönebeck, born on October 26, 1758, at Lübben, in Lower Lusatia, was originally destined for the surgical profession, but felt himself so irresistibly drawn towards music that all attempts to hold him back from it failed through his opposition. In the fourteenth year of his age he was made town musician in his native place. During his fifteenth year he devoted himself, mostly alone, to the learning of various instruments. Then he went as assistant to the town band of the Silesian town of Grüneberg. There he had the opportunity of hearing a travelling violoncellist, whose performances so inspired him that he forthwith resolved to devote himself to cello playing, with which until then he had never occupied himself. He was his own master. After two years of energetic work, Schönebeck went as cellist into the private band of a Count Dohna, though he only remained in it until 1780, preferring to undertake a post which was offered to him as town musician at Sorau. A journey to Berlin procured him the possibility of hearing the violoncello virtuoso Duport, at Potsdam, which incited him to renewed study. Soon after he made, at Dresden, the acquaintance of the French cellist Tricklir,[1] whose playing gave him fresh impulse. From that time Schönebeck led a restless, wandering life, which prevented his attaining to the concentration of his powers. At short intervals he filled, one after the other, positions at the Court of the Duke of Courland, at Sagan; with Count Truchsez, at Waldenberg; and still further at Königsberg. At length, wearied with a musical life, he returned home and devoted himself to husbandry, but did not long persevere with this, and resumed again his artistic career. In the year 1800 he performed at Leipsic, where his pleasing cello compositions, and his playing "with a fine intonation, and rare finish," met with applause, as Gerber remarks.

Joh. Georg Rauppe, born in July, 1762, at Stettin, devoted himself in early youth to cello playing, and under the elder Duport attained to the rank of a master. His studies ended, he travelled through North Germany as well as Denmark and Sweden. In the year 1786 he betook himself to Amsterdam, and there fulfilled the duties of first cellist in the German Opera as well as at concerts. While in that position he died on June 15, 1814. His playing was famed for the beauty and power of his tone, as well as for readiness and purity of rendering.

---

[1] See the next section.

CHRISTIAN FRIEDRICH BAUERSACHS, born on June 4, 1767, at Pegnitz, in the principality of Anspach, was not only unusually clever on the violoncello, but also played the basset-horn with great skill. He travelled through Hungary and Italy, and then also in Germany, giving concerts with good success. Yet he did not succeed in gaining a permanent post. He therefore gave up music as a means of livelihood, and devoted himself to a miner's career. On December 14, 1845, he died at Sömmerda.

JOSEPH ALEXANDER, who, in 1800, lived at Duisburg, and worked there, is worthy of mention on account of two books of Studies, which however are long since obsolete. They consist of a violoncello school, published in 1801, and of an "Air avec xxxvi Variations progressives pour le Violoncelle avec le doigté en différentes clefs, accomp. d'un violon et d'une basse" (1802).

JOHANN GOTTFRIED ARNOLD, born on February 1, 1773, in the Würtemburg town of Niedernhall, died July 26, 1806, at Frankfort-on-the-Main, was the son of a school teacher. He early applied himself to music, and chiefly to the violoncello, so that at eight years of age he attracted notice by his performances. In 1785 his father placed him under the tuition of Lüngelsauer, the town musician. With whom he studied for five years. At the expiration of that time Arnold found employment with his uncle, who was Court and town musician at Wertheim. During this period he pursued, alone, with great zeal, his cello studies, but at the same time did not neglect theoretical study. After some fruitless attempts to make himself known as a soloist beyond his native place, he visited Regensburg, where just then the violoncellist Max Willman, mentioned above, was residing. He gave Arnold, during some few months, instructions on the cello, the first which he had received on this instrument. In the year 1796 he had the opportunity, in Hamburg, of hearing Bernhard Romberg and learning from him. Very soon after Arnold was established in the theatre orchestra at Frankfort. At the same time he gave private lessons. He was esteemed by his contemporaries as a great violoncello virtuoso, whose playing, on account of its "enchanting tone," was excellent, not only in *Allegro*, but also in *Adagio* passages. Amongst the German violoncellists of the last century an amateur deserves mention, who so distinguished himself, that he may properly be counted among the artists of his instrument. It was the PRINCE CHRISTIAN VON WITTGENSTEIN-BERLEBERG. He was born on December 12, 1753, and in his youth occupied himself eagerly with singing and clavier playing. In more advanced years he learnt the violoncello and succeeded so well that he was heard with the greatest applause publicly at a concert in Wetzlar. He maintained towards the end of his life a private band. This patron of art died October 4, 1800.

These distinguished men up to this period, with few exceptions, endeavoured, besides their practical work, to create by their compositions a literature for their instrument. They wrote concertos, sonatas, and works with variations, in considerable numbers.[1] These productions were substantially increased by other musicians who were not cello players.

Before all, the most prominent are PHIL. EMANUEL BACH and JOSEPH HAYDN.

The former composed a Violoncello Concerto, the latter several pieces of the same kind. What a lively interest Haydn, especially, took in the violoncello is proved by the fact that he used it as an obbligato in two of his Symphonies. The first of them (B flat major) appears with the title, " Symphonie Concertante à Violon, Violoncell, Flutte, Hautbois et Basson obligés," as Op. 81 ; the other, called " le Midi," was written in 1761.[2] Therein the violoncello is employed as a solo instrument, chiefly in the Adagio, the close of which ends with an elaborate cadenza for violin and violoncello. The cello part in the above-mentioned "Sinfonie Concertante" contains striking difficulties, especially where it is employed in the higher tones.[3]

---

[1] Fétis has mentioned the greater number of these compositions in the respective articles of his " Biographie Universelle des Musiciens."

[2] It is to be found in Carl Bank's recently published Haydn Symphonies in score. Compare also Pohl's " Haydn Biography," I., 229 and 285.

[3] Recently has come out a Duet (D major) in three movements for violin and violoncello, by J. Haydn, which he must have composed during his residence in London for a certain William Forster. These compositions recall, not only in respect of form, Tartini's manner, so that one is induced to look upon them as Haydn's early work, which he wrote down from memory as a recollection.

Amongst other composers of that period who composed Concertos for the violoncello, we will only mention PAUL WRANITZKY, IGNAZ PLEYEL, FRANZ ANTON HOFMEISTER, FRANZ CHRISTIAN NEUBAUER, LEOPOLD HOFFMANN, and JOHANN LUDWIG WILLING. There were also amateurs who attempted compositions of this kind, such as ERNST LUDWIG GERBER, the author of " The Historical-Biographical Dictionary of Musicians," and CHRISTIAN FERD. DANIEL SCHUBART, who, though he had a musical education, was however really by vocation an author. Further Joh. Geog. Albrechtsberger, Joseph Eybler, F. A. Hoffmeister, C. G. Neubauer, Ignaz Pleyel produced Duets for two violoncellos, violin and cello, or for viola and violoncello. There is also in existence a Cello Sonata with un-figured Bass by the contrabassist Christian Spurni (Spourni), who, born in Mannheim, was, during the years 1763-1770, member of the orchestra of the Italian Opera in Paris, and then of Her Majesty's in London.[1]

The greater number of these compositions, whether emanating from violoncello players or not, are interesting only in so far as from them may be gathered what position German violoncello playing held in the second half of the last century. We have now only to state that the technique at the end of the period mentioned had made great progress, and that Germany, as compared with Italy, even taking into consideration certain cello pieces by Boccherini, was not behindhand. A universally current method for the manipulation of the fingerboard and also for bowing had indeed not yet been attained in either of the two countries. The testing in every way of the executive capabilities of the violoncello naturally followed, as well as discovering the various combinations for playing double stops, the formation of passages and ornaments, and the endeavour to develop and present them in a manner suitable to the nature of the instrument. This tedious work must on the outset have necessarily led to productions in which the question of imagination would not be taken into consideration. In fact, it is with few exceptions of very little value, and as further the figures and runs are antiquated, the compositions in question can awaken no real

---

[1] This has already been mentioned. Page 49.

sympathy. But these trial stages which cello composition had to pass through were necessary in order to arrive at a literature of artistic worth.

III.—FRANCE.

Amongst the first noteworthy French violoncellists the brothers Abbe must be mentioned. They were music masters of the parish church of Agen under their own names of Philipp Pierre and Pierre de Saint Sevin. As such, in conformity with the regulation of that time, they had to wear the "collet" of the Catholic priests over their dress, on account of which they were called shortly Abbé, or l'Abbé. They retained this name, with the addition of "l'Aîné" and "Cadet," after they had given up their posts in Agen and had entered the Paris Opera Orchestra as cellists in 1727.[1] This is all that is known about them.

There is more information extant concerning Berteau.[2] This artist, born at the beginning of the eighteenth century at Valenciennes, was esteemed by his contemporaries as of eminent talent—indeed, as a genius. In his youth he travelled through Germany, and during this time he applied himself with vigour to gamba playing, under the direction of a Bohemian of the name of Kozecz, and acquired great proficiency. However, after he became acquainted with the superiority of the violoncello, and had heard a solo piece for it by Franciscello,[3] according to Fétis, he went over to that instrument. His progress was so remarkable that he was ever without a rival, and was looked upon as a wonder on his return to Paris, for he also performed unusually well on the flageolet, the playing of which had been little developed. In the year 1739 he was heard for the first time at the " Concert Spirituel "[4] in a solo of his own composition, and aroused great enthusiasm. The result was a frequent appearance at these concerts. His chief strength lay in the production of

---

[1] Compare with p. 52 of this book.

[2] His name was written in various ways—viz., Bertaut, Bertault, Bertaud, and Berthaud. The above is the right way.

[3] Franciscello must accordingly have written for the cello.

[4] The " Concert Spirituel," which was the oldest concert institution of the French capital, was founded in the year 1725.

an extraordinary richness of tone. He wrote for the violoncello four Concertos as well as three Sonatas with bass
accompaniment. His death took place in 1756. Berteau was
looked upon as the founder of the French school of violoncello
playing. Fétis asserts as a proof of this that as pupils he
educated CUPIS, JANSON, TILLIÈRE, and the elder of the
brothers DUPORT, who were the propagators of his beautiful
tone as well as his melodious manner of rendering.

JEAN BAPTIST CUPIS, born in 1741, in Paris, received his
first lessons from his father, and in his eleventh year became
Berteau's pupil. Before he had passed the second decade of
his life he was already esteemed as one of the cleverest
cellists in France. He was soon received into the Opera
Orchestra in Paris, and, indeed, with the distinction that he
was associated with those members of it who had to accompany
the solo singers.

In the year 1771 he gave up his connection with the opera
in order to undertake some concert tours. He visited a great
part of Germany, remained some time in Hamburg, and then
went to Paris and Italy, where he married the songstress
Gasparini. In 1794 he was in Milan. From that time
nothing more is known about him. The requisite information
concerning his pupils, Jean Henri Levasseur and Bréval, will
be given farther on.

Cupis composed two Concertos and a couple of pieces with
variations, of which the second, for two violoncellos, appeared
only as a "Posthumous work" after his death. Besides these,
he wrote a violoncello school. It bears the title "Méthode
nouvelle et raisonnée pour apprendre à jour du violoncelle, où
l'on traite de son accord, de la manière de tenir cet
instrument avec aisance, de celle de tenir l'archet, de
la position de la main sur la touche, du tact, de l'étendue du
manche, de la manière de doigter dans tous les tons majeurs et
mineurs, etc. Paris, Boyer."

Berteau's second pupil, JEAN BAPTISTE AIMÉ JOSEPH JANSON,
was born at Valenciennes in 1742. At twenty-four he was
heard for the first time as solo-player at the "Concert
Spirituel." In 1767 he went as accompanist to the heir-
apparent of Brunswick to Italy, and remained there till 1771.
He then returned for a few years to Paris, after which he

travelled in Germany. From Hamburg, where he remained until 1783, he visited Denmark, Sweden, and Poland. He everywhere reaped great applause for his performances, which were distinguished for their broad and fine tone. In the year 1789 he again found himself in Paris. The value that was set upon his playing there is proved by his being offered the post of teacher of the violoncello at the Conservatoire, which was founded in the year 1795. He died September 2, 1803. Of his violoncello compositions, Fétis mentions three Concertos (Op. 3), three Concertos (Op. 7), both with a bass; six Concertos with orchestra (Op. 15), and six Sonatas with bass (Op. 4).

Janson had a younger brother, whose Christian names were LOUIS AUGUSTE JOSEPH, whom he instructed as a skilful cellist, after his father had prepared him for it. In 1789 he was given a place in the Parisian Orchestra, which he held till 1815. He died a few years later. He was born on July 8, 1749. He only published six Sonatas for the violoncello with bass.

JOSEPH BONAVENTURE TILLIÈRE, of whom neither the day of birth nor death is known, was about 1760 in the service of the Prince de Conti, after he had finished his studies under Berteau. He had the reputation of being a clever player. His published works consist of six Sonatas for violoncello and bass, nine Duets for two violoncellos, of which three appeared as Op. 8, and also of a violoncello school, published in 1764 : "Méthode pour le Violoncelle, contenant les principes nécessaires pour bien jouer de cet instrument." This work appeared in several editions.

Berteau's best pupil was JEAN PIERRE DUPORT, called the elder,[1] whose father was a dancing master. He was born in Paris, November 27, 1741. He was heard at twenty years of age, with unanimous applause, in the "Concert Spirituel." At the same time (1761) he was appointed one of the private musicians of the Prince de Conti. He gave up the post in 1769 in order to travel. He first went to England, two years later he visited Spain, and in 1773 he went to Berlin, where he remained, as Frederick the Great engaged him for his chamber musician as well as for the opera. He was at the same time teacher to the future King Frederick William II.,

---

[1] Compare pp. 77 and 83 of this book.

who named him in 1787 superintendent of chamber music. From that time Duport no longer worked in the Opera, but only played at Court. On December 31, 1818, he died at Berlin. Duport published, in 1787,[1] at Berlin, six Sonatas for violoncello and bass, as well as three Duets for two violoncellos, known as Op. 1.

Gerber, who had the opportunity of hearing this artist in 1793, in Berlin, gives an enthusiastic account of his playing. He especially commended his strong, full tone, and his powerful bowing. According to Fétis, however, his younger brother, JEAN LOUIS, surpassed him, and he seems to have been remarkably gifted. He had at first chosen the violin as his instrument, but took up by preference the violoncello, when he saw the artistic success of his brother, whose pupil he became. He very soon acquired considerable reputation by his appearance at the " Concert Spirituel " and at the " Société Olympique," formerly known under the name of "Concerts des Amateurs"; and also by his connection with the house of Baron Bagge, so much frequented at that time by native and foreign artists of note.

When Viotti came to Paris, either at the end of 1781 or the beginning of 1782, and Duport heard him, he took his characteristic style of playing as his model, and his performances gained considerably thereby. He undertook his first concert tour to London in company with the English cellist, Crosdill, who was connected with him, and he there met with a most animated reception. This journey kept him six months away from Paris. But he did not remain then long at home. The ominous events which, in 1789, preceded the Revolution caused him, like a great many others, to fly from Paris. He betook himself to his brother in Berlin, where he soon found employment in the Royal orchestra, to which he was attached for seventeen years. During this time he had many pupils, whose names unfortunately are unknown. His pupils of French nationality—Rousseau, Levasseur, and Platel—will be noticed later.

The events of 1806, so unfortunate for Prussia, obliged Duport to leave Berlin. He returned again to Paris. But

---

[1] Fétis says 1788. The title-page, however, of this Sonata bears the date 1787, by the engraver's own hand.

during his long absence he had been forgotten, and he had to gain for himself another public.

A single public appearance in the year 1807, in which he was supported by the assistance of the singer, Colbran, Rossini's future wife, was sufficient for this. He could not, however, attain to any certain or decided position again by reason of the entire change of circumstances little favourable to Art in Paris. This obliged him to enter the service of Charles IV. of Spain, who had been dispossessed by Bonaparte, and who was then at Marseilles. But this connection came to an end in 1812, when Charles IV. went to Rome, and Duport consequently was obliged to return to Paris. He took part in three concerts, and in spite of his advanced age of sixty-five years, had so great a success that he was named solo cellist to the Emperor and teacher at the Conservatoire. He lost the latter post on the re-organization of the above-named Institution in the year 1816. He remained, however, in his position at Court, which meantime had been changed from an imperial to a monarchical one. But only three years after he succumbed to a liver attack, on September 7, 1819. He was born on October 4, 1749.

Louis Duport was the author of a tolerable number of cello compositions. They consist of four books of Sonatas with bass accompaniment, three Duets for two violoncellos, and eight "Airs Variés" with orchestra or quartet accompaniment. Besides these he composed, in connection with Bochsa, nine Nocturnes for harp and violoncello, a "Fantasie" for piano and violoncello in conjunction with Rigel, and a Romance with piano accompaniment. As his *chef d'œuvre* must be distinguished: "Essai sur le doigter du violoncelle et la conduite de l'archet, dédie aux professeurs de violoncelle." This comprehensive instruction book, for which the materials were collected by degrees during a long period of years, was published by Duport during his residences in Berlin and Potsdam. In the preface he says: "I have treated with minute detail the subject of double-stops, and this I have done for two reasons: the first is that until now nothing concerning them has been written,[1] and they are so important for a good player; the

---

[1] This must not be taken word for word, for Corrette, in his violoncello school, gives directions with regard to double stopping, though very insufficient.

second, because they have so often served me as an argument, for without an established mode of fingering, double notes are impossible. In the course of this work things will be met with of which the performance is difficult, but nothing will be presented which is really impracticable. I am not writing a useless theory. I have put down no scales, no figures, no passagès, no exercises, without having repeatedly tried them myself. I caused them to be repeatedly played by my brother, who was formerly my master, and will ever remain so, as well as by the best of my pupils in Berlin and Potsdam. I am therefore thoroughly convinced that the work contains nothing that may not with ease be clearly and distinctly carried out, and what at first appears impracticable will be practicable for those who will give themselves continuous trouble, and make a point of practising a regular course of fingering.''

It is evident that Duport devoted himself with the greatest care to the working out of his book of instruction (which must be accounted a violoncello school) in order to bring about distinctness in the finger technique, not until then fully settled. For that time it was a meritorious undertaking. A new edition of it, brought out by the violoncellist, A. Lindner, is a proof that the work, in spite of its age, is not quite without value. It is only to be regretted that the original text has not throughout been faithfully adhered to, and that in parts it has been suppressed. The editor should have reproduced the work in its original form, and have enunciated his own dissenting opinions in observations.

Of more value for our present purpose than Duport's work just mentioned are his Twenty-one "Exercices," which contain much that is worthy of consideration and of acquisition. Duport left a son who, for a long time, belonged to the orchestra at Lyons, but then opened a piano manufactory in Paris. The splendid Stradivari cello, which he inherited from his father, he disposed of to the violoncello virtuoso, Franchomme, for 25,000 francs.

Amongst Duport's pupils, FREDERICK ROUSSEAU, born January 11, 1755, at Versailles, must be mentioned. He was member of the Parisian Opera Orchestra in 1787. In 1812 he retired from his position and established a music school in his native town. He was of special importance in the musical life of Paris as having been one of the founders of the Concert Institute of the "Rue de Cléry," formerly so popular. Amongst his compositions he published six "Duos concertants" (Op. 3 and 4) as well as a "Potpourri" for two violoncellos.

Taking up the chronological thread from Berteau, we have next to mention the cellist CHARLES HENRI BLAINVILLE, who was born in a village near Tours, in the year 1711, and died in Paris, in 1769. The intimate circumstances relating to his life are unknown. Only so far is certain, that he enjoyed the protection of the Marquise de Villeroy, who received musical instruction from him, and that apparently through the influence of this lady he obtained the position of a creditable "Maître de Musique" in Paris. Blainville published several theoretical works and a few compositions, amongst them two Symphonies, but nothing for his own instrument.

The cellist NOCHEZ, born between 1720 and 1730, is known as a pupil of Cervetto and Abaco.[1] In his early years he travelled in Italy and was then member of the comic opera in Paris, from which he went to the orchestra of the grand Opéra in 1749. In 1763 he received the appointment of royal chamber musician. He died in 1800 after a year spent in retirement. Nochez is the author of an article on the violoncello which appeared in print in de La Borde's "Essai sur la musique ancienne et moderne" (Paris, 1780).

Concerning the violoncellist EDOUARD, only the following notice is found in Gerber: "A violoncellist living in Paris, in 1737, was an extraordinary artist on his instrument, and was much commended by Telemann" (Ehrenpforte, 367).

CLAUDE DOMERGUE, born at Beaucaire in 1734, seems to have been remarkable among French violoncellists, although he never left his home. That Duport, when he was travelling in the South of France, stopped at Beaucaire solely in order to make Domergue's acquaintance is sufficient proof of his unusual skill in execution. During the disturbances of the

---

[1] See pp. 51 and 54 this book.

Revolution he unhappily ended his days, with thirty of his fellow citizens, on the scaffold, in 1794.

To the Paris Opera orchestra belonged FRANÇOIS JOSEPH GIRAUD, the violoncellist, from 1752-1767. Besides this he was chamber musician. He wrote a volume of Sonatas for his instrument. Further, he occupied himself with vocal composition, and also wrote for the stage.

The next to be mentioned is JEAN TRICKLIR, already named, of German extraction, born at Dijon in 1750, who passed only his youth in France. Destined by his parents for the church, he went to the seminary of his birthplace. In his leisure hours he occupied himself with cello playing. His partiality for it increased by degrees as he advanced in skill, and in his fifteenth year he embraced the resolution of devoting himself to the art. For this object Tricklir went to Mannheim, where he remained several years and reached a master-pitch by zealous study under the direction of experienced teachers. After he had been several times to Italy, he was received in March of the year 1783 as a member of the Court band at Dresden, to which he belonged as a highly appreciated artist until his death on November 29, 1813. His published compositions consist of seven Concertos and six Sonatas for violoncello. It must also be noticed that Tricklir thought to have discovered by a "Microcosme Musical" a sure means of keeping stringed instruments continually in even, pure tune. It was, however, an illusion, and this imaginary invention disappeared as quickly as it had originated.

A remarkable scholar of Tricklir's was DOMINIQUE BIDEAU, or BIDAUX, as he called himself in his violoncello school. He belonged to the orchestra of the " Théâtre Italien " in Paris. His compositions in relation to the violoncello are " Six duos pour Violon et Violoncelle " (Op. 1 and 2), Paris, 1796; " Trois grands divertissements concertants pour violon et violoncelle," " Un air ecossais varié avec quatuor," " Deux duos faciles pour deux violoncelles," and some other things of the same kind. The title of his violoncello school runs thus: " Grande et Nouvelle Méthode raisonnée pour le Violoncelle, composée par Dominique Bidaux. Paris, 1802."

A contemporary of Bidaux, PIERRE FRANÇOIS OLIVIER AUBERT, born 1763 at Amiens, also brought out a violoncello

method.[1] He received his first musical instruction in the
"maîtrise" of his native town, but he learned cello playing by
himself, without any other assistance. After his arrival in
Paris, he found a place in the orchestra of the "Opéra
Comique," to which he belonged for twenty-five years. His
cello method was, as Fétis remarks, the first good instruction book which followed after the insufficient preparatory
works by Cupis and Tillière.

Aubert wrote for his instrument twelve Duets in four parts,
as Op. 3, 5, 6, and 7 ; some Studies, besides three Sonatas,
Op. 8 ; and lastly, eight Sonatas.

A second violoncellist of the same name, who was commonly
called AUBERTI, worked in the orchestra of the Paris Commédie
Italienne. He died in the year 1805. Of his compositions
six Solos for the violoncello (Op. 1) appeared, and six Duets for
two violoncellos.

F. CARDON was a member of the Paris Opera orchestra in the
middle of the last century. He educated his nephew, PIERRE
CARDON, born in 1751, who at the same time studied singing
under Richer. The latter seems to have been his chief
occupation, since he became a singer in the Royal Chapel in
1788, and gave singing lessons. He was, however, also
engaged as a teacher of cello playing.

ESPRIT AIMON, born at Lisle (Vaucluse), in 1754, is also distinguished as a clever violoncellist. He conducted for a long
time the music of the Danish Minister, Count Rantzau; he then
settled down in Marseilles. In the year 1828 he died in Paris.

The cellist, PIERRE FRANÇOIS LEVASSEUR, born at Abbeville,
in 1753, was intended for the church, and received for that
end a liberal education. He decided, however, in the eighteenth year of his life for art. A certain Belleval directed for
three months his practice on the violoncello. This instruction,
however, does not seem to have satisfied him, for he preferred
to be his own master. When he came to Paris, in 1782, he
received a few lessons from Duport the younger,[2] whose tone

---

[1] Fétis says that Aubert published "deux méthodes de violoncelle," but
immediately after speaks of one "livre élémentaire" of the same author, so
that it may easily be concluded the first assertion was an error.

[2] Fétis says from the elder Duport. This is, however, impossible as he had
already settled in Berlin, in 1773, from which place he did not again absent
himself.

and style he adopted. In 1789 he played at the "Concert Spirituel" some of his master's solo pieces, and later he appeared at the concerts of the "Théâtre Feydeau." From 1785-1815 he was a member of the Opera orchestra. Soon after his retirement from this he died. The compositions which he published were twelve Duets for two violoncellos in two volumes.

There was another cellist, LEVÁSSEUR, about ten years younger, who sprang from another family so-called, and whose Christian name was JEAN HENRI. He seems to have been more remarkable than his namesake mentioned above. He was born in 1765 in Paris, was a pupil of Cupis, and belonged consequently to Berteau's school. After he had pursued his studies with the former artist, he profited for some time by the instruction of the younger Duport. He was then received into the Paris Opera orchestra, to which he belonged as first violoncellist until 1823, the year of his death. He was also for some time active as a teacher at the Conservatoire. He likewise had a place at the Court Music of Napoleon, and from 1814 in the Royal band. That he was amongst the first in rank who belonged to the violoncello school of the Conservatoire, under the direction of Baillot, is a proof of the repute in which he was held in Paris. Of his own compositions, he only left a set of Sonatas with bass, two sets of Duets, and a volume of "Exercices."

Levasseur's most prominent pupils were LAMARE and NORBLIN.

JAQUES MICHEL HUREL DE LAMARE, born on May 1, 1772, in Paris, died on March 27, 1823, in the town of Caen, where he possessed some property, was the son of poor parents and got his scientific as well as his artistic education together with the Pages of the Court Music. In his fifteenth year he began, under the direction of the younger Duport, violoncello playing, for which he developed an extraordinary talent. Before he had reached seventeen years of age, he left the Pages' Institute and returned to his parents. In 1794 he found a place in the orchestra of the Théâtre Feydeau. The then famous concerts of this institution gave him the wished-for opportunity of making himself known as a solo player. His excellent performances procured for him very soon the reputation of first French violoncellist of his time. The Committee of the Paris Conservatoire hastened to secure him as a teacher. But he desired to go out into the world, and at the beginning of 1801 he went to Germany. At Berlin he was brought into intimate relations with Prince Louis Ferdinand, and played a great deal with him; as a mark of distinction he presented him with a ring on condition that he would exchange it with one that Lamare himself wore. From Germany Lamare went to Russia. He lived there alternately at St. Petersburg and Moscow until 1808. During this period he was not only soloist at the Imperial Court, but was also active in giving concerts. On his return to France he took the route through Poland and Austria. In April, 1809, he returned to Paris and soon organised a concert in the Odéon without, however, exciting in any way his audience, which determined him not to play publicly again. He only allowed himself to be heard in private circles, where great admiration for his playing was conceded to him. He must have been an excellent performer in ensemble and also in quartet playing. In 1815 he married a lady of fortune. From that time he only pursued his art for pleasure. On March 27, 1823, he succumbed to an affection of the larynx.

Lamare wrote nothing for his instrument. He was destitute of any gift of form. The compositions published in Paris under his name, consisting of four violoncello Concertos, Duets, and an "Air varié" for violoncello, originated probably from the opera composer Auber, who was an intimate friend of Lamare. Of the Concertos, the one in A minor is the best.

LOUIS PIERRE MARTIN NORBLIN was the son of the French painter, Norblin de la Gourdaine, of some repute in his time, who, in 1772, selected Warsaw as his permanent residence and there married a Polish lady. The artist just now mentioned, born on December 2, 1781, was the offspring of this union. In 1798 he went to Paris for the sake of the Conservatoire and was first Baudiot's and then Levasseur's pupil. In the year XI., according to the reckoning of the French Republic—that is, 1803—he received the first prize at a competition of the directors of the above-named Institution for his performances in solo playing. Six years later, 1809, he was appointed to the orchestra of the " Théâtre italien," and, in 1811, solo violoncellist in the orchestra of the Grand Opéra. In this position he remained until 1841. Besides this, he gave instructions at the Conservatoire from January 1, 1826, as successor of his master, Levasseur; on June 5, 1846, he gave this up, in order to withdraw into private life. He died on July 14, 1854, at Château Connautre, in the Department of the Marne.

Norblin was highly estimated, not only as a soloist, but also as a delicate, tasteful quartet player. For many years he took the violoncello parts in the Baillot String Quartets. He gained special distinction from the musical world of Paris, for having assisted in the foundation of the Conservatoire Concerts, called into existence by Habeneck, in 1828.

His son and pupil, EMILE, born April 2, 1821, was a skilful violoncellist, who received the Conservatoire prize. He, however, devoted himself more to teaching than solo playing.

Cupis's pupil, JEAN BAPTISTE BRÉVAL, already mentioned, born, in 1756, in the Department of the Aisne, so quickly developed his talent that he was able very early to appear at the " Concert Spirituel " with brilliant success. He was a member of the Paris Opera orchestra from 1781 to 1806. In 1796 followed his nomination as teacher of violoncello playing at the Conservatoire. From this he was released in 1802, as the number of the pupils at the Institution was not large enough to keep him employed. Towards the end of his life Bréval retired to Chamouille, a village in the neighbourhood of Laon. He shortly after died there, at the end of the year 1825.

Bréval published for the violoncello seven Concertos, five sets of Duets, three Sonatas with bass, and twelve " Airs variés." Besides these he wrote two Concertantes, Quartets, Trios, and an instruction book under the title " Méthode raisonnée de Violoncelle," which appeared in Paris in 1804. His cello pieces were formerly much in request, but have been long obsolete. As a player Bréval had a finished style, but in his rendering lacked force and energy.

Of similar kind is the verdict regarding the pupil of the

elder Janson, CHARLES NICOLAS BAUDIOT, who was born on March 29, 1773, at Nancy, and died in Paris on September 26, 1849. Fétis, who had heard him, says that his rendering, though of great neatness and purity of tone, was cold and without spirit. It appears that he possessed an extraordinary talent for teaching, for he was, in 1802, the successor of his master at the Conservatoire, and worked there until the year 1822 when he accepted a pension. He had an official post in the Treasury as well as his artistic occupation.

In 1807 he was unfortunate in exciting the ridicule of an audience, at a concert given by the famous Catalani, in which he took part. The occasion was of a very harmless nature. In the said concert a Symphony of Haydn was played, and Baudiot had a solo to perform immediately after. It was a "Fantaisie" on the *Andante* of the German master's Symphony which had just been executed, and of the performance of which the soloist had no suspicion, as he entered the hall when his turn came. Scarcely had Baudiot begun Haydn's Theme when the public, who thought he wanted to have a joke, burst out into hearty laughter. The artist, who was at a loss to explain the demeanour of his audience, and ignorant of the connection of affairs, became excited and played out of tune, whereupon the laughter was repeated with renewed vigour. Having lost his self-control, and being on the point of fainting, he left the platform, supported by a fellow artist. Baudiot wrote for the violoncello two Concertos and two Concertinos, as well as a great number of other compositions, consisting of Duets, Potpourris, Fantaisies, Nocturnes, Sonatas, with bass accompaniment, and transcribed besides violin pieces by Lafont and Beriot. He was also the author of a method for his instrument, and under the direction of Baillot, and with the co-operation of Levasseur, he took part also in the production of a violoncello method for use in the Conservatoire.

Of Baudiot's pupils, SCIPION ROUSSELOT, born at the beginning of our century, deserves notice. During his attendance at the Conservatoire, he received also instruction in composition from Reicha. At the completion of his studies the first prize was allotted to him (1823). Rousselot went later on to England. Besides several chamber music compositions and a Symphony, there appeared by him three Sonatinas, some books of Variations, and a "Morceau de Salon" for violoncello.

A fellow student of Baudiot's, under Janson the elder, was PIERRE LOUIS HUS-DESFORGES, grandson of the violin virtuoso, Jarnowick. Hus-Desforges was born at Toulon in 1778, where his mother, Jarnowick's daughter, was performing as an actress. At the age of eight his parents confided him to the boys' choir of the Cathedral at La Rochelle. As he had occupied his leisure hours with trumpet blowing, he accepted the duty of trumpeter (1792) to the 14th Regiment in order to join in the campaigns of the Revolutionary Army. Four years after he lost a finger of his right hand by a musket ball and was consequently invalided. He now tried his fortune as cellist, for during his sojourn at La Rochelle he had acquired some facility on the violoncello. He succeeded in being appointed to the theatre orchestra. In the course of six months he relinquished this and chose Paris as his residence. Here he was received into the Conservatoire and assigned to the pupils of Janson. After his release from the Conservatoire, Hus-Desforges led, like his grandfather Jarnowick, a perpetually changing life. In the year 1800 he went as head of the orchestra with a French opera troupe to St. Petersburg, in 1810 he returned and made some concert tours in France, in 1817 came back to Paris and undertook the functions of first cellist at the Theatre "Porte Saint Martin," in 1820 went to Metz and founded there a music school, made fresh journeys, and in 1828 was the head of the orchestra at the "Théâtre du Gymnase," but at the end of a year asked for his dismissal. He did the same again when in 1831 he had succeeded in obtaining the office of Director of the orchestra at the Theatre of the Palais Royal. He spent the end of his chequered career in the little town of Pont-le-Roi, near Blois, as teacher at the music school there, where he died January 20, 1838.

Hus-Desforges was a clever, skilful violoncellist, but he did not belong to the number of prominent, practised artists of his time. His tone was weak and his performances lacked force and brilliancy, as Fétis remarks. His violoncello com positions, which were formerly somewhat liked, consisted of four Concertos and nine Airs with variations, entitled " Soirées Musicales," four Duets, and two Sonatas with bass. Besides these he wrote a violoncello method.

Of far greater importance to the art of violoncello playing was Duport the younger's pupil, NICOLAS JOSEPH PLATEL, who was born in the year 1777 at Versailles, and received his first musical instruction in the Institution of royal pages. There was then no attempt at violoncello playing, but about the tenth year of the boy's age the inclination for it was developed. Louis Duport, who discerned a disposition favourable to it, devoted himself with special zeal to his training. These relations were broken off, when Duport, at the end of 1789, left France in order to seek a position in Berlin. From that period Platel was thrown for a long time upon his own resources. In the year 1793 he was drawn into close relations with Lamare, who sought in every way to forward him. In 1796 Platel became a member of the orchestra of the " Théâtre Feydeau." He was deprived of his post on account of a love affair with an actress of that institution, with whom he went to Lyons at the end of 1797. When he returned to Paris in 1801, he appeared several times at concerts with great success. He was then reputed the best violoncellist in Paris, and the absence of Duport and Lamare abroad stood him in good stead.

Platel might now have made his fortune in the French capital. However, on account of the carelessness of his disposition and his unpractical nature, he knew not how to turn his opportunities to advantage. In 1805 he left Paris in order to undertake a concert tour, but at Quimper, where he made the acquaintance of a cello playing dilettante, he remained quite two years. He then finally came to the resolution of again beginning his wanderings. When he had appeared in concerts at Brest and Nantes with great success, he went North with the intention of visiting Holland and thence Germany. This plan, however, was not carried out. Platel settled himself down, on the way to the former place, at Ghent, remained there giving lessons several years, and then went to Antwerp. An opera troupe was there at the time who engaged him as first violoncellist. About six years later he undertook the same function in the theatre at Brussels. This was the turning-point which decided Platel's destiny. The

Prince of Chimay engaged him for the Royal Music School of
the Belgian Court, which was opened in 1831. By accepting
this office, to which he devoted himself until his death on
August 25, 1835, he became the founder of the Belgium school
of violoncello playing, from which emanated, under his
direction, such artists as Batta, Demunck, and Servais.

Platel's compositions consist of five Concertos, of which the
last is entitled "Le Quart d'heure," also of three books of
Sonatas with bass accompaniment, and eight "Airs Variés"
of "Caprices ou Préludes," and six Romances with piano
accompaniment. Besides these he wrote six Duets for violoncello and violin, and three Trios for violin, viola, and
violoncello.

We must mention here three French cellists of the second
half of last century, whose master is not known—namely,
Chrétien, Haillot, and Raoul.

GILLES LOUIS CHRÉTIEN, born in 1754 at Versailles, and
died in Paris, March 4, 1811, at the age of twenty-two found
a position as Royal band musician. He possessed great
readiness and a good tone, though he played without expression. He lost his place by the Revolution, but was indemnified in 1807 by being received into the Imperial orchestra.
He does not seem to have occupied himself with composition,
but as a writer on music, though without much success.

HAILLOT belonged to the orchestra of the "Comédie
Italienne," and was also engaged in private teaching. By his
arrangements of operas in the form of duets he supplied the
wants of amateur cello players.

Finally, JEAN MARIE RAOUL, an enthusiastic friend of art—
who besides his official position as crown lawyer and, later, as
Justice at the Paris Cour de Cassation, cultivated zealously
the violoncello, on which he distinguished himself—must be
mentioned in this place as the author of a violoncello school.
It appeared under the title of "Méthode de violoncelle,
contenant une nouvelle exposition des principes de cet
instrument." Raoul composed also some Sonatas and "Airs
variés" for his favourite instrument. His efforts, supported
by Vuillaume, the well-known Parisian violin maker, to
restore the gamba to practical use were in vain. Raoul was
born in Paris, in 1766, and died there in 1837.

When we survey the progressive development of violoncello playing from its commencement to the close of the eighteenth century under all aspects, the following facts are presented to us : violoncello playing was taken up, as we saw, in the first half of the seventeenth century, and even before, by the Italians. It was at first used only as an orchestral instrument and as a harmonised accompaniment of recitative singing in the place of the gamba. But in the second half of the seventeenth century there were some Italian artists, as GABRIELI, ARIOSTI, and BONONCINI, who endeavoured to elevate the violoncello to the rank of a solo instrument. Then appeared FRANCISCELLO, who worked with uncommon success to the same end. By the last three named artists violoncello playing was presented to the German nation with the idea of artistically treating it, while in France Giov. Battista Struck, called Baptistin, exercised an influence in the same direction.

In both these countries this new branch of Art soon received a great impulse by means of native talent. The Germans brought to it more that was empiric, the French what was methodic—consequently at the beginning, it must be acknowledged, the latter gained a certain advantage. It is very noteworthy that they made great efforts to arrange systematically and establish the technique of violoncello playing by instruction books and methods, and Corrette led the way with his violoncello school, published in 1741, which was followed in the course of the second half of the last century by similar works by Tillière, Cupis, and Müntzberger.[1] In Italy and Germany, as far as one can see, the first attempts at instruction books for the violoncello were initiated after Corrette and Tillière had published their Schools.

But in spite of the laudable efforts which were made, especially in France, to establish the science of cello playing on a sure and suitable basis, it made very slow progress. A substantial hindrance existed from the circumstance that the method of violin playing, which, at the time, had already reached a high state of cultivation, had been in a measure used

---

[1] Tillière's violoncello school appeared in 1764, and those of Cupis and Müntzberger, to all appearance, came out before 1800.

as a model without taking into consideration the important difference in the dimensions of the fingerboard in the two instruments. Not only had the fingering of the diatonic and chromatic scales, but also the principles of the so-called positions, been transferred from the violin to the violoncello. With reference to the first point, the necessary directions were given by description in the Method of Corrette. As to the latter point it must be observed that for the lower portion of the fingerboard four different positions were adopted analogous to the technique of the violin. To this position-theory, which has come down to the present time and is treated of in some of the old as well as the new violoncello schools, no special authority, strictly speaking, should be attached.[1] For the violin it has to a certain extent a meaning, as on that instrument it is possible to play a complete scale on all parts of the fingerboard without moving the hand. On account of its wider dimensions the violoncello admits of this only by the help of the thumb position, with the exception of the C major scale by using the open strings. But even here, where an indication of position would be applicable, it is not usual. Evidently there is something inconsistent in this.

There was a singular conjuncture with regard to finger technique in the use of the thumb, as we have already seen from Corrette's violoncello school. The fourth finger was excluded from co-operation as soon as the use of the thumb was introduced, because it was thought that it was too short. This view of it prevailed up to the end of last century. In the method published by the Belgian violoncellist, Müntzberger, it is literally said : " When the fourth position has been passed over, only three fingers are used." Later indeed, where Müntzberger speaks of the use of the thumb, he somewhat

---

[1] Here is an example or two : Alexander in his cello school, which appeared in 1801, takes up quite arbitrarily an " ordinary," a " half," and a " whole," as well as a " mixed " THEORY OF FINGERING, and Fr. Kummer divides the finger-board into " whole " and " half " positions. Müntzberger says in his cello school, which appeared apparently in 1800, he wished that people could accustom themselves to say to the pupil as for the violin : " take this or that position." Here is given a distinct indication of the application of the violin positions. In other cello schools, on the contrary, there is no reference to positions.

Duport, however, makes use of positions 1st, 2nd, and 3rd, &c., throughout his volume.—(Tr.)

modifies this rule, since he remarks : " Many professors, when using the thumb, do not need the fourth finger. I am of opinion that its use should not be rejected, in that he, who by nature is endowed with a long finger, can make it available in certain cases."

In exceptional cases, therefore, Müntzberger advocated the use of the little finger when playing with the assistance of the thumb. But it is evident from his expression that the use of it was not usual at the end of the last century. This is undoubtedly to be ·gathered from the "Méthode de Violoncelle," published conjointly by Baillot, Levasseur, Catel, and Baudiot. In it is the following observation : " The use of the fourth finger in the different positions of the thumb was not known to the older violoncello teachers of France. It has only been introduced a few years, since the necessity for it has been felt." As this violoncello school was in 1804 accepted as an instruction book for the Conservatoire by a resolution of the General Committee, it is clearly evident that in France at least the fourth finger had for the most part remained unused until shortly before the close of the last century. The cause of this was plainly an incorrect manipulation. Concerning the practice pursued in Germany during the second half of the last century with regard to the fourth finger, Joh. Bap. Baumgartner's Tutor, mentioned page 69, would alone be able to give an explanation, if it were still extant. With some probability, however, it may be assumed that the same opinion was held in reference to it as on the other side of the Rhine. The influence of France on German violoncello playing in the second half of the last century made itself felt in other ways This was chiefly through the means of the brothers Duport The succeeding sections will show in what way the furthe1 cultivation of this branch of the art progressed.

The

Art of Violoncello Playing

In the Nineteenth Century.

IV.—ITALY.

THE most important epoch of Italian violoncello playing came to a close with Boccherini. His early withdrawal from his native land caused a loss all the more sensibly felt because there was no one of equal importance to compensate for him in the further development of the art, from the point to which he had attained both in its executive and productive aspect. This task fell principally to Germans, French, and Belgians, whilst Italy was deprived of the position of pre-eminence in regard to violoncello playing which she is asserted to have held for a long time in the previous century. The same phenomenon consequently was repeated here as in regard to violin playing.

Already towards the end of the eighteenth century Art, and especially instrumental music, in which the Italians had accomplished so much that was praiseworthy, fell into decline on the Apennine Peninsula—although Italy brought out some important productions, particularly in the department of opera compositions. The Musical Almanack for Germany, of 1783, contains the correspondence of an anonymous German artist who travelled in Italy in the year 1782. It is there said : " At Naples I found in the Conservatoire[1] a veritable horror. Caffaro[2] is here with Milico, whose music gave me the most pleasure. As for the rest it is all miserable, heavy, modern Italian opera music, as well as in the churches. I hoped to find a great deal at Venice, but it is no better there. Above all, the execution in the whole of Italy is less good than formerly. . . . But what astonishes me most is the extraordinarily little appreciation of music in Italy now. It is almost a miracle to see people of position who have a love of music. It created a great sensation when we gave concerts in Rome which were frequented by sincere admirers and friends.

---

[1] In the last century there existed in Naples four Conservatoires. But in 1806 they amalgamated into one musical Institute.

[2] Caffaro, opera and church music composer, was Director of the Neapolitan Conservatoire della Pietá. Milico was then famous as a stage singer.

Instrumental music is at such a low ebb that it is almost beneath any criticism."

At the beginning of the present century things were not changed in this respect. Louis Spohr, who was in Italy in 1816, expresses himself in his autobiography concerning the condition of music there much in the same manner as the anonymous writer cited above, and, a little later, Felix Mendelssohn Bartholdy likewise.

Under these conditions it cannot excite surprise if Italy in consequence did not produce so many representatives of violoncello playing in the highest sense of the word as hitherto.

Luigi Venzano must be mentioned as one of the first distinguished Italian cellists of this century. He was born in Genoa about 1815, and was solo cellist in the orchestra of the Theatre Carlo Felice, as well as teacher at the musical institute of his native town. He died on January 27, 1878. As a composer he devoted himself to vocal and stage compositions.

An incomparably more important player than the preceding artist, or his countrymen to be subsequently mentioned, is Alfredo Piatti, born at Bergamo on January 8, 1822, and not in 1823, as Fétis says. His father, who died on February 27, 1878, and who early instructed him in music, was not a singer but a violin player.[1] The boy soon decided for the violoncello, on which he received his first lessons from his great uncle, Zanetti, who was engaged as music master at Bergamo.

Later he was sent to Milan for the benefit of the Conservatoire. Here the excellent violoncellist, Merighi, conducted his further education. Piatti attended the above-named Institution until September, 1837, after having appeared previous to this date at one of the concerts with decided success. In April, 1838, he gave a concert of his own in the Teatro della Scala, at Milan, with the profits of which he supplied himself with the means of undertaking a concert tour. Soon after he was heard very favourably at Venice and Vienna. In the latter town he remained some time ; then he returned to

---

[1] See my work, " The Violin and its Masters." 2nd Ed., 365.

Italy and gave concerts at Milan and Padua. In 1843 he went to Munich and joined in a concert with Liszt there. In the following year he presented himself at Frankfort-on-the-Maine, Berlin, Breslaw, and Dresden, when he afterwards visited Paris. In 1845 he was in St. Petersburg, where his performances met with unusual appreciation. Having returned to Milan, the post of teacher was offered to him, in 1846, at the Conservatoire. He did not, however, accept the offer, but established himself in the same year in the English capital, which from that time he has only left occasionally, either to undertake concerts or journeys to recruit his health. In London he soon became one of the most distinguished artistic celebrities, and he still remains in full favour with the public. His performances are proportionably marked by fine tone, the greatest purity, tasteful rendering, as well as by a perfect mastery of all technical difficulties. He is not only the most important cellist in England, but belongs altogether to the highest rank of artists of the present time. He wrote for his instrument two Concertos (Op. 24 and 26), a Concertino (Op. 18), a " Fantasia romantica," Capriccios (Op. 22 and 25), a " Sérénade Italienne " (Op. 17), " Airs Baskyrs " (Op. 8), as well as a long list of other works, consisting of Themes with variations and drawing-room pieces of various kinds. Further he has brought out new editions of old cello compositions and six Sonatas by Boccherini. He has also published original songs with violoncello obbligato.

Two other pupils of the Milan Conservatoire are GUGLIELMO QUARENGHI and ALESSANDRO PEZZE. The first, born on October 22, 1826, in Casal Maggiore, was pursuing his studies during the years 1839-1842. Arrived at maturity he was first violoncellist at the Teatro della Scala, at Milan, and from 1851 he gave instruction also at the Conservatoire to which he was indebted for his education. In February, 1879, he took the place of Boucheron as Choirmaster at the Cathedral. He enjoyed this position only a few years, for he died February 3 or 4, 1882. Amongst his compositions the most noteworthy are—Six Capriccios, a " Chant elégiaque," with piano accompaniment ; two Romances, a Scherzo, " Un pensiero al lago," and some Fantasias on *Motifs* from Italian operas.

ALESSANDRO PEZZE, born 1835, at Milan, received from his father, a clever dilettante, his first musical instruction, after which, in 1846, he went to the Conservatoire of his native town. Merighi directed his violoncello studies. After he had been for some time first cellist at the Teatro della Scala, he was engaged by the English impresario, Lumley, for Her Majesty's Theatre in London. Pezze belonged to it until 1867, in which year the theatre was destroyed by fire. Later this artist was employed in the orchestras of the Philharmonic Society and Covent Garden. He is still living in London.

The Naples Conservatoire produced GAETANO BRAGA, born on June 9, 1829, at Guilianuova in the Abruzzi. He was originally destined for the church, but the inclination for music came out so strongly that he could not be kept back from it. His parents now wished that he should be educated as a singer; he, however, decided for the violoncello, on which Gaetano Ciandelli directed his studies. He soon became a pupil of Mercadante for composition. In the year 1852 he had finished his studies at the Conservatoire. Soon after he undertook a concert journey to the North of Italy, and from thence to Vienna, where he formed a connection with Mayseder, and was a member of his String Quartet for a short time. In 1855 he betook himself to Paris, where he was much in request as a favourite solo player. He is at present living in Florence. As a composer Braga devoted himself by preference to stage compositions. For the violoncello he only wrote a Concerto, and some smaller pieces with piano accompaniment, and a Serenade for voice with cello accompaniment.

Other Italian violoncellists at the present time worthy of notice are—RONCHINI and G. MAGRINI in Milan, PINI in Venice, SERATO in Bologna, TOSCANINI in Parma, SBOLCI and CASTAGNOLI in Florence, FURINO in Rome, CENTOLA in Naples, MONTECCHI (who lives at present at Rennes in Bretagne as a music teacher), and MATTIOLI, now in Cincinnati.[1]

---

[1] In spite of every effort, I have not succeeded in gaining any more details concerning the above violoncellists.

V.—GERMANY

GERMAN violoncello playing had, during the second half of last century, found unusual opportunities for expansion in consequence of the demand for numberless competent artists for the various princely households, as well as for the larger towns. Amongst the cellists mentioned in the second part of this work, there were already some specially prominent personages to distinguish. The branch of art, however, to which this book is devoted first received a really important and sustained impulse through means of BERNHARD ROMBERG. This artist acquired for German violoncello playing a significance similar to that which Louis Spohr gained for German violin playing, only with this difference—that the latter master was far superior to the former as a composer. While certain violin compositions of Spohr (not to speak of his other works), on account of their intrinsic worth, are calculated to appear in concert programmes, and will presumably do so in the future, the cello pieces by Romberg have already for some time completely disappeared from them. Yet they have, from a scholastic point of view, proved to be of value even to the present day. In regard to this, what Romberg did for the cultivation and perfecting, as well as the fine manipulation of his instrument, merits for him the appellation of founder of the German school of violoncello playing. His Concertos and concert pieces have been of more importance, however, for taking such a direction than his violoncello school, which by no means belongs to the best instruction books of the kind, and is a proof that a man can be a distinguished teacher—and Romberg was in any case this—without having the capacity for the production of a thoroughly satisfactory instruction book. The examples and music pieces in Romberg's violoncello school are indeed excellent, but some of the maxims which he enunciates seem peculiar, and he goes too much into extraneous matter, instead of bringing forward the more substantial principles with the necessary precision and accuracy.

It is noteworthy that Romberg advocated a simplified notation for violoncello music. Primarily (besides the bass clef), in Italy and Germany, only the tenor clef was used, and the alto clef in France. But as the compass of violoncello playing was more and more extended up to the high parts of the scale, by the use of the thumb positions, keys used for the discant and violin were added. Boccherini, for the notation of many of his compositions, made use altogether of five clefs, sometimes indeed in one and the same piece—as, for example, at the opening *Allegro* of his Concerto (C major). There was nothing arbitrary in this procedure. Boccherini had far more in view the object of giving to the player starting-points for the finger positions to be used in each case. In his later compositions, however, he abandoned this, as the use of so many different clefs had its inconveniences; and he restricted himself to the use of the bass, tenor, and violin clef. This notation was subsequently generally accepted, particularly also by Romberg, and is still in use up to the present time. In opposition to the earlier favourite manner of writing the notes—by the use of the violin clef an octave too high for the violoncello, as is the case in Mozart's and Beethoven's compositions—Boccherini, by the application of the clefs mentioned, wrote everything as it would sound. By this means he gained the advantage that he was not obliged to make so much use of ledger lines in the writing of his passages—which were continually moving in the soprano part—as he must have done if he had followed the custom of his contemporaries and had adhered to the higher system of notation. It is readily understood why Romberg in his cello school should declare himself in favour of the change introduced by Boccherini, for he also, with special predilection, made use of the higher regions of the fingerboard for his playing; wherefore it was said of him that his handling of the violoncello was often after the manner of the violin. From this point of view it is thoroughly rational that Romberg, in regard to notation, should follow the example given by Boccherini. In later times the too frequent and continuous use of the soprano clef—in which a broad, energetic volume of tone, full of expression, is nearly excluded—has been abandoned without, however, being neglected entirely; while to the most beautiful and effective clef—namely, the tenor—has been accorded its right place.

BERNHARD ROMBERG was the son of the bassoon player,

Anton Romberg, of some note in his time, and was born on November 11, 1767, in the village of Dinklage, near the little Prussian town of Quakenbrück. It is unknown whom he had as teacher for the violoncello. It was probably an orchestra musician in Münster, to which place his parents had removed their home. In any case, Romberg's talent caused him to make the most of it, for before he had passed his youth he was able to undertake with his cousin, Andreas Romberg,[1] who was about the same age, a concert tour which led them through Holland, and was extended to Paris, where they were both heard with such success in the house of Baron Bagge[2] that they were engaged in 1787 for the "Concert Spirituel." After his return from Paris Romberg devoted himself eagerly to progressive studies, and at the same time worked in the orchestra at Münster.

Münster belonged then, as is known, to the Electorate of Cologne. The Elector Maximilian Franz, who on his accession to his dominions (April 27, 1784) resided often in the Westphalian town, had his attention drawn to the two Romberg artists, and engaged them for his Royal band at Bonn. The announcement of the appointment bears the date of December 19, 1790.

When the Elector, in the autumn of the following year, went to reside at Mergentheim, then the seat of the German order—whose Grand Master he was—he caused about twenty members of his band to follow him from Bonn. Amongst them, besides Beethoven, who in addition to his office as organist was also tenor player at the Court, were also the two Rombergs. In one of the musical entertainments which took place in the apartments of the Elector, Bernhard Romberg was heard in a Concerto. Boszler's Musical Correspondence of the year 1791 contains a notice of it in which is said[3]: "Romberg, the younger, combines in his violoncello playing extraordinary rapidity with charming rendering; this rendering is the more marked and decided when he is heard in

---

[1] This artist was a violinist, and was born on April 27, 1767, at Vechta, in Oldenburg, and died on November 21, 1821, as Hofkapellmeister, in Gotha.

[2] Bagge was a Prussian Chamberlain, who then lived in Paris, built a house there, and acted the part of an art patron. He died there in 1791.

[3] This notice is by the Court Chaplain of Hohenlohe in Kirschberg, Carl Ludwig Junker.

connection with the greater number of violoncellists. The tone which he produces from his instrument is, moreover—especially in the expressive parts—extremely clear, firm, and penetrating. Taking into consideration the difficulty of the instrument, a thoroughly marked purity of tone, in the extraordinarily quick rendering of the *Allegro*, must be attributed to him in the highest degree. Yet this after all is mere mechanical readiness; the connoisseur has another standard by which he measures the greatness of artists; and this is, the manner of playing, the perfection of expression or the spiritual interpretation. Once on this point, the connoisseur will pronounce in favour of the expressive *Adagio*. It is impossible more deeply to penetrate into the more delicate hues of feeling—impossible to colour them with more variety—to enhance them, moreover, by greater light and shade—impossible to hit more exactly the very tones through which this feeling has utterance, tones which appeal more directly to the heart than Romberg succeeds in doing in his *Adagio*."

" How acquainted he is with all the beauties of detail, which lie in the nature of the piece in the peculiar kind of expression to be given, and for which the composer has no signs for recognition? What effects he is able to produce by the *crescendo* of his tone, swelling up to the strongest *fortissimo*, and then again by its dying away to a scarcely audible *pianissimo !!* "

From this enthusiastic announcement we must conclude that Romberg's playing at that time—he was in his twenty-fourth year—showed already a high degree of perfection. It is therefore quite conceivable that he cherished the wish of obtaining a position in life adequate to the merit of his performances, for in Bonn he received only a yearly salary of 600 florins, and, moreover, the existence of the Cologne Electorate, the complete dissolution of which was accomplished in the autumn of the year 1794, had fallen into a very doubtful condition from the time of the appearance of the revolutionary army on the Rhine (October, 1792).

Romberg therefore accepted with his cousin, Andreas, at Easter, 1794, an engagement at the Schröder Theatre in Hamburg, but he did not long remain there. Three years later they undertook together a concert journey into Italy;

gave concerts on their return at Vienna, supported by
Beethoven, and again betook themselves to Hamburg, whence,
after a two years' residence, Bernhard Romberg visited
London. He next travelled in Portugal and Spain, in 1800
returned again to Paris, and performed this time at the
concerts of "La Rue de Cléry" and the "Théâtre des Victoires"
with such great success that he became teacher at the
Conservatoire. Romberg does not, however, appear to have
felt comfortable in this position, for after two years he
withdrew from it and again turned to Hamburg. In 1805 he
responded to an invitation to be solo cellist at the Berlin
Hofcappelle. The calamities of war, which broke over Prussia
in the following year, compelled him once more to become a
wanderer. He next visited the Austrian States. After the
conclusion of the peace of Tilsit, he found himself again in
Berlin, remained there up to the year 1810, and then undertook a journey through Silesia, Poland, and Russia. At
St. Petersburg he met with Ferd. Ries, and in conjunction
with him gave concerts in the Southern provinces of the
Czar's dominions. The artists wished to arrange a visit to
Moscow, but were prevented by the memorable burning of the
Kremlin which compelled the French army to retreat. They
then turned to Stockholm, and from thence went to Copen-
hagen and Hamburg. Here they separated—Ries went to
London, which he reached in March, 1813, and Romberg took
his way by Bremen to Holland and Belgium. From the
latter country he again visited Paris for a short time.
Returned to Germany, Romberg prepared for a second journey
to Russia. On this occasion he lingered two years at Moscow.
After he had been, from 1815-1819, in the service of the Berlin
Court, he chose Hamburg as his settled residence. Wherever
Romberg played his highly finished performances excited
great enthusiasm. In this his violoncello compositions—
which were entirely in accordance with the taste of that period
in a virtuoso point of view, and which, moreover, were distinguished by their solid quality above all other cello
compositions of the time—had a substantial share.

During his many journeys through European countries,
Romberg had collected national airs, of which he availed himself in various ways for his compositions under different

names. Amongst them are to be found Caprices on Swedish, Polish, Moldavian, Wallachian, and Spanish songs, as well as a "Fantaisie" on Norwegian and a "Rondo brilliant" on Polish melodies, besides four books of Variations on Russian national airs. He further wrote ten Concertos, three Concertinos, a Fantasia with orchestra, Polonaises, as well as Duets and Sonatas, with bass accompaniment for the cello. He was also very productive in the sphere of chamber music, and composed also for the stage. These last compositions have, however, not survived him, while, on the other hand, his cello pieces, as already noticed, maintain even at this time a certain value for teaching.

There have been certain famous artists who in advanced age, in spite of a considerable decay in their capacity for performance, have unwisely indulged the inclination of still endeavouring to attract admiration. Bernhard Romberg was one of these. In his seventy-third year he again had a desire to visit Paris in order—though not in public—to appear in artistic circle' as a solo player. The failure which he experienced appears to have had a prejudicial effect on his health, for he died soon after his return home, on August 13, 1841.

Romberg promoted the advancement of German violoncello playing chiefly by his activity as a soloist, and also by his compositions, for, on account of his many concert journeys, which led him sometimes in one direction and sometimes in another, he had not sufficient leisure for continuous and regular teaching. A few young artists, however, enjoyed the benefit of his instruction. Of these we will mention only here his nephew, Cyprian, and Julius Schapler. Some others will be noticed farther on.

CYPRIAN ROMBERG, born in 1807 (according to other accounts, 1810), in Hamburg, made himself known, after he had finished his studies, by his journeys in Germany and Austria, and was then a member of the Imperial band at St. Petersburg. In Hamburg, where he spent the last years of his life, he was, unfortunately, drowned while bathing in the Elbe in 1865.

JULIUS SCHAPLER was born on August 21, 1812, in Graudenz.[1] He received his musical education in Berlin.

---

[1] Not 1820 in the Hartz, as is elsewhere said.

B. Romberg was at first his master for the violoncello, on which also he received instruction from the pensioned chamber musician, Hansmann.[1] After his education was concluded Schapler was heard as solo player in the Opera House at Berlin, as well as in the Gewandhaus at Leipsic, with great applause. He declined offers for engagements, which were in consequence proposed to him, as he wished to make himself known by concerts. Soon after, however, when the position of solo player in the Court band of the Duke of Nassau was offered to him he accepted it. In Wiesbaden, besides his official duties, he was much occupied with composition. The fruits of it were not only several cello pieces, but also three greater chamber music works— namely, a String Quartet, a Trio for piano and violoncello, as well as a Quintet for piano, violin, tenor violoncello, and contra-basso. These last compositions were all crowned with success. A warm and appreciative critique of the String Quartet appeared in 1842 from the pen of Robert Schumann, in his musical paper.

The unquiet year, 1848, caused the Duke of Nassau to dismiss the members of his Kapelle (without pensions). Schapler returned to his home and created for himself a lucrative field of work as music teacher in Thorn, to which he devoted himself for many years. At the present time he is living privately in Berlin.

Schapler belonged in his prime to the best violoncellists of Germany. With fine tone-rendering he had complete mastery over his instrument. Unfortunately, he did not succeed, after his departure from Wiesbaden, in obtaining a post worthy of his excellent performances.

While Bernhard Romberg was raising to a position of high honour the art of violoncello playing in Germany, several important centres were forming for it in Dresden and Vienna.

The Dresden Court, which had always done a great deal for music, was continually taking into consideration the means of attracting into its neighbourhood distinguished instrumentalists; and if for some time a succession of foreign, but specially

---

[1] Page 77 of this work.

Italian artists found a place there, a certain amount of gain was the result in connection with it—for the artist youth of Germany received thereby a progressive impulse to their own endeavours. The Dresden Court orchestra had already, in the last century, a distinguished reputation, and this was more and more enhanced by the continual influx of talented and highly gifted musicians. As regarded the violoncello especially, it gained not long after the beginning of our century an exemplary representative in DOTZAUER. From that time until the present day Dresden has remained an important centre for violoncello playing.

JUSTUS JOHANN FRIEDRICH DOTZAUER, born on January 20, 1783, at Häselrieth, near Hildburghausen, was the son of a minister there. Instructed early in music, he devoted himself to the piano, violin, and violoncello playing. The latter soon gained the ascendancy, and as the inclination for an artistic career showed itself decisively in him, his father sent him, in the year 1799, to Kriegk,[1] at Meiningen, under whose direction he studied two years. After the expiration of that period he found a post in the Meiningen Kapelle until 1805, when he went to Leipsic, and from 1805-1811 he was a member of the orchestra.

From Leipsic he visited Berlin. Here he heard Romberg, with advantage for the pursuit of his studies. In the year 1811 he accepted an honourable position in the Dresden Court orchestra, to which he belonged, from 1821-1850, as first solo cellist. He then lived in retirement, which he enjoyed for ten years. He died in the place where he had successfully worked for so many years on March 6, 1860.

Dotzauer was also well-skilled in composition, and attempted it in various forms. He wrote an Opera, Overtures, Symphonies, a Mass, and several chamber pieces. All these productions have long been forgotten. Not so his violoncello works, which consist of nine Concertos, three Concertinos, two Sonatas with bass, Variations, Divertissements, Potpourris, and a great number of Duets, some of these at least are still prized as objects of study. This is especially the case with regard to his books of instruction, to which belong two violoncello

---

[1] P. 78.

schools,[1] as well as a number of exercises of various kinds.[2] Amongst these the most commendable on account of their excellence are the eighteen "Exercices d'une difficulté progressive" (Op. 120), for beginners (with the exception of the two last numbers), and the "Twenty-four Daily Studies for the acquiring and keeping of Virtuosität." The latter work is in every respect by far the best of Dotzauer's many studies. He also published a School for Flageolet playing (Op. 147). His performances combined the gifts of great solidity and fascinating sweetness. Of his two sons, the younger, Carl Ludwig, devoted himself to the violoncello under the direction of his father. In 1820 he was member of the Hofkapelle at Cassel. He was born on December 7, 1811, at Dresden.

Dotzauer was distinguished not only as an executant artist but also as a teacher. The most remarkable of his scholars are—Kummer, Schuberth, Voigt, and Drechsler.

FRIEDRICH AUGUST KUMMER was born on August 15, 1797, at Meiningen. His father, an accomplished oboist, belonged to the Ducal band there. At the beginning of the century he entered the Kofkapelle at Dresden, and here his son, who at first had taken up his father's instrument, became Dotzauer's pupil. When his education was completed on the violoncello, Kummer should have been admitted into the Dresden Kofkapelle; but as there was just then no vacancy for his instrument he was obliged for a while to content himself with being received as oboist. This was in 1814. Three years ater he was enrolled among the cellists. By diligently prosecuted studies, Kummer gradually reached such a high degree of artistic cultivation that when Dotzauer was pensioned, he was appointed in his place as first violoncellist of the Royal band. In 1864 he celebrated his fiftieth Jubilee, and then gave himself up to his well-deserved retirement. During his long tenure of office he displayed a most extraordinary activity as soloist, quartet, and orchestra player, as well as teacher. In the latter capacity he worked both privately and

---

[1] The first of these appeared at Schott's, in Mayence; the other, for " Elementary instruction," at Haslinger's, Vienna.

[2] Concerning Dotzauer's violoncello compositions, Philipp Roth's " Guide to Violoncello Literature " may be consulted with special reference to their degree of difficulty.

at the Dresden Conservatoire, to which he belonged, until his death, which took place on May 22, 1879. At the same time he wrote a good deal for his instrument, a Concerto, two Concertinos, instructive Duets (some easy and others more difficult), Variations, Etudes, Caprices, Studies (amongst them, daily ones), diverse musical "Divertissements," which were formerly much in request amongst dilletanti, some of which are still used as subjects for the practice of youthful players. He also produced a violoncello school. It is at present the most generally used work of the kind, short and clear, though only extending to a moderate degree of difficulty; finally, Kummer published a useful compendium : "Repertorium and Orchestral Studies," containing important and difficult cello pieces from oratorios, symphonies, overtures, and operas. Kummer's playing bore the stamp of great precision and correctness, united to powerful and solid intonation. His technique "was in every point thoroughly cultivated, but to acquire the 'finesses' of a virtuoso he was of too simple a nature, which was better calculated to occupy itself with the sphere of music in its intellectual aspect than in brilliant display. All that he produced on his instrument was most correct and defined, in which he was greatly assisted by his quiet and cautious temperament. He was unable indeed to raise himself to the height of poetical inspiration and unrestrained warmth of expression, though he never did violence to a good composition. His manner of rendering was always strictly objective and according to rule. Amongst Kummer's pupils Cossmann and Julius Goltermann are prominent.

BERNHARD COSSMANN, born on May 17, 1822, in Dessau, studied at first under Theodore Müller, the cellist of the formerly famous Müller String Quartet, at Brunswick, and then under Kummer. During the years 1840-1841 he worked in the orchestra of the Grand Opéra in Paris, after which he went to London. In 1848 he was engaged as solo player for the Leipsic (Gewandhaus) Concert, in 1852 taken to Weimar by Franz Liszt, and in 1866 appointed teacher of cello playing to the Conservatoire at Moscow. From 1870 to 1878 Cossmann lived privately in Baden-Baden and only appeared to play at concerts. When the Conservatoire at Hoch was founded in

1878, the office of teacher of his instrument was entrusted to him, which post he now occupies. Coszmann belongs to the best cellists of the present time. He has a fine, distinct tone, manages the fingerboard with ease, and is not only a distinguished solo player but also an excellent quartet player. Amongst his compositions the most worthy of notice are a Concert piece with piano accompaniment, three " Fantasias " on *Motifs* from the " Freischütz," " Tell," and " Euryanthe," six Solos in two parts, a Swiss Melody and a Neapolitan Canzonet, three Pieces (Op. 8), Etudes de Concert (Op. 10), and Violoncello Studies.

JOHANN AUGUST GOLTERMANN, born on July 25, 1825, in Hamburg, after he had perfected himself under Kummer, was appointed to the Prague Conservatoire, to which he belonged from 1850 to 1862. In the latter year he exchanged this employment for that of first solo cellist in the Stuttgart orchestra. In 1870 he was pensioned, and on April 4, 1876, he died. He was an able artist in his branch of it.

The next pupil of Dotzauer to be mentioned is CARL SCHUBERTH, born on February 25, 1811, in Magdeburg. He received at first, from a musician of his native town named Hesse, six years' instruction, and then repaired to Dresden to Dotzauer, with whom he remained two years. On his return home he made his *début* with success as a soloist at a concert organised by Catalani, in Magdeburg. At the end of 1828 he undertook a concert tour to the North. The destination was Copenhagen, where, in the spring of 1829, he arrived and made a prolonged sojourn. Later on Schuberth occupied the position of first violoncellist at the Magdeburg Theatre, gave it up, however, in 1833, and undertook, in the autumn of the same year, a journey through Western Germany and Belgium. From the latter place he visited Paris. In the following year he went to Holland, and during the season of 1835 he was heard in London. Schuberth then went to St. Petersburg, where he found, as elsewhere, a brilliant reception, and immediately a permanent position, for he was not only named Director of the Imperial band, but also Inspector of the Music School affiliated to the Court Theatre and Director of Music at the University. He filled these posts until 1863, in which year death overtook him during a journey for the benefit of his health, on July 22, at Zurich. Schuberth's playing was exceedingly clever, but in expression more elegant and ornamental than impressive. His cello pieces give evidence of this, which, with the exception of a Concerto, belong to the description of so-called conversazione music ; but they have not survived their author. Amongst his pupils the most remarkable is Carl Davidoff.[1]

CARL LOUIS VOIGT, the third of Dotzauer's pupils above-mentioned, was born on November 8, 1792, at Zeitz ; he was the son of the organist at St. Thomas's Church, Leipsic, Joh. Georg Hermann Voigt. He played several instruments, and amongst others the violoncello also, on which his grandfather, Johann Heinr. Viktor Rose,[2] had given him instruction at Quedlinburg. Besides his work as organist, he played the violoncello with the orchestra of the theatre in the Gewandhaus at Leipsic. He imparted to his son what he knew and was able to do as cellist, who, in order to perfect himself, studied under Dotzauer's direction some time, and in 1811 took the latter's place in the Leipsic Orchestra, to which he had belonged since the winter of 1809-1810. Voigt filled this post until his death, which took place on February 21, 1831. His violoncello compositions extant, consisting of Sonatas, Duets, Exercises, and a diversity of Drawing-room Pieces, are feeble, but may be used for instruction—as, for example, the three Sonatas (Op. 40).

CARL DRECHSLER, finally, born on May 27, 1800, at Camenz, in the kingdom of Saxony, early studied violoncello playing. He began his career as a military musician at Dessau. At the same time he assisted as cellist in the orchestra there. Through the recommendation of Friedrich Schneider, who discerned the young man's talent, the Duke of Dessau granted him the means, in 1824, of placing himself under Dotzauer's direction for further cultivation. After this he undertook a long concert tour. The great success of this caused his name to be well known, with the result that, in the year 1826, he was permanently established in the orchestra at Dessau, with. the title of Concertmaster.

Drechsler's performances were characterised as much by

---

[1] See under the violoncello players of Russia.
[2] See page 72.

faultless purity and refinement as by feeling and tasteful rendering. His playing was not powerful, but pleasing by its grace and delicacy. He was everywhere received with welcome, and, as he responded to all that was demanded as an excellent leader of his instrument in the orchestra, he was an eagerly sought guest at all musical festivals. After he was pensioned, in 1871, he chose Dresden as his residence. He did not, however, long enjoy the amenities of retirement, for he died in the year 1873.

His son, LOUIS, born on October 5, 1822, at Dessau, formed himself under the direction of his father as a clever violoncellist. He lived and worked as such for a long time in Edinburgh.

Drechsler, the father, was an excellent teacher. Through him Dessau was for a time affiliated to the Dresden school of cello playing, in which he educated excellent artists, amongst whom the best known are Lindner and Grützmacher.

AUGUST LINDNER,[1] born on October 29, 1820, at Dessau, after he had completed his studies, was appointed, in the year 1837, to the Kofkapelle at Hanover, to which he belonged until his death (June, 1878). He enjoyed the reputation of a distinguished violoncellist. Of his compositions we must mention a Concerto (Op. 34), Nine Drawing-room Pieces (Op. 18), Six Fantasias (Op. 38), Divertissements for young cellists (two parts, Op. 32), Concert au Salon (two parts), Three Paraphrases on *Motifs* from Meyerbeer's "Huguenots" and "Le Prophète," as well as Verdi's "Ernani" (Op. 12), and a long list of Opera Potpourris. Besides these, Lindner produced a new edition of L. Duport's "Essai sur le doigter du Violoncelle." [2]

His pupil, BERNHARD THIEME, born on June 11, 1854, in Altenburg, began his musical career after he left school, under the town musician at Penig, in Saxony, and when at eighteen he returned home from there, he received cello instruction, for a short time, from the Kapellmeister, Toller. He very soon found employment in the Berlin Orchestra. He then went, as first cellist, with the Fliegen Orchestra, for

---

[1] Not to be confounded with the excellent cellist, Wilhelm Lindner, who was Chamber Musician of the Grand Duchy of Baden, and died on August 19, 1887.

[2] Compare p. 91.

a summer, to St. Petersburg, in the same capacity; a few months later he entered the Bückeburg Kapelle. He was subsequently occupied in the Hofkapelle at Hanover for two years, and during this period he enjoyed the excellent teaching of Aug. Lindner. Since 1879 he has filled the place of solo cellist in the town orchestra at Baden-Baden.

The Dresden school of cello playing, founded by Dotzauer, and continued by Kummer, received a still greater forward impulse through FRIEDRICH WILHELM LUDWIG GRÜTZMACHER.

This far-famed artist, whose efficiency was a great ornament to the Dresden "Kapellinstitute," was born on March 1, 1832, in Dessau, and after he had learned from his father, who was an esteemed member of the Ducal band, the elements of music, benefited from the instruction of Carl Drechsler. Thus the teaching of Dotzauer, whose pupil Carl Drechsler was at the place whence it had emanated, was further developed—a most valuable gain for the artistic life of the Court of Saxony.

Grützmacher came to Leipsic in the year 1848, fundamentally well prepared for his vocation, and entered a private choral society in order to be thoroughly conversant with the necessary routine in orchestra playing. He was soon invited to take part in the Gewandhaus and the Euterpe Concerts. In the latter he made his *début* at the beginning of February, 1849, as solo player, with Variations by Franchomme. The first violoncellist of the Leipsic Gewandhaus was a certain Wittmann. As, however, his performances did not fully satisfy, Bernhard Cossmann was engaged in 1848 for the solo parts and for the cello teaching at the Conservatoire. Then when Cossmann responded to the invitation to go to Weimar, Grützmacher took his place, although at the same time he was a regular member of the opera orchestra. From that period he was the chief representative of his instrument in Leipsic. Not the less however did he strive indefatigably to progress in his Art, keeping unceasingly in view the goal of perfection. How well he succeeded in reaching it is proved by the dominant position which he gained and maintained. Julius Rietz, who was himself an able violoncellist, and had had during his Directorship in Leipsic many opportunities of observing Grütz-

macher's extraordinary executive capacity, rated him very
highly, and was in the habit of admiringly expressing himself
with regard to the incomparable, exemplary and thorough
training of his left hand. It is, therefore, the more intelligible
that he made him every offer possible in order to gain him
for the Dresden Hofkapelle, after he had undertaken its
direction. This happened in 1860, and in the same year
Grützmacher was summoned to Dresden as Kummer's successor. From this time he travelled through Germany,
Holland, England, Austria, Hungary, Italy, Denmark, Sweden,
and Russia, and was received everywhere with triumph; but
he was also distinguished in many ways at the place of his
work. In course of time he received from the King of Saxony
the title of Chamber Virtuoso, later he was appointed Royal
Concert leader, and on his twenty-fifth jubilee of service he
was honoured far and wide in manifold ways.

In Grützmacher's playing were happily united the endowments of a finished mastery of complex technical difficulties
and delicate manner of expression, more especially in the
rendering of *Cantilena*. He is not only a virtuoso of the first
rank, but also an excellent interpreter of classical chamber
music. For this latter qualification the foundation had
already been laid by a careful musical education under his
father's roof, to which Friedrich Schneider had substantially
contributed. He pursued his theoretical studies under the
direction of this master.

Grützmacher published a great number of compositions.
Those which have had the widest circulation are the two
Concertos, Op. 10 (A minor) and Op. 46 (E minor); the Hungarian Fantasia (Op. 7), the Nocturne (Op. 32), the Scherzo (Op.
30), the Transcriptions of Classical Music (Op. 60), the "Daily
Studies," the Twenty-four Studies (Op. 38), as well as three
Songs with Violoncello obbligato (Op. 50). He added con-
siderably to the enrichment of violoncello literature by his
transcriptions of Haydn's, Mozart's, Beethoven's, and Schu-
mann's Sonatas, as well as of two of Beethoven's Violin
Romances, and of Schumann's "Kinderscenen." He further
arranged for the Violoncello the Thirty-six "Songs without
Words" of Mendelssohn, about twelve selected Piano pieces by
Schumann and Chopin, the Violin Sonata (Op. 19) and the

128 THE ART OF VIOLONCELLO PLAYING

Romance (Op. 44) by Rubinstein, the "Pensées fugitives"
by Steph. Heller and Ernst, and many other pieces of music.
Grützmacher also brought out new editions of classical and
modern compositions, with the addition of careful annotations.
We must here mention the two Gamba Sonatas of Joh. Seb.
Bach, as well as his six Violoncello Suites; a Gamba Sonata
by Handel and by Phil. Em. Bach, six Boccherini Sonatas
with the addition of a piano accompaniment, a Sonata by
Bonifazio Asioli, some Violoncello Compositions of Beethoven,
Mendelssohn, Schumann, and Chopin; a "Thème Russe
varié" by Ferd. Ries, the ten Concertos and six easy Instruction Pieces for Violoncello by Bernhard Romberg, as well as
twelve Exercises by Dotzauer (Op. 107), with the addition of
a second violoncello part.

In a special manner Grützmacher is deserving of merit by
his highly successful method of instruction in violoncello
playing. Even during his active work in Leipsic he formed
several excellent cellists, whose names are Leopold Grützmacher, Kahnt, Wilfert, Hilpert, and Hegar.

LEOPOLD GRÜTZMACHER, a younger brother of the cello
master already mentioned, born on September 4, 1835, at
Dessau, was taught cello playing first by Drechsler and then
by his brother, while Fr. Schneider conducted his theoretical
education.

Leopold Grützmacher belonged successively to the Theatre
and Gewandhaus orchestras in Leipsic, to the Court band
at Schwerin, to the orchestra of the German National Theatre
in Prague, and to the Meiningen Court band. From the
latter he was called, in 1876, to Weimar, as solo cellist to
the Grand Ducal Kapelle. Like his brother he was also
distinguished by the title of "Chamber Virtuoso" and "Concertmaster." He published for the violoncello two Concertos (Op.
6 and 9) and several smaller, pleasing, and well worked out
compositions.

Leopold Grützmacher educated his son, whose Christian
name was Friedrich, as a cellist. He has already afforded
agreeable proofs of his executive capacity in his public
appearances, and is a member of the Weimar Royal orchestra.

MORITZ KAHNT, born on April 27, 1836, in Löbnitz (near
Leipsic), received instruction in his parents' house from his

seventh to his fourteenth year not only on the violin and the piano, but also on several wind instruments. Later he devoted himself by preference to violoncello playing, in which he was Grützmacher's pupil for three years in the Leipsic Conservatoire. During the same time he received instruction at the above-named Institution in composition and the organ. From the year 1855 he has been first cellist of the Concert Orchestra, as well as teacher in the school of music at Basle. Besides his post as organist he superintends the direction of a Musical Union there.

BRUNO WILFERT, born on July 26, 1836, at Schmalzgrube, in Saxony, began his education first as violinist under the town musical director at Kirschberg (in the neighbourhood of Zwickau), then went with him to Glauchau, and there began cello playing. Twice a week he journeyed, with his violoncello under his arm, to the town of Zwickau, three hours distant, in order to get instruction from the violoncellist, Fr. Herrmann, a pupil of F. A. Kummer, who belonged to the town orchestra. Later on he became Grützmacher's pupil at Leipsic. By his unceasing industry Wilfert succeeded so well that in the year 1864 he was appointed solo cellist to the German Theatre at Prague. Since the foundation of the Prague Musical Union (1876) he has belonged as a co-operating member to the Quartet Society. The cello compositions of Wilfert which have appeared are Two Pieces (Op. 1), Hungarisch (Op. 2), Fantasia on Airs from the "Masked Ball" (Op. 3), Two Drawing-room Pieces (Op. 4), and a "Nocturne" for four Violoncellos (Op. 5).

FRIEDRICH HILPERT, born March 4, 1841, at Nuremburg, went to the Leipsic Conservatoire, was there pupil of Grützmacher, and having finished his studies found an appointment in the Karlsruhe orchestra. He then went to Zurich, where he made the acquaintance of the distinguished violinist, Jean Becker (who died on October 10, 1884); with him, in 1866, in connection with the Italians Masi and Chiostri as second violin and tenor, he founded that artistic union which, as the "Florentine String Quartet," attained to such great reputation on account of its excellent performances. In 1875 Hilpert separated from his Quartet companions in order to take the place, hitherto filled by Röver, which had been offered to him in the Grand Opéra and the Conservatoire at Vienna. After the lapse of a year, he gave up this appointment again, and became, under the title of Chamber Virtuoso, a member of the Meiningen Hofkapelle, and was employed as soloist in the concert tours under the direction of Hans v. Bülow. When he relinquished this undertaking, he entered the Royal orchestra at Munich, to which he still belongs. Hilpert is reckoned one of the best German cellists of the present day. The publication arranged by him of a collection of " classical studies " by Couperin, Rameau, Bach, and Martini are worthy of notice.

EMIL HEGAR also, born on January 3, 1843, at Basle, received his education, like the above-named cellists, from Grützmacher, at the Leipsic Conservatoire. In the year 1866 he was appointed, on account of his much esteemed performances, first Violoncellist of the Academy Orchestra, as well as teacher at the Conservatoire at Leipsic. Compelled by a nervous affection to abandon entirely, a few years later, Violoncello playing, he devoted himself to the study of singing, and became a singing master. He worked with success as such in the school of music in his native town. The loss which cello playing sustained in him is proved by his pupil,

JULIUS KLENGEL, one of the most excellent and purest violoncello players of the younger generation. He was born on September 24, 1859, at Leipsic, and is now working in his native town as first cellist in the Gewandhaus Concerts and as teacher at the Conservatoire. Klengel has not only made himself known outside the sphere of his work by his remarkable playing, but also as a most attractive composer for his instrument. Amongst his works we will mention only the compositions published, as Op. 1, 3, 4, 5, 7, 9, 10, 11, 15, and 20. Of those of his works not numbered must be named a collection of " Unsere Lieblinge," which contains "the most charming melodies of ancient and modern times," cleverly arranged with piano accompaniment.

A second pupil of Hegar's is HERMANN HEBERLEIN, who also had the advantage of Carl Schröeder's and Bernhard Coszmann's instruction. Born on March 29, 1859, at Marckneukirchen, in the kingdom of Saxony, Heberlein went, from

1873-1877, to the Leipsic Conservatoire. In the last years of that period he gave concerts in South Germany, and finally was appointed to be solo cellist at the town theatre of Königsberg. In 1883 he undertook the office of teacher of his instrument at the music school there. He wrote " Elementary Studies " for the Violoncello, " Practical Cello Studies " (2 books, Op. 5), Variations for the Violoncello, with piano accompaniment (Op. 2), Two Cello Pieces (Op. 3), four Pièces de Salon (Op. 6), and also published a Violoncello school.

The favourable results which had been attained in Leipsic by Friedrich Grützmacher in the training of his pupils made him very soon the most attractive teacher in Germany. As already mentioned, after he had accepted the flattering invitations made to him to go to Dresden, pupils came to him from all parts. Only the most famous amongst them are noticed below.

OSCAR EBERLE, born June 5, 1841, at Krossen, on the Oder, received from his father, who was town music director, his first instruction on the cello. At fourteen he had already made such progress that he was taken into the Bilse Orchestra, which at that time had its headquarters at Liegnitz. He belonged to it for five years, in the course of which he was also employed as soloist in the concerts of the Society. He was then for two years Grützmacher's pupil in Dresden; advancing rapidly under his direction, he attained to artistic maturity. In 1867 Eberle was summoned to Rotterdam as teacher to the music school there, as well as solo cellist at the concerts given by the " Matchappy tot bevordering der Toonkunst." He was immediately engaged as soloist for the German Opera at Rotterdam. He retired from the latter post in 1886. Eberle is an honorary member of the Concert Society, with which he worked, as well as of the Society of Students, " Sempre crescendo," at Leyden, a proof of how highly his talent is appreciated in Holland.

RICHARD BELLMANN, born on June 8, 1844, at Freiburg, in the kingdom of Saxony, at first benefited by the instruction of F. A. Kummer, and then went through a course under Grützmacher, after having for three years frequented the Conservatoire at Dresden. He then went to Paris, in order to study composition under the direction of Franchomme. This connection, however, did not last long, as Bellmann was soon summoned to the Grand Ducal Kapelle at Schwerin, as first solo cellist. His performances met with such high appreciation that he was distinguished by the Grand Duke with the bestowal of the title of Chamber Virtuoso. In 1878 Bellmann gave up his position at Schwerin, which he had occupied for twelve years, took up his residence at Bonn, and was engaged chiefly as a concert player. A short time after was formed at Cologne the Heckmann String Quartet, which gained such reputation in recent years during its tours in Germany, England, and Italy, which Bellmann joined, and to which he still belongs as a special ornament.

Bellmann must be considered one of the most accomplished violoncellists of the present time, not only as a soloist, but also as a quartet player. With complete technical training, his playing is distinguished by its exemplary purity, rarely fine tone, its elegance, and its noble and accurate musical rendering.

EMIL BOERNGEN spent his youth in Emden, where his father was music director. He was born on February 2, 1845, at Verden. He received his first instruction in music from his father. He then began the study of violoncello playing under the direction of the chamber virtuoso, C. Mattys, in Hanover. He obtained, however, his higher education under the direction of Grützmacher, and had the benefit of his tuition for three years. In 1870 Boerngen went to Helsingfors. He there undertook the post of cellist at the theatre. At the same time he was frequently a much appreciated player both as soloist and in quartets. Two years after he accepted the invitation to Strasburg Theatre as solo cellist. After several years of activity he relinquished his post and went to Salzburg, where he was engaged for the Mozarteum. Since 1875 he has been teacher of violoncello playing at the Royal Music School at Würzburg. In consideration of his successful work at that Institute, in 1883 he received the title of Professor as a mark of distinction. During his official activity he was also occupied as solo and quartet player.

RICHARD VOLLRATH was born on December 16, 1848, in the Thuringian town of Sonneberg, belonging to Saxe-Meiningen, where his father filled the office of town musician. The boy early tried several instruments, till he at length showed his preference for the violoncello.   His first teacher was the royal chamber musician, Roda, at Rudolstadt.   During the years 1865-1867, he studied under the direction of Grützmacher. Having fulfilled his military term at Coblenz, Vollrath belonged, from 1871-1873, to the Royal orchestra at Ems as cellist.   In the following winter he joined the Mannsfeld first orchestra at Dresden.   He made use of his residence there to renew his studies under Grützmacher.   He then went as first cellist for two years into the Wiesbaden orchestra.   Since September, 1876, he has belonged in the same capacity to the Municipal orchestra at Mainz.   Besides his official post he is also prominent as a solo player and an appreciated teacher.

CARL. FRIEDR. WILH. FITZENHAGEN was educated under the guidance of Grützmacher as a violoncello virtuoso of eminent rank.   This distinguished artist was born on September 15, 1848, in the little town of Seesen, in Brunswick, where his father was music director.   He early began his practice—in his fifth year on the piano, in his eighth on the violoncello, in his eleventh year on the violin.   Besides these instruments, he learned by degrees several wind instruments in order to take part in his father's musical entertainments when a vacancy occurred in his orchestra.   By means of this many-sided capacity, Fitzenhagen gained, even in early youth, a certain routine in musical matters which, later on, stood him in good stead.

Fitzenhagen received the first regular cello instruction, besides making progress in piano and violin playing, from the Ducal chamber musician, Plock, in Brunswick.   But he soon made his appearance there as soloist.   His really serious study, however, was in the beginning of October of the year 1862, when he became Theodore Müller's pupil. After a lapse of three years, Fitzenhagen was heard by the Duke of Brunswick in the Theatre Royal.   The trial performance was so satisfactory that the Duke, in order to forward him in his artistic career, released him entirely from military service. Patrons of high standing immediately supplied him with the means of prosecuting his cello studies under Grützmacher. This occurred in May, 1867.   A year later, notwithstanding his youth, he was named a member of the Hofkapelle of Saxony.

From that time he frequently made his appearance as a solo player; took part, in 1869, in the general musical gathering in Leipsic, and in 1870 at the Beethoven Festival. Franz Liszt wished to gain him for the orchestra at Weimar, but Fitzenhagen preferred to accept an offer made to him to be Professor at the Imperial Conservatoire in Moscow. From that time he has developed an uncommonly active and successful artistic capability as a concert player as well as chamber music performer. He gained striking results in his professorial relations, for he is at present looked upon as the cello master of greatest repute in Russia. The best of his pupils will be mentioned in the last section of this book.

After Fitzenhagen had been appointed Concertmaster to the Russian Imperial Musical Society, the direction of the Moscow Music and Orchestral Union, which organises annually some concerts, was made over to him some three years ago.

Fitzenhagen was very industrious as a composer. Besides a String Quartet, which gained the prize of the St. Petersburg Chamber Musical Union, he wrote four Cello Concertos, a Suite for Violoncello and orchestra, a " Fantasia " on *Motifs* from Rubinstein's " Dämon," with orchestra; a long list of drawing-room pieces, amongst them twelve little pieces which embraced a Quarto, a Ballade with orchestra, and a book containing technical Cello Studies.

ALBERT PETERSEN, born on October 23, 1856, in Lubeck, after he had studied under Grützmacher, was first cellist in the private bands at Dresden, Kreuznach, and Cassel; accepted engagements for America and Pawlowsk, near St. Petersburg, and has since filled for ten years the position of solo cellist in Magdeburg, as well as that of cello master at the Musical Institute there.

CARL MONHAUPT, born on March 9, 1856, in Hamburg, began his musical studies with piano playing. In his fifteenth year he decided for the violoncello, of which he learnt the elements from the cellist named Katerbaum, of the Central Hall orchestra of his native town. In 1872 he betook himself to Sondershausen, in order to pursue his studies under the direction of his brother Fritz,[1] who at that time belonged to

---

[1] He is now member of the Royal Theatre Band at Cassel. No information about him could be obtained.

the Royal orchestra of Sondershausen as first cellist. Here he remained three years, when he went to Dresden in order to perfect his education under Grützmacher's guidance. At the present time he is first violoncellist of the Musical Society and of the Orchestral Union at Berne, as well as teacher at the music school there.

OSCAR BRÜCKNER, born on January 2, 1857, at Erfurt, received his first cello instruction from the Concertmaster, Herlitz, in Ballenstedt, after he had been prepared by his father for the musical career. But he completed the most important part of his studies under Fr. Grützmacher, in Dresden, where he also received instruction in the theoretical portion from Felix Dräseke.

After he had finished his course of study, Brückner undertook concert tours in Russia, Poland, and Holland. Wherever he was heard he was marked by well-merited success. Besides his clever "technique" he made a great impression by his broad and full tone. From 1882-1884 he was engaged as violoncellist at the Grand Ducal Court Theatre in Neustrelitz. On retiring from this post he received the title of Chamber Virtuoso. Since 1886 he has been solo cellist at the Theatre Royal, Wiesbaden. At the same time he takes part in the Violoncello teaching at the Wiesbaden Conservatoire.

Brückner's official successor in Neustrelitz, OTTO KÖHLER, was born December 21, 1861, at Neuhaldensleben (in the district of Merseberg). He went to school at Chemnitz and having performed his military service, he entered the Regiment of Life Grenadiers at Dresden. He there remained until 1882, in order to perfect himself, under Grützmacher, in Violoncello playing, which he had already pursued by himself. In January, 1883, Köhler was engaged for the Kapelle of the Duke of Coburg Gotha. He remained two years at this post, during which he went through a theoretical course under the direction of the Court Kapell-meister, Langert. In 1885 he was offered the post of solo cellist at Neustrelitz. In this position he is at present.

A German-American is also amongst Grützmacher's pupils. EMIL SCHENK, born at the beginning of the sixties at Rochester, North America. In 1879 his father, a native of

Baden, who had settled as music teacher in the above-mentioned American town, sent him to Dresden to complete his studies under Grützmacher's direction. He made rapid progress, and soon attracted the attention of the Dresden musical circle to so great a degree that at the end of the same year he was appointed to the Hofkapelle there. His engagement, however, was only temporary, for as soon as Schenk had completed his studies under Grützmacher, he returned to America. On his frequent public appearances in New York he has had brilliant success. The well-known Director of the Philharmonic Concerts, Theod. Thomas, did not let the favourable opportunity escape of gaining over the highly gifted young artist as solo cellist for his orchestra. He attained to ever-increasing appreciation and popularity. But as Thomas so frequently undertook tours with his orchestra in the States of the Union, this occupation became at length too irksome to him; he released himself from the contract, and from that time, encouraged by the sympathy of the public, he lives in New York as an independent artist, and works not only as a concert player, but also as a teacher of great repute.

Another excellent pupil of Grützmacher is HUGO BECKER, son of the famous Violinist who founded the Florentine Quartet, but who unhappily died in the flower of his age, in 1884. Hugo Becker was born on February 13, 1863, at Strasburg, in Alsace, and at the beginning of the sixth year of his life received instruction from his father on the piano and the violin. When he was nine years old, he heard a Violoncello played in church, and this made such an impression on him, that he decided in favour of that instrument. A pupil of Menter's, the cellist Kündinger, of Mannheim, whither Becker's parents had gone in 1869, undertook his education. At fifteen he had made such progress, that the place of second cellist was offered to him in the orchestra of the Mannheim Court Theatre, which he accepted. At the end of nine months he gave this up in order to go through a course under Grützmacher, from whose instruction he benefited for five months. Having returned home, his father undertook his further tuition, and used to play to him studies and concert pieces on the Violin which greatly assisted his progress in regard to their comprehension and rendering. The circumstance that he was constantly hearing in the parental home a great deal of chamber music in the best manner and himself took part in it, was of great value for the young man's musical education. In the year 1880 Jean Becker resolved to undertake concert tours with his son Hugo and his brother and sister JEANNE (a pianist) and Hans (tenor), during which the young Cello virtuoso, then seventeen years of age, gained his first laurels. While the Becker family quartet was performing in London, Hugo Becker had the opportunity of being brought a good deal in contact with Piatti, which was not without producing some influence on his playing. The practices at the De Swert Violoncello Concerts, under the direction of their founder, also contributed to his progress.

For two years, from October, 1884, till the autumn of 1886, Becker filled the office of solo cellist at the Frankfort Opera. From that time he accepted no other post, in order to leave his time quite free for concert engagements. Frankfort-on the-Main has continued to be his place of residence. We must mention that he has the title of Grand Ducal Chamber Virtuoso of Baden.

KARL LÜBBE, born on February 11, 1839, in Halberstadt, began his musical career as a member of the regimental band at Magdeburg, was appointed to the Grand Ducal Berneburg orchestra at Ballenstedt, and came to Dessau on the union of the Anhalt Duchies. As he showed himself very assiduous the Duke of Dessau granted him the means of perfecting himself still more under the guidance of Grützmacher. He gained great dexterity and skill, but was inclined to the various experiments of a virtuoso, which he carried out also in his compositions. His cello pieces have not been published. After Drechsler was pensioned Lübbe became his successor as first Violoncellist in the Court Chapel at Dessau. He died in his prime on January 7, 1888.

HUGO JÄGER took his place, born on May 17, in Warmbrunn. He profited by the instruction of Popper and Grützmacher, became then a member of the Hofcapelle of the Prince of Hohenzollern, in Löwenberg, and after relinquishing this was employed in Ems, Altenburg, and

Brunswick.   Since 1874 he has belonged to the Ducal band in Dessau.

AUREL V. CZERWENKA, born on December 31, 1860, at Karánsebes, in the Hungarian state, Szoreny, was first a pupil of the Steiermark Musical Union at Gratz. In 1882 he came to Dresden and frequented the Conservatoire as a pupil of Grützmacher, under whose direction he afterwards studied privately. On the completion of his education he worked for a time as first cellist in the Mannsfeld orchestra in Dresden, and then he undertook the office of solo cellist at the Land Theatre, as well as that of teacher at the Steiermark Musical Union at Gratz. His performances show genuine artistic talent and training.

Two other pupils of Grützmacher's must be here mentioned concerning whom there is very defective information. The first to be considered is THEODOR KRUMBHOLZ, who unfortunately died while still young. He was first Violoncellist at the Stuttgard Court Kapelle, with the title of Royal Wurtemburg Chamber Virtuoso.

H. RUHOFF became, after he had finished his studies, first cellist at the Theatre Royal at Pesth, but was obliged to give up his place on account of a nervous affection, and still lives as a music master at Zurich, where he teaches chiefly at his brother's Musical Institute.

A. HEYN, born in Dresden, is exclusively a pupil of Grützmacher. After his training he was first occupied in the orchestra of German Opera at Rotterdam. He is now working as first Violoncellist in the Grand Ducal band in Darmstadt. As regards the Violoncellists, Smith and Rüdinger, who were likewise Grützmacher's pupils, information will be given among the Dutch and Danish cellists. As a third pupil of Drechsler—

KARL SCHRÖDER, born on December 18, 1848, in Quedlinburg, must be here noticed with distinction. He had already made such progress in cello studies at fourteen years of age that he, was able to be received into the Hofkapelle at Sondershausen. After he had joined his brothers in forming a string quartet, which was distinguished by his performances, he accepted, in 1873, the place offered to him as first cellist in the Brunswick Kapelle. Only a year later, however, he consented to go as first representative of his instrument to Leipsic, and he also superintended at the same time the cello instruction in the Conservatoire there. From Leipsic Schröder went, in 1881, as Hof-Capellmeister to Sondershausen. He worked at this post for five years; he then undertook the direction of German Opera in Rotterdam. Thence he went, in 1887, as Hof-Capellmeister to Berlin. Since the autumn of 1888 he has been occupied as Capellmeister at the Stadt-Theatre at Hamburg.

Schröder published the following Cello compositions: Three Concertos (Op. 32, 36, and 55), three concerted pieces (Op. 38, 51, and 56), an Allegro di Sonatina (Op. 13), Pieces of National Airs (Op. 14), a Song without Words (Op. 15), and a Nocturne (Op. 42). Besides these he produced a Violoncello school (Op. 16), a school of scales and chords (Op. 29), a school of shakes and staccatos (Op. 39), a practical course for Violoncello playing, as well as a long series of Etudes and Exercises. The latter bear the Nos. 22, 25, 35, 40, 44, 45, 46, 48, and 57. He also edited orchestral and concert studies as well as five classical pieces.

The same continuity of Violoncello playing as that of the Dresden school cannot be traced in Vienna because, though at the beginning of our century several cello masters were actively working at the same time, a similar connection did not exist amongst them as in Dresden. But the Austrian capital had the advantage of a richly endowed musical life by means of the heroes of instrumental music, which had a quickening and progressive effect on all branches of executive art, and specially on Violoncello playing. Although this influence was not confined to Vienna alone—since the works of these highly-gifted men, after their publication, spread over an ever-widening circle—still the musical world of Vienna was the chief gainer thereby.

It was at the source and therefore had the opportunity of knowing and studying the creations of these master composers at first hand. We need only recall the Schuppanzigh Art Society, which practised and produced Beethoven's Quartets before they were published. The Violoncello was represented at the end of last century and the beginning of the present one by Anton Kraft and, later, by Joseph Linke. For the first Beethoven composed the Cello part of the Triple Concerto (Op. 56). The Sonatas (Op. 5, 69, and 102) of the great master may be here mentioned as important works of Violoncello Literature.

ANTON KRAFT was born on December 30, 1752, in the little Bohemian town of Rokitzan. After his school education was finished he entered the University of Vienna, in order to study law. There he soon began his musical career, and, as he had already diligently practised Violoncello playing in his father's house, and had acquired remarkable proficiency, he did not find it difficult to procure a position in the Imperial Hofkapelle. Joseph Haydn, to whom he was introduced as clever, appointed him, in 1778, to the orchestra of the Prince Esterhazy. As, however, this artist-patron died at the end of September, 1790, the band was done away with, and Kraft returned again to Vienna, where, in the year 1793, by his conjunction with it, the Schuppanzigh String Quartet was founded, which used to play every Friday morning in the house of Prince Lichnowsky. Kraft was himself occupied, however, until 1795, in the band of Prince Grassalkowitz, and later on in that of the Prince Lobkowitz. He died at Vienna on August 20, 1820.

Of Kraft's compositions were published—six Sonatas for Violoncello, with Bass (Op. 1 and 2) ; three concerted Duets for Violin and Violoncello (Op. 3) ; a Violoncello Concerto, with orchestra (Op. 4) ; two Duets for two Violoncellos (Op. 5 and 6), and a Divertissement with Bass.

Amongst Kraft's pupils his son, Nicolas, and Birnbach must be mentioned.

HENRICH AUGUST BIRNBACH, born 1782 at Breslaw, went in 1792 to Berlin, and there learnt Piano and Violoncello playing. The year 1802 found him at Vienna, where he enjoyed the instructions of Kraft and was employed in the opera orchestra. Two years later Count Lubomirski engaged him for his private band in Galicia. But in 1806 he returned to Vienna, and in 1812 he accepted an engagement as first Violoncellist at the Theatre of Pesth. From 1822 to 1824 he remained at Vienna, occupied himself zealously with the " Chitarra coll' arco," invented by a certain Stauffer, wrote a

Concerto for it, and played it in a public assembly. In the year 1825 he at length received an appointment in the Hof-kapelle at Berlin. He seems to have belonged to it until his death.

NICOLAS KRAFT, born at Esterhazy, in Hungary, on December 14, 1778, began his musical practice in his fourth year, on a large tenor which he possessed, something like a Violoncello. Two years later he played a solo before the Prince Esterhazy, which his father had written specially for him with this object in view. At eight years of age he made a tour, accompanied by his father, and performed at concerts favourably in Vienna, Presburg, Dresden, and Berlin. On his return, the young Kraft sought to fill up the gaps in his general education, which, until then, had been neglected, and this took up five years. During the time he only occupied himself with his instrument as a recreation. In 1796 he entered with his father into the Lobkowitz band. The prince, who took a great interest in the youth, and cherished the wish that he should cultivate still further his art, granted him the means of going through a course with Louis Duport at Berlin. This happened in the year 1801. He afterwards went to Holland, in order to be heard there. Prince Esterhazy meantime desired his speedy return, so that he could not pursue farther the journey he had begun. On his way home, he went to Leipsic, Dresden, and Prague, exciting great enthusiasm everywhere by his performances.

˙ Nicolas Kraft was engaged in the year 1809 as solo cellist for the Imperial Opera, but retained also his connection with Prince Lobkowitz, who offered him a permanent salary, under the condition that he should never play anywhere without his permission, except in his Palace. This, however, did not continue, because the Prince fell into serious money difficulties from the year 1811, and was no longer free to dispose of his ruined fortune. But Kraft was indemnified in another manner. At the Congress of Princes in 1814, he played before an assemblage of crowned heads in Vienna, and the King of Wurtemburg experienced such great pleasure at his performances, that he named him his Chamber Virtuoso. He now settled at Stuttgard, and thence took a journey, in 1818, to the Rhine, which he extended as far as Hamburg. Here he became acquainted with Bernard Romberg, who gave him every encouragement, and showed it by giving with him two concerts publicly, when he went to Stuttgard in 1820. In the year 1824 Kraft wounded the first finger of his right hand, on account of which, after futile attempts at curing it, he was obliged to retire. He spent his pension in Stuttgard, where he died on May 18, 1853. Kraft composed for his instrument four Concertos, nine Duets (three of which are marked as "Divertissements"), a Polonaise, a Bolero, a "Scène pastorale," a "Rondo à la chasse," and two Fantasias, of which one is an arrangement of airs from the "Freischütz." Nicolas Kraft had a son whose Christian name was FRIEDRICH, whom he likewise educated as a clever cellist. He was born on February 12, 1807, in Vienna, and belonged to the Stuttgard band as chamber musician. Nothing further is known of him.

About the same time as Anton Kraft, Friedrich's grandfather, JOSEPH LINKE, the violoncellist already mentioned, was at work in Vienna for some years as a distinguished quartet player. He was born on June 8, 1783, in the Silesian town of Trachenberg, received his first instruction from his father, and after his death pursued his studies under a certain Oswald. In his twelfth year he went to the Dominicans at Breslaw, there his teachers in cello playing were Lose and Flemming; for theory he studied under the organist Hanish. Lose was a member of the theatre orchestra, and when he relinquished the post Linke took his place. He remained there, however, only until 1808, when he went to Vienna. He was engaged immediately by Schuppanzigh for the house quartet of Count Rasoumowski, which existed until the year 1816. After the dissolution of this Society, Linke was attracted to Croatia by the family of Count Erdödisch. Two years later he again appeared in Vienna, in order to work at the theatre there as soloist. Thirteen years later he received an appointment in the same capacity at the Imperial Grand Opera. His death took place on March 20, 1837.

Linke's published cello compositions consist of a Concerto, three books of Variations, a Polonaise, a "Rondoletto," and a "Caprice" on Rossini airs. Whilst the elder Kraft and Linke, whom Beethoven likewise held in great esteem, represented in

Vienna violoncello playing from a purely artistic point of view,

Joseph Merk did so more especially on the virtuoso side. This artist, born on January 18, 1795, at Vienna, who was originally to have been a violinist, and had already in his younger years made great progress, had the misfortune to be bitten so severely by a dog that, even after the wound was healed, he was never able again to bring his left arm into the requisite position for violin playing. He therefore took up the Violoncello, on which he received instruction from Philippe Schindlocker.[1] Under his direction, Merk made such rapid progress that already after the lapse of a year he was engaged as quartet player by a Hungarian magnate. He remained at this post two years, when he made a tour through the Austrian dominions in order to make himself known in a wider circle. In 1816 he was appointed first Violoncellist to the Grand Opera at Vienna. Three years later he entered the Imperial Kapelle, and, in 1821, the Professorship for the Violoncello was entrusted to him at the Vienna Conservatoire, which institution later on acquired such importance in regard to instrumental music. He retained the latter office until 1848. In 1834 the Emperor named him his chamber virtuoso. Soon after he undertook a prolonged tour, visited Prague, Dresden, Leipsic, Brunswick, Hanover, Hamburg, and from the last-mentioned town went to London. In Vienna, Merk enjoyed great favour. " He was," C. Hanslick says, in his " History of Vienna Concerted Music " (p. 245), " indefatigable as an industrious concert-giver, and continually encouraged by public sympathy. He frequently performed at Concerts with Mayseder, whose compositions he played by preference, and might properly be called the Mayseder of the Violoncello. . . . Merk also performed, as cellist, in Böhm's quartet productions. As virtuoso he soon surpassed Linke as well as Friedrich Wranitzky. The latter, who was a son of the violinist and Kapellmeister, Anton Wranitzky, held a respectable position among the Viennese cellists of that period, and, about his twentieth year, frequently played Duets with his brother, the violinist, Anton Wranitzky, at concerts."

---

[1] See page 69 of this book.

Merk died in Vienna on July 16, 1852. Of his Violoncello compositions were published—one Concerto, one Concertino, one Adagio and Rondo, one Polonaise, four books of Variations, " Vingt Exercices " (Op. 11), and Six Etudes (Op. 20). Formerly these compositions were much played, but, in course of time, they have gradually gone out of fashion, like most of the Cello productions of that period.

Amongst Merk's numerous pupils, the most remarkable are—Böhm, Träg, Marx, and the Dutchman, Franco-Mendez.

KARL LEOPOLD BÖHM, born November 4, 1806, at Vienna, profited by Merk's instruction in the Conservatoire there. He was successively member of the orchestras of Josephstadt Theatre and of the Vienna Theatre. In September of the year 1824 he went to Donaueschingen, where he was appointed musician to the Prince of Fürstenburg. Thence he undertook a successful concert tour to Switzerland and Germany. When in August, 1849, he was released from his engagement in the Donaueschingen Kapelle, he went to Strasburg and entered the theatre orchestra, and also undertook a series of concerts at Vichy. At the beginning of 1851 the amateur Prince of Fürstenburg recalled some of the members of his former band, in order to organize some chamber music. Amongst them was Böhm, who now concluded his artistic career at Donaueschingen. Of his Cello compositions he published a Concerto, Duets, Fantasias, Variations, Polonaises, and some smaller pieces.

ANTON TRÄG, son of a Viennese composer, Andreas Träg, was born in 1818, at Schwechat, near Vienna; began his musical education at six years of age, and went to the Conservatoire at Vienna as a pupil of Merk's. On February 28, 1845, he was engaged as teacher of Cello playing for the Conservatoire at Prague. Ten years later however he gave up the post and returned to Vienna, where he died on July 7, 1860. Träg devoted himself by special preference to classical music. He had abundant opportunity of occupying himself with it in the Palace at Clam. Of his pupils,

HEINRICH RÖVER distinguished himself, who was born May 27, 1827. Röver belongs to the number of those violoncellists who were at first violinists. As early as eight years of age he decided in favour of the violoncello. Fétis says of him :

"He was about 1863 the cleverest player of his instrument in Vienna." Of his compositions may be cited—Iydll (Op 1), Mazurka (Op 8), and "Sérénade du Savoyard" (Op 11). Röver died in 1876.

JOSEPH M. MARX, born in 1792 at Würzburg, where he also received his musical education, began his artistic career as member of the Theatre orchestra at Frankfort-on-the-Main, whence he went to Vienna, in order to study under Merk. Later on he worked in the Stuttgard orchestra, until he was appointed first Violoncellist at Carlsruhe. He finally was musical director there, and died while working in this capacity on November 11, 1836. His daughter, Pauline, made her appearance on the stage as a singer during the years 1830-40. Concerning FRANCO-MENDEZ, see the Cello players of Holland.

To the best Viennese violoncellists about the middle of our century belongs CARL SCHLESINGER, born on August 19, 1813. The violin was originally his instrument. After the lapse of three years he devoted himself to the Violoncello. Who his master was is unknown. In 1838 he was appointed solo cellist to the Pesth National Theatre. He gave up this place in 1846, as the opportunity presented itself of entering the Imperial Opera orchestra in the same capacity at Vienna. In 1862 the office of cello teacher at the Conservatoire there was committed to him. Schlesinger's most noted pupils are: Udel, Sulzer, Hummer, and Hegyesi.

CARL UDEL, born on February 6, 1844, at Warasdin, in Croatia, was early directed to the study of music by his father, who was Kapellmeister, and went in September, 1859, to the Conservatoire at Vienna. He next occupied himself there with violin playing under the guidance of Professor Carl Heissler. Twelve months after he took up the Violoncello, and for five years received instruction from Schlesinger. In 1867 he was first Cellist at the opera in Pesth; a year later, however, he returned to Vienna and was engaged there, in 1869, for the orchestra of the new opera house. By degrees he rose in his profession, and in May, 1876, he entered the Conservatoire as substitute for Röver, whose duties were then performed by Hilpert for a year. After the resignation of the former, Udel was again elected in his place. In 1878 Cello instruction at the Conservatoire was divided between him and Hummer, who in the interval had been nominated first Cello player of the Imperial Hofkapelle. Hummer received the three upper and Udel the three lower classes. After three years of work the latter obtained the title of Professor. On account of an injured hand, Udel was obliged to give up his place as member of the opera house, since when he has not played in public. He now devotes himself entirely to teaching.

Joseph Sulzer, born on February 11, 1850, at Vienna, emerged in 1869 from the Conservatoire as one of Schlesinger's best pupils, and was engaged for the Italian Opera, and as master for the Conservatoire at Bucharest. He remained there four years. In 1875 Sulzer received an appointment in the Vienna Opera orchestra. Illness, brought on by over-exertion, compelled him for three years to withdraw from his employment in the orchestra. On his recovery he still further endeavoured to perfect himself, in which the friendly advice of Popper was of service to him, and in 1880 he was appointed solo player at the Imperial Opera. At the same time he gave concerts and taught. He belonged to the Helmsberg Quartet from 1882 to 1885. Sulzer published various compositions and productions for the Violoncello at Breitkopf & Härtel's, and D. Rahter's, and Cranz'.

Reinhold Hummer, born on October 7, 1855, at Linz, on the Danube, began his career with violin playing very early at Vienna, where he was brought up, and pursued it with great eagerness for six years. Then an ardent desire was awakened in him to learn the Violoncello. He forthwith began the study of that instrument at the Vienna Conservatoire under Schlesinger's guidance. At his death, H. Röver became his master. On the whole he was four years at the Conservatoire. His progress was so rapid that he carried off the first prize against his fellow students by unanimous consent. After he had left the establishment to which he was indebted for his education, he immediately received an appointment in the opera orchestra to which he has belonged since the year 1873. Four years later he was appointed teacher at the Conservatoire, and in 1878 solo Cellist in the Imperial Court band; he was also given the title of Professor.

Besides his official employments, this much-favoured artist worked at Vienna and elsewhere as concert and quartet player.

Hegyesi will be mentioned among the Hungarian violoncellists.

As an older pupil of the Vienna Conservatoire (1835 to 1839), JOSEPH HUBER must be mentioned, who was born about 1816 at Vienna. According to Fétis, he was heard during the years 1836 and 1837 at the Conservatoire Concerts. Several of his Violoncello compositions appeared at Vienna.

A succession of excellent German cellists emanated from the Prague Conservatoire, opened in the year 1811. At this Institution JOHANN NEPOMUK HÜTTNER, born on January 1, 1793, was actively engaged as Violoncello teacher from 1822. He pursued his studies under J. Zimmermann. After they were concluded Hüttner joined the orchestra at the Pesth Theatre. Two years later he went to Lemberg. Thence he undertook, in 1820, a concert tour in Poland and Russia, after which he was appointed to the Prague Conservatoire, and the place of first cellist was immediately given to him at the theatre. His playing was distinguished by remarkable skill and delicate tone. In the *Adagio* his rendering was full of feeling. Hüttner was specially appreciated as a quartet player.

Hüttner formed an excellent cellist in his pupil, FRANZ HEGENBARTH, born on May 10, 1818, at Gersdorf, in Bohemia. On May 1, 1831, he entered the Prague Conservatoire, and remained there as student until May 16, 1837. Count Kinsky provided him with the means for his artistic education. In May, 1865, the Professorship at the Prague Conservatoire was given to Hegenbarth ; it had until then been in the hands of Moritz Wagner, Goltermann's successor. He devoted himself to this until his death, which occurred on December 20, 1887.

Besides several other compositions, Hegenbarth wrote a Violoncello school, though nothing at all of his has been published. Amongst his pupils the following are distinguished : Lang, Grünfeld, and Wihan.

ANTON LANG, born on November 10, 1850, at Carlsbad, from his tenth year played both the Piano and Violin, but decided at thirteen in favour of the Violoncello. In 1865 he became Hegenbarth's pupil in the Prague Conservatoire. When his training was ended Lang was employed as solo player in several concert orchestras. Since 1877 he has been attached to the Grand Ducal Kapelle in Schwerin as first cellist, with the title of " Kammer Virtuoso."

HEINRICH GRÜNFELD, born on April 21, 1855, at Prague, went to the Conservatoire there, and profited by the instructions of Hegenbarth. In 1873 he became solo cellist at the comic opera at Vienna and filled this place for two years. In 1876 he went to Berlin, where he worked as teacher of his instrument. From time to time he undertook some successful concert tours in Germany, Russia, and Austria, with his brother Alfred. Everywhere his beautiful tone and his tasteful rendering were appreciated.

HANS WIHAN, born on June 5, 1855, at Politz, in Bohemia, is likewise a pupil of the Prague Conservatoire, which he frequented from 1868 until 1873. At the end of this period he studied for awhile under the direction of Davidoff. His excellent performances procured for him the position of first Violoncellist in the Hofkapelle at Munich, which he filled for eight years with honour. In the spring of 1888 he was nominated to the Professorship of the Prague Conservatoire as successor to his master, Hegenbarth.

Another of Hüttner's pupils, SELMAR BAGGE, must be cited, born on June 30, 1823, at Coburg.[1] He received his musical education from the year 1837 at the Prague Conservatoire, and after he had pursued a course of composition under Simon Sechter, became a teacher of the theory at the Vienna Conservatoire. He relinquished this post in the year 1855, and from that time was chiefly engaged in composition, until in 1868 he was summoned to Basle as Director of the music school.

Amongst Hüttner's pupils there is also a gifted dilettante, Joseph Edler von Portheim, born on January 6, 1817, at Prague. For many years he has deserved the thanks of the

---

[1] Fétis erroneously says that Bagge was born in Bohemia, about 1815.

musical world in his native town by his zealous encouragement of chamber music, not only in his hospitable house, frequented by native and foreign artists, but also abroad. Since the foundation of the Prague Chamber Music Society (1876), he has been at the head of the undertaking, to which he devotes his indefatigable care.

Three other pupils of the Prague Conservatoire must be noticed in this place. EBERT, CABISIUS, and POPPER. They all had the benefit of Joh. August Jul. Goltermann's[1] instruction, who from 1850-1862, as successor to Träg, was teacher at the above-named establishment. (See page 123.)

LUDWIG EBERT, born on April 13, 1834, at Schloss Kladrau, in Bohemia, began early his musical training in the home of his father, who was royal treasurer of Windischgratz, and was sent in 1846 to Prague in order to study at the Conservatoire.

At first he received instruction from Träg. But when he went to Vienna, Ebert studied two years more under Goltermann's direction. From the autumn of 1852 until Easter, 1854, he was cellist at the opera in Temesvar, and was then engaged as first performer of his instrument for the Oldenburg Hofkapelle, where he worked up to the year 1874. Invested with the title of Concertmaster by the Grand Duke, as a mark of distinction, Ebert, in the same year, accepted the offer of being first cellist of the Gürzenich orchestra in Cologne, and teacher at the Conservatoire of the Rhenish metropolis. In this place he remained until April 1, 1888. At present Ebert is living at Wiesbaden, where he devotes himself to teaching. He has published " Four pieces " for Violoncello and Piano in the form of a Sonata (Op. 3), and three " Charakterstücke " (Op. 7).

JULIUS CABISIUS, born October 15, 1841, at Halle-on-the-Saal, received his first instruction from his father. During the years 1855-1861, he studied under Goltermann at the Prague Conservatoire. He then became a member of the Court Kapelle at Löwenberg and Meiningen. From the latter place he was summoned, in 1877, to be first Cellist in the royal band at Stuttgard.

---

[1] Not to be confounded with Georg Eduard Golterman, to be mentioned farther on.

DAVID POPPER, born on June 18, 1845 or 1846, in Prague, soon gained for himself, after leaving the Conservatoire of his native town, a remarkable reputation during the concert tours, which he began in the year 1863 as an excellent and cultivated solo player. He received special honour, in 1865, at the Carlsruhe Musical Festival, and in 1867, in Vienna, where, from 1868, he was engaged as first cellist at the Imperial Opera. In 1873 he gave up this post, in order to undertake, in company with his wife, the famous pianist, Sophie Menter, some concert tours, which led him into Germany, France, England, and Russia. He is at present teacher at the Pesth Conservatoire. Popper's playing is distinguished by its very pure and extremely clever technique, as well as by a refined, graceful manner of rendering. He published for the Violoncello two Concertos (Op. 8 and 24), two Suites (Op. 16 and 50), as well as a considerable number of smaller drawing-room pieces, which are in much favour among cellists.

In Berlin, as we saw, a great influence was exercised by France through the brothers Duport,[1] but in consequence of the political events of the years 1806-1807, which were the cause of so much suffering in Prussia, it was almost paralysed, for Louis Duport returned to France on the outbreak of the war declared by Napoleon Buonaparte ; and his elder brother, who on account of his advanced age could no longer occupy himself with Violoncello playing, went at the same time into retirement. It is, however, possible and even probable that the Violoncellist,

JOHANN FRIEDRICH KELZ, born on April 11, 1786, at Berlin, if he did not actually take regular lessons from him, was able to profit by his occasional advice.[2]

---

[1] Also the two Maras (father and son) had an important effect on Violoncello playing in Berlin, though not so great as that of the brothers Duport. Concerning the elder and younger Mara, the necessary details will be given in speaking of the Bohemian violoncellists.

[2] Fétis contests this, for he says: "The German biographers of Kelz affirm that he (Kelz) was advised by Duport ; but this is erroneous, as at this time (1811) Duport was no longer in Berlin." This could only refer to L. Duport, for his brother remained until his death in the Prussian capital.

His first years of study were spent by Kelz chiefly with the town musician, Fuchs, under whose direction he occupied himself with well-nigh every kind of musical instrument, amongst which the Violoncello attracted him most. His uncle, Ad. Friedrich Milke, who was himself not a bad cellist, assisted his progress on that instrument. He also provided for his reception into the band of Prince Frederick August of Brunswick-Öls, to which he belonged, from the year 1801, for four years. When this prince died, in 1805, Kelz returned to Berlin, and was nominated, in 1811, Royal Chamber Musician. In 1857 he went into retirement, and died in January, 1862. He must have been much in request as teacher of his instrument. His compositions, the number of which it is pretended extend to about three hundred, are of a very superficial description, and have long fallen into oblivion.

More remarkable than Kelz in Violoncello playing was MORITZ GANZ, who was born at Mayence in the year 1804, and learnt the elements of music from his father. In Violoncello playing he made further progress under the Bohemian Cellist, Stiastny, who at that time was residing at Frankfort-on-the-Maine. Ganz then joined the orchestra at Mayence until, in 1826, he was appointed first Violoncellist in the Berlin Kapelle. During this engagement he undertook, in the years 1833-1837, concert tours to Paris and London. In appreciation of his performances he received from the King of Prussia the title of Concertmaster. His playing, which gave proof of solid cultivation, was artistic and in every respect made an advantageous impression, without, however, electrifying. His compositions are unpretending, and consist of Concertos, Duets, and Variations.

Among the pupils educated by Ganz the most remarkable are—Rietz, Lotze, Giese, and Klietz.

JULIUS RIETZ, born on December 28, 1812, at Berlin, had, besides Ganz, also Bernhard Romberg for a short time as master, and developed so rapidly that, as early as sixteen years of age, he was received into the orchestra of the Royal Stadt-Theatre of his native town.

Six years later he went to Düsseldorf, and worked as assistant-director at the theatre managed by Immermann, with Mendelssohn at its head; when the latter retired he undertook the sole conduct of the opera, and became also, when Mendelssohn was summoned to Leipsic, town Music Director. He filled this place until 1847, in which year he went to settle at Leipsic, in order to work as "Capellmeister" at the theatre. His work so greatly increased at Leipsic—for he not only undertook the direction of the Academy of Singing, but also, in 1848, the conducting of the Gewandhaus Concerts—that he was obliged more and more to neglect cello playing.   In Dresden, whither Rietz went in 1860 as Court Kapellmeister, he almost entirely discontinued performing. In private circles only he now and then caused his instrument to be heard, as his time was wholly taken up by his official occupations, as well as by the direction of the Dresden Conservatoire, which was given over to him, and by the editorial labours connected with the publication of the collected works of the great classical composers, set on foot by Breitkopf and Härtel.   In the midst of this varied artistic activity he died on September 17, 1877.

Rietz's Violoncello playing was of an able but simply deserving kind and was limited entirely to the more classical sphere of music.   His compositions consist of two Concertos and a Fantasia with orchestral accompaniment.   He produced the latter on February 15, 1844, in the Gewandhaus, at Leipsic.

WILHELM LOTZE, born on January 17, 1817, at Berlin, acquired the first elements of cello playing under the royal chamber musician, Töpfer (1865), and then Ganz was his master.   In 1837 he received an appointment in the Royal Kapelle of his native town, and from 1838-1852 belonged to the excellent Zimmermann String Quartet.   Lotze was pensioned in 1872.

JOSEPH GIESE, born on November 24, 1821, at Coblenz on the Rhine, undertook concert journeys through France and Switzerland after he had for some time profited by the instruction of Ganz; he then went to the Hague, where he became teacher at the Royal School of Music and first Violoncellist at the French Theatre.   He educated a large number of pupils.   Amongst them we shall mention only his son,

Fritz Giese, who was born on January 2, 1859, at the Hague. At ten years of age he was so forward that he was able publicly to perform Romberg's second Concerto. He completed his studies under Grützmacher in Dresden and under Jacquard in Paris. After he had made a journey through Sweden and Denmark, he was for a year soloist in the Amsterdam Park orchestra, and then entered, as a member, into the Mendelssohn Quintet Club of Boston. As one of the chief supporters he took part for a long time in the annual concert journeys of the Society, which extended to North America and Australia. At present he is living as a soloist at Boston.

The fourth of the above-mentioned pupils of Ganz, Magnus Klietz, born on April 29, 1828, at Altenkirchen, on the Island of Rügen, began his musical career at fourteen as a pupil of the Greifswalder town music director, Abel. After a year's instruction on the violin and various wood-wind instruments, he decided on learning the Violoncello, which he chose as his principal instrument. In 1848 he went to Berlin to the Concertmaster Ganz, pursued his studies under him for a year, and then selected Hamburg as his settled place of residence. In 1850 he was appointed first cellist at the Stadt-Theatre as successor to Joh. Aug. Jul. Goltermann. In this position he remained seventeen years, giving lessons as well. He then joined the Philharmonic orchestra and was one of the founders of the Quartet Union now existing in Hamburg.

After him, as a remarkable Berlin violoncellist, must be mentioned Julius Stahlknecht, born on March 17, 1817, in Posen. Both Drews and Wranitzki were his masters. Their method of instruction must have been good, for as early as twenty-one years of age (1838) Stahlknecht was so far educated that he was admitted into the Berlin Hofkapelle. He undertook later, in company with his brother Adolf, who was a respectable violin player, a concert tour; and with him and the addition of the pianist Carl Albert Löschhorn, from 1844 or 1846, he gave for some years, Trio Soirées, which were very popular with the Berlin public. After the death of Ganz he stepped into his place with the title of " Concertmeister." In 1881 he was pensioned. He had as his successor the Cello virtuoso, Louis Lübeck. Of Cello compositions he published two Concertos and several smaller pieces besides—as, for example, Divertissements (Op. 3), a Fantasia (Op. 6), Three Pieces with Piano (Op. 8) and a " Sérénade Espagnole " (Op. 11).

Stahlknecht formed an excellent cellist in ALBERT RÜDEL, who was born on February 29, 1840, at Wittstock in East Priegnitz, where his father was musical Director. During the years 1859-1867 he pursued his studies at Berlin, under Stahlknecht. On June 1, 1867, he was appointed Royal Chamber Musician, and in the year 1880 solo Cellist of the Hofkapelle. Rüdel often had the honour from that time of being admitted to take part in the Royal Concerts. Kaiser William I. liked his playing, and repeatedly expressed to him his approbation. Amongst Rüdel's compositions for the Violoncello must be mentioned : Romance (B major), Elegie (D minor), Introduction, Andante e Tempo di Valse, four Fantasias for Concert-room, and many little Drawing-room pieces for pupils. All these productions have a piano accompaniment.

Violoncello playing received a fresh impulse in Berlin by the opening, under the direction of Joachim, of a section of the Royal High School, on October 1, 1869, for executive music. The Belgian cellist, JULES DE SWERT, was one of the first to give the necessary instruction at the above-named Institute. WILHELM MÜLLER succeeded him from 1873-1876 in this office. Both masters were, however, at the establishment too short a time to pave the way for any important results. These were first attained by means of Hausmann's appointment, who since the year 1876 has been working as teacher of Violoncello playing at the Berlin High School.

ROBERT HAUSMANN, born on August 23, 1852, at Rottleberode, in the Harz, frequented the Gymnasium at Brunswick, and benefited there, from 1861-1867, by the Violoncello instruction of Theodor Müller, who advanced him considerably. He was then Elève of the Berlin High School for Music, and there prosecuted his studies for three years, under the direction of Wilhelm Müller, nephew of the Brunswick master just mentioned. Finally, he went to Piatti, and under him pursued a course in London, and later on at his property at

Caddenabia, on Lake Como. Shortly after Hausmann took an engagement with Count Hochberg, in Silesia, as Cellist of the string quartet formed by him, and after this was dissolved, in 1876, he was named second master of Cello playing at the Berlin High School for Music; three years later he rose to the position of regular teacher, and from that time he fulfilled the duties alone in his own department. In 1884 he received the title of Professor in acknowledgment of his deserving work.

Hausmann at the present time belongs to the most eminent masters of his instrument. He is not only a distinguished solo player, but also an excellent quartet player, which is evident from the fact that Joachim has chosen him as his usual quartet associate. Of the pupils formed by Hausmann, until now the following have specially distinguished themselves: Roth, Dechert, Prill, Koch, and Lüdemann.

PHILIPP ROTH, born on October 25, 1853, at Tarnowitz, in Upper Silesia, occupied himself in his father's house from his eighth to his twelfth year with violin playing, and then went over to the Violoncello. After he had for some time applied himself to quartet playing with his brothers, he became the pupil of Wilhelm Müller, and later on of Robert Hausmann, at the Berlin High School for Music. He soon took part in the lessons, conducted by Joachim, in quartet and orchestra playing, and also pursued the study of composition under Wihl. Tauberts and Woldemar Bargiel. Settled in Berlin for eighteen years, he only left the capital in order to make concert tours, of which he undertook one three years ago into Russia. He, however, has devoted his powers chiefly to teaching. Roth has also been zealous in the publication of Cello literature. Besides his original compositions, he has published a long list of various kinds of attractive music pieces as arrangements for Violoncello and Piano, as well as a Violoncello school and a "Guide to Violoncello Literature," which latter has also been published separately.[1] This list, which ought to be recommended, will, it is hoped, be continued and completed in later editions without delay.

HUGO DECHERT, born September 16, 1860, in Potschappel,

---

[1] At Breitkopf and Härtel's.

near Dresden, received from his father, who is a musician, instructions in violin playing at six years of age, and from his twelfth year in Cello playing. Until 1875 he profited by the instruction of the chamber musician, Heinrich Tietz, in Dresden. Then began Dechert's practical work. At first he was for a year first Cellist in the orchestra of the Belvedere, on the Brühl Terrace, at Dresden, and then, after some concert tours in Saxony and Silesia, he was engaged at a Concert Orchestra in Warsaw. In 1887 he went to Berlin. There he had the good fortune, by the acquisition of a scholarship as well as by getting free instruction in the High School for Music, to pursue and complete his studies under the direction of Rob. Hausmann. Since 1881 he has belonged to the Royal Kapelle at Berlin, and he is also occupied as a much-appreciated concert and quartet player as well as teacher.

PAUL PRILL, born October 1, 1860, at Berlin, received from his father, a royal Prussian military bandmaster, his first lessons both in piano and violin playing. Later on the musical director, W. Handwerg, undertook his instruction on the piano, and the chamber musician, W. Sturm, the theoretical part. At the same time Paul Prill occupied himself in learning the "Cornet à piston" with his father. Only in his seventeenth year, after he had been performing at concerts with his brother and sister under the conduct of his father in Germany, was fulfilled his cherished wish to devote himself to Violoncello playing. In this the chamber musician, Mahnecke, assisted him by giving him gratuitous instruction. After a lapse of nine months he had made such rapid progress on the Violoncello that, having undergone a previous examination, he was received as a free pupil into the High School for Music. He frequented it for four years, and then entered the so-called master class, conducted by Bargiel, in order to perfect himself in the theoretical department; but at the same time he also benefited further by Hausmann's tuition. He soon found an appointment as solo cellist in the Berlin Symphony Kapelle, as well as in the orchestra of the Italian Opera. From the beginning of September, 1882, until the end of April, 1885, he worked as solo cellist in the "Bilse Orchestra." Such occupation did not suit him for a continuance; he aimed higher, and desired to devote himself to the conducting branch of music. After Bilse had dissolved his orchestra, he found an engagement as Director at the Belle Alliance Theatre, in Berlin. Occasionally also he performed the office of Conductor at the Wallner Theatre. This work, however, did not have the hoped-for result, as there seemed no prospect of a more remunerative sphere of conducting. Paul Prill then determined to accept the place of solo cellist at the German Opera at Rotterdam. With this the advantageous offer was made to him of performing at concerts in and around Rotterdam, yet he did not lose sight of his ambition in regard to the career of Conductor. His wish was fulfilled, for during some time he has been second Kapellmeister of the Rotterdam Opera.

FRIEDRICH KOCH, descended from a well-known Berlin family of painters, was born on July 3, 1862, and began his musical studies in his eleventh, but Violoncello playing only in his fourteenth year. From 1879-1882 he was pupil of the Royal High School of Music, and specially under Hausmann, as well as Succo and Bargiel for theory and composition. In the summer of 1883 he was named Royal Chamber Musician, after he had been submitted to a trial performance. In 1886 he founded, with three of his colleagues, a string quartet, which within a short period has gained a respected position in the Berlin musical world. Of Koch's Cello compositions only two, Op. 1 and 2, up to the present time have appeared.

OTTO LÜDEMANN, born on September 7, 1864, at Bernkastel, on the Mosel, after his father had prepared him, was from 1876-1880 Ebert's pupil in the Cologne Conservatoire, to whom he is indebted for part of his other artistic education. At the beginning of 1880 he went to the Berlin High School of Music, and benefited by Hausmann's instruction, not only in compulsory piano playing but in the theory of music until 1883. In this year he took part in the playing competition for the possession of a vacant cello place in the Royal Prussian Kapelle, in which he succeeded so well that in the autumn of the year 1884 he was nominated Royal Chamber Musician. Besides his official duty he was selected by his master, Hausmann, to be his assistant in the High School of Music, and also commissioned to prepare his advanced Cello pupils for the upper classes—a proof of how highly his performances were appreciated. Amongst others belonging to the older and more modern of Berlin violoncellists are Griebel and Espenhahn.

JULIUS GRIEBEL, born on October 25, 1809, at Berlin, learnt cello playing of his father, who was bassoon player in the Hofkapelle there. As Max Bohrer belonged to it, he also received instruction from him. At the beginning of the year 1827 Griebel was taken into the orchestra and rose to be solo cellist next to Ganz. During the years 1835-1841 he undertook successful journeys to Holland, and later on he visited also Denmark. As chamber music player he found opportunity of distinguishing himself in the Zimmermann Quartet, of which he had been permanent cellist for many years since 1835. He died in 1865.

His pupil, HERMANN JACOBOWSKY, born on October 19, 1846, in Neustrelitz, received instruction in piano playing during his school years from his father, who was clarinetist of the Mecklenburg-Strelitz Court band. At sixteen years of age he decided for the musical profession, chose the Violoncello as his instrument, and went to Berlin in order to take lessons from Griebel; at the same time Rich. Wuerst was his master in theory. In 1864 Jacobowsky entered as solo cellist into the Liebig "Symphonie Kapelle." Six years later he was summoned to Jassy as teacher of cello playing at the music school, but when the Franco-German War broke out he had to hasten to the standard, and took part in the campaign. When it was over, he received a place as Chamber Musician in the Royal orchestra, which had already been promised to him in 1868, consequent on a successful competition.

Jacobowsky has not only made himself known to advantage as solo player, but also in connection with the Soirées in which he takes part with Hans Bishoff and Waldemar Meyer. Besides some Drawing-room Pieces for Violoncello, he published "Tonleiterübungen in fünf Stufen" and twenty-two Elementary Exercises in the first position.

L. ESPENHAHN, born at Sandersleben, was at first member of the Dessau Court band, but entered as assistant into the Prussian Hofkapelle, after he had appeared in Berlin as a solo player. He did not, however, remain in this place, but accepted an invitation to join the private band of the Russian Prince Narischkin.   After the death of the latter, he was again received into the Berlin Kapelle.   Since 1852 he has belonged to the Zimmermann String Quartet, as successor to Griebel.   He was also occupied as teacher in Berlin. Espenhahn died in the year 1879.

For Munich during the first quarter of our century the chief representative of Violoncello playing was PHILIPP MORALT.[1] He belonged to a gifted Bavarian musical family, whose members were employed in the Munich Court Kapelle.   This family possessed in JOSEPH MORALT a second younger Cellist. Nothing further is known about him except the fact of his performing so well that he was admitted into the Leipsic Gewandhaus Concert on January 21, 1847, for solo playing.

JOSEPH MENTER, however, who received his education from the elder of the two Moralts just named, had a greater artistic importance.   Born on January 17, 1808, in the Bavarian village of Daudenkofen, near Landshut, he began as so many of his colleagues did, with the violin, but soon abandoned it to take up the Violoncello.   He had scarcely completed his twenty-first year before he found a position in the Hohen-zollern-Hechingen band.   In 1833 his vocation took him to Munich.   He belonged to the Kapelle there until his death, which occurred on April 18, 1856.   Menter—he is the father of the well-known Piano virtuosa of that name—made himself known outside his sphere of work by concert tours in Germany, Austria, Holland, Belgium, and England, as well as by several Cello compositions, of which a few were published after his decease.

Menter formed several good Cellists, amongst them the best is—

HIPPOLYTE MÜLLER.   He was born on May 16, 1834, at Hilburghausen, and received his first instruction from his father.   His development was so rapid that, at eleven years of age, he already appeared as soloist.   He was assigned to Menter for further cultivation, by whose assistance he became a master of his art.   In 1854 Müller joined the Munich Court Band as first Cellist.   He also undertook the tuition at the

---

[1] See p. 79 of this book.

Conservatoire.   On August 23, 1876, he died at Munich.
His pupil,

GEBHARD GRAF, for fourteen years first Violoncellist in the
Grand Ducal Kapelle at Brunswick, was born on February 4,
1843, at Waal, near Buchloe, in Bavaria, and attended, from
his fifteenth year, the Royal Conservatoire at Munich.   He was
dismissed from it at the end of four years with a certificate
of merit, and then held concerts in Hamburg, Warsaw,
Amsterdam, Frankfort, and Munich.   Later, he was six years as
solo Cellist in the Princes' Kapelle at Sondershausen, worked
with the Bilse Orchestra for one year as first Cellist, and
after that time had elapsed he took an engagement in the
Grand Ducal Kapelle at Strelitz.   Thence he was summoned
to Brunswick.

FERDINAND BÜCHLER is also an excellent pupil of Menter's,
born on March 17, 1817, at Darmstadt, where his father was
Grand Ducal chamber musician.   As his first instructor
he had the Darmstadt Concertmaster, AUGUST DANIEL
MANGOLD, born in July, 1775, at Darmstadt.   He was a very
distinguished artist on his instrument, of the Romberg school,
and belonged to the Darmstadt orchestra from 1814 until his
death, which happened in 1842.   Büchler got on well under
Mangold's training, but went, in order to perfect himself, to
Jos. Menter, whom he had met during the winter of 1838-
1839, at the Munich Quartet Soirées, when he had undertaken
a concert tour to Vienna.   Having returned to Darmstadt
he again found an appointment in the band there to which
he had belonged previous to his absence in Munich, and was
named first Cellist.   An injured arm, which was never entirely
cured, compelled Büchler to withdraw from playing in public
as a soloist, though he still continued as a chamber music
player.   In 1881, after forty-six years' service, he was
pensioned.

Büchler pursued his theoretical studies under the guidance
of the Darmstadt Cantor, Rinck.   They enabled him to compose a few cello pieces which may be favourably distinguished
from amongst others.   This is especially the case with regard
to his five Studies; they are of value particularly for the
purposes of teaching, and consequently are admitted into
many music schools.   Besides these, he wrote two pieces for

four Violoncellos, and transcribed also three pieces from Alessandro Stradella's Cantatas. At present there are now in the press arrangements of twenty-five pieces of ancient and modern masters with the title " Bunte Reihe."

VALENTIN MÜLLER, born on February 14, 1830, at Münster, in Westphalia, studied with Menter, and continued under Servais, in Brussels, in 1848. During his many years' residence in the Belgian capital, he performed for some time the functions of Deputy-Professor at the Conservatoire. In 1858 he betook himself to Paris and filled the place of Chevillard[1] in the Maurin Quartet. Ten years later he accepted a post at Frankfort-on-the-Maine, where he worked as member of the Quartet of the Museum Society, and as master at the Hoch Conservatoire.

JOSEPH WERNER, born on June 25, 1837, at Würzburg, was, in 1852, Elève of the Munich Conservatoire, and educated himself there as Violoncellist under Menter's direction. In the year 1867 he went to Dresden to Fr. Grützmacher in order to become better acquainted with his method of instruction. After he had been solo cellist in the Court Kapelle at Munich, he became teacher at the music school, and later on he received the title of Royal Chamber Musician and Professor, which proves that he was particularly esteemed in the music world of Munich.

In compositions Werner published a Quartet for four Violoncellos, Studies, Etudes, Caprices, Solos, a book of Songs, as well as an instruction book, with Piano accompaniment, under the title of "Practical Violoncello School." With regard to this the Munich Allgemeine Zeitung, of September 12, 1886, remarks: "Concerning this School, which is entirely devoid of theory—i.e., thoroughly practical—there exist a whole list of witnesses from celebrated authorities of that branch of Art, such as C. Davidoff, in St. Petersburg, Jos. Rheinberger, Louis Abel, and so forth, as well as many recommendations (from the Bavarian Ministry of Instruction) and acknowledgments in the musical periodicals of the time on the subject. All are unanimous that the above-named work must be considered in every way the best instruction book amongst those of the

---

[1] See amongst the Belgian Cellists.

highest rank." The Cello School of Werner has gone through five editions already since its appearance.

Amongst Werner's numberless pupils we can only here cite HEINRICH SCHÜBEL, at Carlsruhe; H. SCHÖNCHEN, in Munich; EMIL HERBECK, at St. Petersburg; FRL. MARIE GEIST and CARL EBNER, in Munich. The last-named artist, born on November 6, 1857, in Deggendorf, near Munich, is Royal Bavarian Chamber Musician, and takes part in the Trio Soirées, which are held annually with the co-operation of Bussmayer and Walter, in Munich. His Violoncello compositions, published as Op. 5, 6, 8, 9, 10, and 14, belong to the Salon *genre*.

Meiningen possessed a very distinguished Violoncellist in GUSTAVE KNOOP, who was born at Göttingen in 1805, and was member of the Meiningen Court orchestra. He must have been, in regard to beauty of tone, a successful rival of Romberg. It is related of him that he only married in order to get into his possession a valuable Violoncello which belonged to his wife; that soon after the wedding he set out on a journey with the instrument, and did not return home again. It is a fact that Knoop went to North America in 1843, and on December 25, 1849, he ended his life at Philadelphia.

Of Knoop's pupils two are worth mentioning : Grabau and Mollenhauer.

JOHAN ANDREAS GRABAU, born October 19, 1809, had, after benefiting by Knoop's instruction, Fr. Kummer as his master for a time. He chose Leipsic as his settled residence, but only worked at his vocation until his marriage, which made it possible for him to pursue music for his pleasure only. He remained, however, until his death, which occurred in August, 1886, a member of the Gewandhaus Orchestra. Grabau was less occupied with solo than with quartet playing, in which he was a much esteemed performer.

HEINRICH MOLLENHAUER, born on September 10, 1825, at Erfurt, was from his fourth year taught piano and violin playing, and when only a half-grown boy he made, with his brothers, under his father's guidance, a concert tour through Germany. He later devoted himself, under Knoop's direction, to Violoncello playing with great success. Mollenhauer belonged for three years, from 1853, to the Royal band at Stockholm, and then turned to New York. After he had travelled through the North American States as a Concert-giver, he settled down, in 1867, at Brooklyn, and founded there a music school.

In the sphere of chamber music the best performer was the Cellist of the formerly famous MÜLLER STRING QUARTET, whose name was THEODORE. He was born on September 27, 1802, in Brunswick, and died there on May 22, 1875. He is described as the very soul of the Quartet Band, which with his brothers Carl (1st Violin), Georg (2nd Violin), and Gustave (Tenor), he so carefully kept together for so many years, the most brilliant period of which was from 1831-1855. During this time the brothers Müller undertook journeys into Germany, Holland, Denmark, and Russia, which were crowned with fame. They were also heard in Paris.

As is known, the Müller String Quartet was continued by the sons of Charles, the eldest of the brothers, who belonged as Concert Master to the Ducal Kapelle of Brunswick. The Violoncellist of the junior Quartet Band was—

WILLIAM MÜLLER, born on June 1, 1834, in Brunswick. He had his uncle, Theodore, as his master. After he had been working with his brothers in the Meiningen orchestra, as well as in Wiesbaden and Rostock, he entered the Berlin Court Kapelle as solo cellist, and also undertook the Cello instruction in the Royal High School for Music. In this position he remained three years, when he went to America. From that time there is no more account of him.

His pupil, EUGEN SANDOW, born on September 11, 1856, in Berlin, occupied himself from his sixth to his eighth year, under the direction of his father, with violin-playing; gave it up however in favour of the Violoncello, and had as his next teacher the royal chamber musician, A. Rohne. In 1870 he was taken into the High School for Music, and was there, from 1873 to 1876, Müller's pupil. In April of the year 1879 ensued his appointment as Chamber Musician in the Royal band.

Since the beginning of the present century Hamburg has been distinguished by excellent cellists. Foremost must be brought forward here—

JOHANN NIKOLAUS PRELL. He was born on November 6, 1773, in Hamburg, and earned the thanks of the musical world there especially by the institution of regular Quartet Academies. He died on March 18, 1849. His son—

AUGUST CHRISTIAN PRELL, under Romberg's direction, whose last pupil he was, reached a high degree of art. An extremely beautiful and grand style of playing lent his performance a classic stamp. Already at twelve years old he could perform in public. Four years later the post of Chamber Musician in Meiningen was offered to him, and in 1824 he received a summons to Hanover as first Cellist of the Kofkapelle there, to which he belonged until February 1, 1869, when he went into retirement. He was born on August 1, 1805, and died on September 3, 1885, in Hanau. His fine Amati Violoncello passed into the possession of Grützmacher.

In GEORG EDUARD GOLTERMANN, born on August 19, 1824, at Hanover, A. Ch. Prell formed a distinguished Cellist. He received the last touch from Joseph Menter during his two years' residence in Munich (1847-1849). He there also had instruction in composition from Lachner. After he had made some journeys from 1850-1852, he became music director in Wurzburg, but remained there only a year, for he was summoned, in 1853, to be second Kapellmeister at the Frankfort Theatre, and became in 1854 first Director. Goltermann has also made himself eminent as a composer for his instrument. For the Violoncello, besides seven Concertos, he wrote a tolerable list of Drawing-room Pieces, which have received a considerable degree of favour.

Two other famous Hamburg Cellists are the BROTHERS LEE. The elder, whose Christian name was Sebastian, was born on December 24, 1805, in Hamburg, and was educated by Prell, the father. At twenty-five years of age he made his first *début* as solo player in his native town, as well as in Leipsic, and then undertook a journey, by Cassel and Frankfort, to Paris, where he arrived in April, 1832. He was heard then with approbation in the Théâtre Italien. In 1836 he went to London, and again returned to Paris, in order to join, as solo cellist, in the orchestra of the "Grand Opéra." He devoted himself to this work from 1837-1868, when he returned to Hamburg, and died there on January 4, 1887. Seb. Lee published a considerable number of compositions for his instrument. Amongst them are Divertissements, Fantasias, Variations, Etudes, as well as a great number of easy and more difficult Duets, of which three books, under the title of " Ecole du Violoncelliste à l'usage du Conservatoire de Paris," have been published.

Two scholars of Seb. Lee worthy of mention are BÖCKMANN and BIELER.

Ferdinand Böckmann, born January 28, 1843, at Hamburg, enjoyed Lee's instruction ; and then Magnus Klitz,[1] who was at the time first Cellist at the Hamburg Stadt-Theatre, was his master. In the autumn of 1861 he found an appointment in the Dresden Court band, and was then, for a time, Kummer's pupil. Böckmann is a clever Violoncellist, who made himself known extensively by the editing of old Violoncello music.

AUGUST BIELER, born on May 9, 1863, at Hamburg, began his Cello studies under Lee, in his fourteenth year, and continued them in Leipsic, where he went in January, 1879, to be under Karl Schröder[2] ; at Easter, in 1881, he was received into the Sondershausen band, of which he has been first Cellist since 1885. He is at the same time giving instruction on his instrument at the Conservatoire of Sondershausen. Bieler, who is possessed of a remarkable technique, has distinguished himself both as a solo and quartet player. His tone is powerful and full of energy, but, at the same time, flexible and melodious, his manner of rendering full of expression and extremely musical.

Lee's younger brother, LOUIS, who is reputed to have had great skill in bowing, was born in Hamburg in 1819. He also undertook several journeys, during which he appeared at Leipsic, Cassel, Frankfort, Paris, and Copenhagen. He published and wrote but very few cello compositions; amongst them, " Trois Pièces gracieuses," with piano accompaniment, must have a prominent place.

---

[1] See p. 153.   [2] See p. 138.

Finally, another much valued Violoncellist of Hamburg, ALBERT GOWA, must be mentioned, who obtained his education in the Leipsic Music School, but on the Violoncello especially shared the instruction of F. Grützmacher and Davidoff. He made himself advantageously known by his public appearances, not only in German towns, but also in Copenhagen and London; accepted an engagement from 1867-1868 at the Philharmonic Society in his native town, and at the expiration of this he was appointed solo cellist at the Bückeburg Court; he then returned to Hamburg, where he is still living and working. He was born on April 14, 1843.

Some other German distinguished Violoncellists of modern times are Ripfel, Gross, Bockmühl, Néruda, and Alwin Schröder.

KARL RIPFEL was a character, and moreover in his youth was a so-called piano phenomenon, until the Minister of Baden, de Touche, persuaded him to devote himself to Cello playing, and himself gave him instruction. In regard to the technical branch of his art he made great progress, but he was so nervous that he could never make up his mind, except during his youth, to appear in public. His manner of rendering must have been *bizarre*. Nevertheless he was a distinguished orchestra player; assisted by an extraordinary memory he was able to play the cello part in the opera without music on an occasion when his colleague would not turn over the page at the right moment. He belonged to the Frankfort Theatre orchestra for forty-five years. His grave has the inscription: "Carl Ripfel, of Mannheim, died March 8, 1876, at the age of seventy-seven years." He must accordingly have been born in the year 1799. In the "Signalen für die Musikalische Welt," of March 19, 1876, the following is asserted of him: "Although not known in an extensive circle, he was esteemed by Bernhard Romberg to be the greatest master of technique on his instrument, which he was at last able to manipulate almost as well as Paganini."

Ripfel was also a composer, but never published any of his compositions. When the Violin virtuoso, Jean Becker, asked him to let him have one of his string trios, he was roughly refused.

JOHANN BENJAMIN GROSS, born at Elbing, on September 12, 1809, went in his youth to Berlin in order to devote himself there to the study of the Cello. It was not long before he found a position in the orchestra of the Königstadt Theatre, which he gave up in 1831. He now turned to Leipsic, was often heard there, even in the Gewandhaus, and in 1833 joined the Liphart String Quartet, at Dorpat, at the head of which was Ferdinand David. In 1835 he was engaged for the Imperial Theatre in St. Petersburg as first Cellist, where he continued until 1847. He then returned with a pension to Germany, but soon appeared in St. Petersburg again, the Grand Duke Michael having summoned him to his neighbourhood. He did not long enjoy the pleasures of this intercourse, for on September 1, 1848, he died of cholera. Of his compositions, the number of which extend to about forty, there appeared for the Violoncello a Concerto, Etudes, Duets, Variations, and a variety of Drawing-room Pieces. He wrote also a Concerto for Piano and Violoncello, as well as a Sonata for these two instruments.

Robert Emil Bockmühl, born 1820, in Frankfort-on-the-Maine, died on November 3, 1881, was a clever Violoncellist, and an industrious composer for his instrument. He published about seventy works, consisting of "Fantasias," Variations, Divertissements, and Rondos on opera themes or national songs. Also an extensive book of studies under the title: "Études pour le développement du mécanisme du violoncelle; adoptées pour l'étude élémentaire de cet instrument au Conservatoire royal de musique de Bruxelles, et au Conservatoire de musique de Bavière à Munich" (Op. 17), in five parts. At the beginning of his fiftieth year, Bockmühl settled in Düsseldorf. At that time Robert Schumann was composing his Violoncello Concerto, for which he solicited Bockmühl's advice in regard to the technical questions.

Franz Néruda, born on December 3, 1843, at Brünn, occupied himself from his fifth year with Violin, and from his twelfth year with Violoncello playing, to which latter he eventually devoted himself exclusively. In the year 1855 he appeared publicly for the first time at Ischl. He then made concert journeys in Germany and Russia, during which he attained his twentieth year. In 1864 he was appointed to the Copenhagen Court Kapelle, to which he belonged for twelve years. During this time he was frequently heard as soloist in Copenhagen, as well as in London, where he often took Piatti's place at the Popular Concerts. He also performed at Concerts in Manchester and Liverpool. Latterly he appeared at Vienna. Néruda studied under his father, although he was indebted to Servais for many good hints. He published about thirty of his Violoncello compositions, amongst them a Violoncello Concerto, and some little pieces for Cello with Piano accompaniment. It may be further remarked that he is brother to the famous Violinist, Wilma Néruda.

ALWIN SCHRÖDER, brother to Karl Schröder,[1] was born at Neuhaldensleben in 1855, where his father was music director. He devoted himself to Violoncello playing only, after he had pursued from the seventh year of his age piano, violin, and tenor playing, and had attained to remarkable proficiency in them. In his youth he was engaged in several orchestras in Berlin as tenor performer. During a visit to his father's house he conceived a great desire to take up the Violoncello, and practised on his own account the Cello solo in the Introduction to Rossini's "Tell" Overture. He succeeded so well that his brother Karl, to whom he played it, urged him to occupy himself further with the Violoncello, which he did. In 1875 he had reached such a degree of proficiency that he was engaged in the autumn of the same year as first Cellist for the Liebig Orchestra. This position he exchanged for one in the Fliegen Band. After he had been a member of the Laube Kapelle, he chose Leipsic as his place of residence in 1880, and occasionally took his brother Karl's work in the orchestra. When the latter accepted the post of Royal Kapellmeister in Sondershausen, he was appointed in his brother's stead, together with Klengel,[2] as first Cellist of the Gewandhaus and Theatre Orchestra, as well as teacher in the Conservatoire. Besides this, he is permanent member of the Peter String Quartet. He received the title of Chamber Virtuoso from the reigning Prince of Sondershausen. His playing is famous for its clever technique, fine tone, perfect accuracy, and most expressive rendering. He has been heard in the capitals of Germany, Belgium, and Russia with remarkable success.

---

[1] See p. 138.   [2] See p. 130.·

VI.—FRANCE, BELGIUM, AND HOLLAND.

THE prominent position which the French attained in respect to Violoncello playing in the second half of the last century was maintained by them subsequently. They exercised, however, with few exceptions, no real influence in Germany after the period signalised by Romberg's appearance. On the contrary, this master influenced in a certain way French Cello playing, as appears from a remark in Baudiot's school, mentioned on page 104, that Romberg had introduced the use of the fourth finger in the thumb position. The sign ♀, by which Romberg denoted the thumb position, also was adopted in France, where, as in other places, it had been necessary until then to use a variety of indications for it. In other respects the aim of the French Violoncellists greatly inclined in the virtuoso direction, as was the case with regard to violin playing, whereas in Germany greater stress was laid on the more solidly musical aspect, without neglecting the virtuoso side.

Taking up the thread again from the preceding section with France, the first to be mentioned is

AUGUSTE FRANCHOMME. This artist, who belongs to the most important masters of his department, was born at Lille on April 10, 1808, and learnt the first elements of his instrument from a mediocre teacher of his native town, whose name was Mas. In 1825 he went to the Paris Conservatoire as pupil of Levasseur, and, after the latter retired from his professorship, Norblin undertook his further instruction. Franchomme's great talent developed so rapidly, under the guidance of these two masters, that immediately, during the first year of his attendance at the Conservatoire, he gained the first prize at the musical competition of the pupils of the establishment. He understood how to extract from the instrument a full, sympathetic tone, and possessed with an extraordinary intonation the rare gift of an expressive and tasteful reading. He specially distinguished himself by a charming *Cantilena*. It is easily understood that on his public appearances he always aroused the greatest enthusiasm.

Franchomme filled various places successively in Paris. He at first belonged, during the years 1825 and 1826, to the orchestra of the Theatre "Ambigüe-Comique." He then went over, in 1827, to the "Grand Opéra," but remained there only one year. He belonged for a longer period to the Italian Opera, but he relinquished this position after a few years. Instead, he established regular quartet evenings with the famous violinist, Delphin Alard; and in 1846 he undertook the Cello instruction at the Paris Conservatoire. He died on January 21 or 22, 1884. His compositions, consisting of a Concerto, Nocturnes, Etudes, Variations, and a variety of smaller Drawing-room pieces, have still some value for cello players. His best productions are the Twelve Caprices (Op. 7), which for pieces of that kind have every claim to consideration.

The best known pupils of Franchomme are VIDAL (the younger), JACQUARD, and BARBOT.

LOUIS ANTOINE VIDAL, born at Rouen on July 10, 1820, devoted himself by preference to the literary branch of music after he had finished his Cello studies. By his valuable work, "Les instruments à archet," he attained to a prominent position among the French writers on music of modern times.

The younger JACQUARD, whose Christian name was Louis Auguste, born on December 26, 1832, at Pont-le-Roy, so distinguished himself as a scholar of the Paris Conservatoire, that he gained in 1850 the second, and in 1852 the first prize. He is a permanent member of the Orchestra of the Conservatoire Concerts.

JEAN FRANÇOIS BARBOT, born in 1847 at Toulouse, settled down in his native town after he had completed his studies at the Paris Conservatoire, and is still at the present time working there at his profession as an artist. Other modern French cellists are—BATTANCHON, SELIGMANN, DANCLA, LEBOUC, and JACQUARD THE ELDER. They were all Norblin's pupils.[1]

FELIX BATTANCHON, born on April 9, 1814, in Paris, frequented the Conservatoire of his native town, and studied there under Vaslin and Norblin, who turned him out as a

---

[1] See p. 97.

clever Cellist. After he had worked in various ways as a solo player, he was appointed in 1840 to the orchestra at the Grand Opéra. His compositions consist of Etudes, which are fully adapted to the object in view and of which several books have been published; Caprices, Duets, Trios (for three Violoncellos), and light pieces of various kinds. His Op. 4, which contains twenty-four Studies, has been introduced into the Paris Conservatoire.

HIPPOLYTE PROSPER SELIGMANN, whose name suggests a German origin, was born on July 28, 1817, in Paris, entered the Conservatoire there on December 2, 1829, and had Norblin as his master for the Violoncello, and Halévy for Composition. In 1834 he received the second prize and, two years later, the first prize. After he left the Conservatoire, in the middle of 1838, he played a great deal in public, and in course of time made concert tours through Southern France, Italy, Spain, Belgium, and Germany. For the beauty of his tone he is indebted to a valuable Amati Cello of large size. As a composer, Seligmann only cultivated the lighter kind of music. His Violoncello pieces are no longer used in solo playing.

ARNAUD DANCLA, born January 1, 1820, at Bagnères-de-Bigorre, was likewise Norblin's pupil at the Paris Conservatoire. He was dismissed, in 1840, with the first prize. Dancla distinguished himself especially as a quartet player. In Cello compositions, he published Etudes (Op. 2), two books of Duets, a "Fantasia" on Themes from Auber's "Sirène," "Melodies," and a Cello School, "Le Violoncelliste moderne."

CHARLES JOSEPH LEBOUC, born on December 22, 1822, at Besançon, attended the Conservatoire in Paris, and at first had Vaslin as his teacher for a short time, but subsequently Norblin. He also distinguished himself in playing chamber music. Besides some pieces for Violoncello, with piano accompaniment, he composed a "Methode complète et pratique de Violoncelle."

LEON JEAN JACQUARD, the elder, born on November 3, 1826, in Paris, passed his youth at Pont-le-Roy, near Blois. Hus-Desforges had retired thither, and from him Jacquard received his first cello instruction. When Hus-Desforges died, at the beginning of 1838, a certain Levacq undertook the further direction of Jacquard, until he went to Paris to attend the Conservatoire. Here he was in Norblin's classes. He so distinguished himself amongst his fellow scholars that he received, in 1842, the second prize, and, in 1844, the first.

Jacquard enjoyed the reputation of a virtuoso-trained player. He was, however, much appreciated as a member of the orchestra of the Conservatoire Concerts, as well as of the chamber music concerts instituted by the violinist, Armingaud, in which also the violinist, Mas, and the tenor, Sabatier, took part. It is a proof of his extraordinary ability, that in 1877 he was appointed teacher in that institution as Chevillard's successor, whose pupil he had been. Nine years later (March 27, 1886) death summoned him away.

JACQUES OFFENBACH, the creator of the Stage productions which are known by the name of "Bouffes Parisiens," was born on June 21, 1819, at Cologne, and occupied himself zealously with Violoncello playing in his younger years. Partly to make himself more widely known, and partly to perfect himself on his instrument, he went to Paris in 1842, and shared for a time the instruction of the Vaslin Classes in the Conservatoire. His efforts, however, to succeed as a Cellist were in vain ; according to the opinion of Fétis, because his bowing was inefficient. In fact, he only succeeded in assisting in the orchestra of the Comic Opera. This occupation did not please him for any length of time; he withdrew and undertook the office, in 1847, of *Chef d'Orchestre* at the Théâtre Français. But Offenbach cherished more extensive plans, which aimed at becoming a composer for the theatre. It is known that he successfully attained to this, though not in the way of gaining a very high reputation. Here, however, we are considering Offenbach solely as a Violoncellist. Although he did not perform as such in any very extraordinary manner, yet he possesses claims to be noticed in this place, because he wrote a number of Cello compositions which gained a certain amount of favour. Besides some light pieces he composed a considerable list of Duets.

AUGUSTE TOLBECQUE, whose father was a distinguished pupil of Rudolphe Kreutzer in violin playing, was born on March 30, 1830, in Paris, and went in his eleventh year to the Conservatoire as a pupil of Vaslin. In 1849 he obtained the first prize. Since 1858 he has been living and working at Niort, the chief town of the Department Deux-Sèvres.

Two other French cellists are Lasserre and Boubée.

JULES LASSERRE, born on July 29, 1838, at Tarbes, went from 1852-1855 to the Paris Conservatoire, and was dismissed from there with the first prize. He then successfully undertook journeys in France and Spain. In 1869 he settled down in London as his permanent residence, and became first Cellist in the "Musical Union" as well as in Costa's Orchestra. He wrote several things for his instrument.

ALBERT BOUBÉE, born in 1850, at Naples, was originally destined for commerce, and failing to persevere in this, it was intended he should devote himself to teaching. But neither in this could he succeed, and Boubée finally decided for the musical profession. The enthusiasm excited in him by his cello teacher, Gaetano Ciandelli, and later on by Servais and Piatti's playing, really induced him to pursue the study of music. In 1867 Boubée chose London as his residence, where since then he has become completely naturalised, though from time to time he has accepted engagements abroad. He worked on several occasions with the orchestras at Spa and Scarborough, and travelled in Sweden, Norway, and Denmark as a concert player, but he devotes himself chiefly to the sphere of work which he has made for himself in the English capital. Of his Cello compositions, which consist of several solo pieces, the best known in England is "La Gymnastique du Violoncelliste."

France possessed also a Violoncello virtuoso of reputation about the middle of the century in LISA B. CRISTIANI, whose name really points to an Italian descent. She played with delicate intonation charming little pieces, pleasantly and gracefully, and performed them on her journeys through Germany and Denmark to Russia, and also on October 18, 1845, at Leipsic. The general approbation which was everywhere lavished upon her was substantially increased by her beautiful and imposing appearance. Felix Mendelssohn considered it worth while to accompany her performances on the piano at her Leipsic Concert, and to compose a "Song without Words" for her. She was appointed Chamber Virtuosa by the King of Denmark. In 1853 she died at Tobolsk, of cholera. She was born at Paris, on December 24, 1827.

At the present time the best French cellists are: JULES DELSART, RABAUD (both teachers at the Paris Conservatoire), LIÈGEOIS, LOEB, and BECKER. Information regarding them is lacking up to the present time.

In Belgium and Holland the Violoncello was introduced about the same time as in France, though it made, indeed, but slow progress in both these countries. This may be concluded by the very modest number of Belgian and Dutch Cellists worthy of mention in the last century, of which there are only four to notice. The oldest of these,

WILHELM DE FESCH, born in the Netherlands towards the end of the seventeenth century, was not only cellist, but organist. In the latter capacity he worked at the Antwerp Cathedral until 1725, when he undertook, as d'Eve's[1] successor, the office of Choirmaster. But as he treated somewhat roughly the boys of the church choir entrusted to his direction, he was dismissed in 1731, when he betook himself to London. He was still living there in 1757, as appears from the portrait of him in that year by Lacave. Amongst his published compositions mentioned by Burney as dry and uninteresting, there are also six Violoncello solos printed at Amsterdam (Op. 8). After Fesch,

PETER WILHELM WINKIS must be mentioned. Born in 1735 at Liège, he did not remain at home, but travelled to Germany, where for a few years he was in the service of the Cassel Court, and then (at the beginning of 1788), as Gerber notices, became Chamber Musician and Violoncellist to the "Kapellinstitut" of the Queen of Prussia. He well understood how to accompany with "much taste and observation."

---

[1] Alphonse d'Eve received the appointment of Choirmaster at the Antwerp Cathedral on November 5, 1718, having previously directed during a long period the choir of the church of St. Martin in Courtrai. The announcement of Fétis that d'Eve composed a solemn Mass in the year 1719, for two choirs, with accompaniment for instruments, amongst which there was an obbligato for Violoncello, is a matter of interest to us.

The third Violoncellist of consideration is JEAN ARNOLD DAMMEN (Fétis calls him Jean André Dahmen), who belonged to a large Dutch musical family, was born in 1760, at the Hague, and had the reputation of being a clever player. About 1769 he was living in London. Of his compositions, several books of Duets and Sonatas appeared. In 1794 he was appointed to Drury Lane, and in the years 1796 and 1797 he travelled in South Germany.

Finally we must here mention JOSEPH MÜNTZBERGER. He was of German extraction, and was born in Brussels in 1769, where his father, Wenzeslaus Müntzberger, was chamber musician in the service of Prince Charles of Lorraine, Governor of the Netherlands. Fétis informs us that the young Müntzberger at six years of age played a Concerto before the Prince, on a tenor viol, handled somewhat like the Violoncello. On account of this performance he was induced to have the boy instructed by the violinist, Van Maldere. This account must be erroneous, for Van Maldere died on November 3, 1768, a year before Müntzberger's birth. In his fourteenth year he went to Paris. He there advanced himself—with the sole assistance of Tillière's Violoncello School —so far that he was able to play the most difficult pieces of the Cello literature of that period. In 1790 he accepted a place in the orchestra of the " Théâtre Lyrique et Comique," but after a time gave it up and entered the orchestra of the " Théâtre Feydeau,"[1] of which he became first cellist after Cardon's resignation. Besides this, he was a member of Napoleon the First's band, as well as, later, of the King's. During his official occupation he often assisted at concerts, and specially at those of the " Rue de Cléry," which at the beginning of this century were in great favour with the Parisians. In 1830 he retired on a pension, and died in January, 1844.

Müntzberger, who, during his long residence in Paris, had not only Gallicised himself as an artist, but also in regard to the pronunciation of his name, composed a good deal for the Violoncello—namely, five Concertos, a " Symphonie Concertante," Trios, in which, besides the Cello obbligato, the violin

---

[1] Fétis points out that he was at the Favart Theatre. Müntzberger, however, calls himself on the title-page of the Cello School : " Professeur de Violoncelle au Théâtre Feydeau."

and bass take part ; a great number of Duets, Fantasias, and
Variations; two books of Sonatas, with bass; three of Etudes
and Caprices, as well as a " Nouvelle Méthode pour le Violoncelle." The latter work in all probability appeared before 1800,
as in it, as in Boccherini's compositions, besides the bass and
tenor and violin clefs, the alto and soprano clefs are used,
which do not occur in French books of instruction after this
date.

Violoncello playing received a remarkable impulse in Belgium
towards the middle of our century.   Platel (mentioned already
on p. 101) greatly contributed to this by founding the school of
Violoncello playing which subsequently gained such reputation.
From it came out prominently,

ADRIEN FRANÇOIS SERVAIS, born on June 6, 1807, at Hal,
near Brussels.   He began his career, like so many of his
colleagues, with violin playing, in which his father, who was
a musician in the church at Hal, first gave him instruction,
and under whom he became acquainted with the elements of
theory.   The child's rare talent inspired the art-loving
Marquis de Sayve, who possessed an estate in the neighbourhood of Hal, with so great an interest that he granted him
the means of beginning to study in earnest under the direction
of the first violinist of that time in the Brussels Theatre, of
the name of Van der Planken.   In Brussels, Servais soon
found an opportunity of hearing Platel, whose playing made
a deep impression on him, and excited in him the desire of
devoting himself to Violoncello playing.   In order to become
Platel's pupil, he applied for admission to the Brussels Conservatoire.   His development was so rapid that he surpassed all
his fellow-students, and gained, before the year was over, the
first prize in the competition.   Platel made him his assistant in
the Conservatoire, and at the same time he was placed in the
opera orchestra, to which he belonged for three years.
During this period, however, he did not succeed in gaining
from his fellow countrymen the appreciation which he soon
after gained in Paris.

In the year 1834 Servais went to London.   He acquired
there also remarkable success ; but the applause of the public
did not excite in him self-satisfied content, for when he returned
home he gave himself up to renewed study, by means of which

he attained to the highest degree of masterly performance. In the beginning of 1836 he went to Paris—the following year he travelled in Holland, and in 1839 visited St. Petersburg, where he met with a brilliant reception. Such was the case also when he re-appeared in his native land, and performed at Brussels and Antwerp, after his return from Russia. In the beginning of 1841 he undertook a second journey to the East, in which he aroused great applause at St. Petersburg, Moscow, Warsaw, Prague, and Vienna by his performances. In 1843 he gave concerts again in Holland, and the following year in Germany, after which he again went to Russia. In the winter of 1847 he was in Paris and later on he travelled into Scandinavia. Now a quieter time was in store for him, for in 1848, after he had been nominated solo violinist to the King of the Belgians, he undertook the Professorship at the Brussels Conservatoire, which for a time attached him to the place. At the beginning of 1866 he made another journey to Russia, which he extended to Siberia. It is supposed that by these unceasing efforts Servais laid the seeds of his death, which took place on November 26 of the same year, at his birthplace, whither he had resorted to recruit his health.

Servais was not only a virtuoso of the first rank, but also a thoroughly original artist who was the means of effecting an important advance in Cello playing, by opening out for it new lines. His performance was distinguished by broad, energetic, and rich intonation, as well as by the most careful finish and effective manipulation, for he understood how to bring out into the clearest light all the advantages of his instrument. Many connoisseurs consider him the first cellist of his time; in any case, he competed successfully with his French colleagues, and raised the Belgian school of Violoncello playing to extraordinary reputation.

Servais as a composer for his instrument is well-deserving of notice. Besides three Concertos, he wrote ten Fantasias, with orchestral accompaniment. He united with J. Grégoire in composing fourteen Duets for Piano and Violoncello, and with the violinist Léonard three Duets for Violin and Violoncello, upon opera themes. In conjunction also with Henri Vieuxtemps, a Duet of the same kind was produced. Finally, he composed six Caprices in the Etude form, which, however, are not so attractive as many of his other Cello pieces. Amongst these the " Souvenir de Spa " and Variations on Schubert's Sehnsucht Valses have had the widest circulation.

Of the numerous pupils whom Servais formed, the best known are—Meerens, Deswert, Fischer, and Bekker.

CHARLES MEERENS, born at Bruges on December 26, 1831, is the son of a clever flutist, who in 1845 settled in Antwerp, where young Meerens received his first Cello instruction from Joseph Bessems. Later, a certain Dumon, in Ghent, was his teacher. Having returned to his birthplace, Bruges, he founded an amateur musical society, " Les Francs-Amis," and superintended a music warehouse established by his father. In 1855 he went to Brussels in order to study music under Servais's direction, but subsequently devoted his chief attention to writing on music, especially in relation to acoustics.

JULES DESWERT, the most prominent pupil of Servais, and altogether one of the best of Belgian cellists, was born on August 1, 1843, at Louvain, and made himself a name, after having completed his studies under Servais, by several concert journeys. In 1865 he stopped at Düsseldorf, and was for a time engaged there. Three years later he entered the Weimar Hof-kappelle as first Cellist, whence he was summoned to Berlin, in 1869, with the title of Concertmaster, as solo cellist of the Royal band and teacher in the High School of Music. He gave up this in 1873 in order to devote himself to composition. After he had remained a few years in Wiesbaden, he chose Leipsic as his residence in 1881. Besides two operas, of which the one called " The Albigenses " was brought out in 1878 at Wiesbaden, and the other, " Graf Hammerstein," in 1884 in Mayence, he wrote three Cello Concertos, as well as an important number of Drawing-room Pieces, re-edited a collection of old Violoncello music and arrangements of classical compositions, and published three books of Etudes under the title of " Le Mecanisme du Violoncelle." He also produced a Cello school, which was brought out by Novello, in London. Servais also formed a very distinguished artist in the Cellist,

ADOLPHE FISCHER, born November 22, 1850, in Brussels, whose name implies a German origin. His father, who worked in the Belgian capital as conductor, and founded the first Society for men-singers, prepared him for attending the Brussels Conservatoire. His education, under the guidance of Servais, went rapidly forward. At sixteen years of age the first prize was conferred on him. After his studies were completed, Fischer chose Paris as his residence, and soon met with general appreciation. Since then he has undertaken several concert tours in the larger towns of Germany.

The violoncellist, P. R. BEKKER, born on May 23, 1839, in the Dutch town of Winschoten, was pupil of the Brussels School of Music from 1852-1855. He progressed so far under Servais that he soon received the first prize at the playing competition. Bekker sought and found a sphere of work as music teacher at Utrecht. A testimony to the excellence of his performances is the circumstance that, in 1861, he was granted the title of solo Violoncellist by the King of Holland. He did not, however, long enjoy the fruits of his industry, for he died in 1875.

Servais educated also the elder of his two sons, whose Christian name was JOSEPH, as a very good cellist. From 1869-1870 he belonged to the Weimar orchestra. In the year 1872 he was nominated professor of his instrument at the Brussels Conservatoire. He was born November 23, 1850, at Hal, the home of his father, where he died August 28 or 29, of the year 1885.

Returning to Platel's pupils, we have, after the elder Servais, FRANÇOIS DEMUNCK (De Munck) to mention, who was born on October 6, 1815, in Brussels, where his father was teacher of music. Instructed by him in the first elements of the art, he entered the Conservatoire of his birthplace as a boy of ten years of age, and soon had Platel as his master. In 1834 he left the Institution with the first prize, and in the following year he was nominated as his master's assistant. When the latter died a few months after, Demunck was appointed his successor. His star was gradually in the ascendant. Fétis says of him that, about 1840, the hope was cherished that he was destined to be at the head of the Violoncellists of his time, for his playing was distinguished not only by the opposite fine qualities of energetic and delicate intonation, but also by an expression full of feeling, and ease in surmounting all difficulties. This hope was not, however, to be fulfilled. Demunck fell into relations which had a paralysing effect on the work of his profession. He neglected more and more the study of the Cello ; consequently his performances were deprived of their precision and brilliancy ; and, further, he ruined his health. Notwithstanding this he still excited some consideration in London. Soon after, in the year 1845, he resigned his official work, in order to perform at concerts, in company with a singer, in Germany. His performances, however, no longer came up to the cherished expectations. In the year 1848 Servais stepped into Demunck's place as teacher at the Brussels Conservatoire, which induced him to go to London, and labour for a time in the orchestra of "Her Majesty's" Theatre. But only too soon the results of his dissolute life became apparent. He fell into doubtful circumstances, and, broken in body and mind, he returned, in the spring of 1853, to Brussels, where, on February 28 of the following year, he died.

Demunck published only a "Fantasia" with variations on a Russian theme (Op. 1).

Of his two sons he brought up the younger, by name ERNEST, as cellist, who was born in Brussels on December 21, 1840. As early as eight years of age he was able to appear as a solo player in his native place, and at ten in London. He then became, for a time, Servais's pupil in the Brussels Conservatoire. Later, in company with Julien, he travelled all over Great Britain, then settled in London, but in 1868 went to Paris, was there for two years member of the Maurin String Quartet, and accepted, in 1871, the invitation made to him to be first Cellist of the Weimar orchestra. His work for many years suffered impediment from an injury to his left hand. Since his marriage with Carlotta Patti he has resided in America.

As one of the elder Demunck's pupils deserving notice, GUILLAUME PAQUE must be mentioned, born at Brussels on July 24, 1825. At ten years of age he became a pupil of the Conservatoire, where, during a course of six years, he received his entire artistic training. Dismissed from the institution with the first prize, he entered the orchestra of the Royal Theatre in his native town. After he had belonged to it for some years, he took up his abode in Paris, with the intention of permanently settling there. But an offer which he received in 1840, of entering, as solo cellist, the Italian Opera at Barcelona, induced him to leave the French capital. Scarcely had he arrived at Barcelona, when the Professorship of the Musical School was committed to him. In 1849 he played before the Queen of Spain in Madrid, and in 1850 he travelled in the South of France giving concerts. In the same year he fixed his residence in London, where he gained popularity as a chamber music player. He found his particular sphere of work as solo cellist at the Royal Italian Opera, as well as teacher at the London Academy of Music, until his death on March 3, 1876. Amongst his compositions he published several " Fantasias," Variations, and Drawing-room pieces.

The elder Demunck had a second famous pupil in

ISIDORE DESWERT, not to be confounded with the Violon-cellist of the same name already mentioned. Isidore Deswert, the son of a musician established at Louvain, was born there on January 6, 1830, and, after he had completed his studies at the Brussels Conservatoire, he received the first prize at the playing competition. In 1850 he found a position as teacher at the music school of his native town, and six years later he was invested with the office of solo cellist at the "Théâtre de la Monnaie," in Brussels. Since December 3, 1866, he has been occupied as Director of the Violoncello Class at the Conservatoire there.

Of Platel's pupils we have still to mention Batta and Van Volxem.

ALEXANDER BATTA, born on July 9, 1816, at Maestricht, received from his father, a singing master, his first instruction in music, and at first practised violin playing. After some time his father was appointed " professeur de solfège " at the Brussels Conservatoire, and in consequence the family Batta took up their abode in the Belgian capital. There the talented boy heard the Cello master, Platel, play, and the desire of emulating him was awakened. He succeeded in inducing his father to let him share Platel's instruction at the Conservatoire. By persevering industry he succeeded in gaining the first prize with Demunck at the competition of his class in 1834.   In 1835 he went to Paris, where he found a good reception.   This decided him to make it his home.

At this time the tenor, Rubini, was flourishing in Paris. All vied in doing him homage, and Batta became such an unbounded admirer of him, that he copied his manner of rendering.   It is known that instrumentalists can learn a great deal from good singers.   Rubini, however, with all the advantages of his manner of singing, had the failing of making excessive contrasts of *forte* and *piano* without the use of intermediate gradations, in order to produce startling effects upon the public.   Batta appropriated this merely for the sake of attaining an easy effect, and therefore became for a time the recognized darling of the Parisian public, and especially of the ladies, whom he knew how to captivate by his sweetly coquettish style of playing.   He naturally possessed also valuable artistic qualities, but an apparently virtuoso tendency ever after clung to him.

Batta published a respectable list of Drawing-room pieces and transcriptions, as well as a Concerto and a couple of Concert Etudes for his instrument.   These productions were for a time made use of by violoncellists : now they have ceased to excite any interest.

J. B. VAN VOLXEM, born on November 30, 1817, at Uccle-lès-Bruxelles, became, in 1833, a student of the Brussels Conservatoire as a pupil of Platel.   At the competition he gained the second prize for Cello playing and composition. Later on he was Chorus Director in the Brussels Royal Theatre. Since then he has by preference devoted himself to chorus singing, and has deserved considerable merit for its diffusion in Belgium.

Three other Belgian violoncellists must be added to those artists already mentioned, namely : Chevillard, Warot, and Vieuxtemps, of whom the first-named is distinguished as by far the most important and most famous.

PIERRE ALEXANDRE FRANÇOIS CHEVILLARD, born on January 15, 1811, at Antwerp, received—after he had been prepared for the musical profession in the parental home—his higher education, as a pupil of Norblin, in the Paris Conservatoire, to which he belonged from March 15, 1820, until the year 1827.   Dismissed from thence with the first prize, he undertook the duties of solo cellist in the orchestra of the "Théâtre Gymnase." In this position, which afforded him abundant leisure for pursuing the study of composition under Fétis's direction, he remained until 1831. He then became member of the orchestra of the Italian Opera. In the year 1859 he undertook the Professoriate at the Paris Conservatoire in Vaslin's place.

Chevillard distinguished himself not only as a trained virtuoso player, but also as a musician animated by a high artistic aim, which he proved by his efforts to introduce the last String Quartets of Beethoven into Parisian musical circles, for whom these magnificent "tone poems" had until then been an unknown world. After repeated fruitless attempts, which failed on account of the insufficient intelligence of his associate players, he at length succeeded by means of the artists Maurin, Sabattier, and Mas, who had the same aim in view, in gaining the requisite force by which he was able to carry out his ideas. At first the quartet confederates established private performances before a few connoisseurs only. By degrees, however, the number of the audience increased, so that they ventured on a public hearing, which took place in the Pleyel Saloon. During the years 1855 and 1856 the four players undertook tours in Germany in order to perform the last Beethoven Quartet at Cologne, Frankfort, Darmstadt, Leipsic, Berlin, and Hanover. Everywhere they found the appreciation which they deserved. In the year 1868 Demunck the younger joined the Quartet in the place of Chevillard, who died at the end of 1877.

Chevillard's cello compositions were a " Concerto, Quinze Mélodies, Morceaux developpés pour Violoncelle et Orchestre ou Piano," a " Fantasia " on Themes from Marino Falliero " Lamenti, Adagio and Finale," and " Andante et Barcarolle." Besides these he published a Cello school which bears the title : " Méthode complète de Violoncelle, contenant la théorie de l'instrument, des gammes, leçons progressives, études, airs variés et leçons pour chacune des positions."

CONSTANT NOËL ADOLPHE WAROT, born on November 28, 1812, at Antwerp, began early the practice of music on the violin, but gave up this instrument in favour of the violoncello. In 1852 he was appointed teacher at the Brussels Conservatoire. Besides a Violoncello School, which was introduced as a work

of instruction to the Art Institute mentioned, he wrote Duets
for two Violoncellos, and an " Air Varié " with piano accompaniment. He died on April 10, 1875, at the place of his work.

Concerning JULES JOSEPH ERNEST VIEUXTEMPS, the younger
brother of the celebrated Violin virtuoso of the same name,
nothing more is known than the fact that he was for a long
time solo cellist at the Italian Opera in London, and that he
is at present solo player in Hallé's Orchestra at Manchester.

Amongst the Dutch Violoncellists we have—

ANDREAS TEN CATE, born in 1796, at Amsterdam. He was
originally destined for a commercial calling, but at the age of
fourteen he decided for the musical career, and became Jan
Georg. Bertelmann's pupil. In his riper years he devoted
himself chiefly to composition for the stage. He wrote,
however, some instrumental pieces ; amongst them a couple
of Violoncello Concertos. He died on July 27, 1858.

JACQUES FRANCO-MENDÈS, who descends from a Portuguese
family settled for a long time in Amsterdam, has exercised a
great, indeed the greatest influence on Dutch cello playing.
He was born in 1816[1] in the said town, and in his earliest
years began the practice of music. He received instruction
from Präger on the Violoncello, from Bertelmann in theory,
and, in order to educate himself still further in cello playing,
he went to Merk, at Vienna, in 1829.

Until then Franco-Mendès was undecided as to whether he
should pursue music for his pleasure or as his career. He
soon decided for the latter, and undertook with his brother
Joseph, who was a gifted violin player, a journey to London
and Paris in the year 1831. He made his *début* in the
former city at a concert given by Nepomuk Hummel and on
his return to Amsterdam he received from the King of
Holland the title of Chamber Violoncellist. In 1833 the
brothers Franco-Mendès undertook together a concert tour
in Germany, and were heard with success in Frankfort,
Leipsic, and Dresden. In the following year Jacques was
nominated first solo Cellist of the King of Holland. In 1836

---

[1] Fétis gives the year of his birth 1812. His brother, Joseph, was born
1816.—(*Tr.*)

he again went with his brother to Paris. The latter died in 1841, and this loss so heavily affected Jacques that for a long time he could not resolve to undertake any more art journeys but played only at a few concerts in the chief towns of Holland. In 1845 the desire was again aroused in him of making further efforts. He took part, in that year, in the musical festival which was held at Bonn to celebrate the unveiling of the Beethoven memorial, but on account of the overwhelming number of musical productions he gained no success. In 1860 he took up his permanent abode in Paris. As a composer, Franco-Mendès proved that to a certain extent his aim was worthy of respect, for he occupied himself with chamber music in its more serious aspect. He wrote two Quintets and a String Quartet, one of which was distinguished by receiving a prize from the Netherlands " Society for the advancement of Music." He has also composed a long list of Drawing-room pieces for his instrument, amongst them a grand Duo for two Violoncellos, an Elégie, "Fantasias," "Caprices," and more pieces of the same kind; some of them are still performed, as, for example, the Adagio (Op. 48).

Among Franco-Mendès' pupils,

CHARLES ERNEST APPY must be cited, who, springing from French parentage, was born on October 25, 1834, at the Hague. His father was a tenor player in the Royal band, but went away with his family to Amsterdam, where his son at fourteen years of age began with piano playing under Richard Hol. A year after he gave it up for the Violoncello, on which the Belgian, Charles Montigny, and later, Merlen, the first cellist at Amsterdam, gave him instruction. He received the final finish from Franco-Mendès, under whom he also studied composition.

Appy began his work as a musician in 1851, as member of the Concert orchestra at Zaandam. He soon received invitations to the provincial towns of his Fatherland to assist as a solo player at concerts, and in 1854 he was engaged for six months by Joseph Gungl, as solo cellist for Scotland. Two years later he was member of the Amsterdam Park orchestra, as well as of the orchestra of the " Felix Meritis " Society. In 1857 he worked for six months at the concerts of the London Crystal Palace, and after his return he joined the orchestra of the " Cäcelia " Society in Amsterdam. From 1862 he has belonged to the String Quartet of the excellent violinist, Franz Coenen, for nine years, by which means he has enjoyed the opportunity of playing with distinguished artists, such as Ernst Lübeck, Alfred Jaël, and Madame Clara Schumann.

In the year 1864 Appy was appointed Cello teacher to the "Maatschappij tot Bevordering van Toonkunst," in which office he remained till 1883. During this time, in 1871, he went for six months to New York, in order to join in the Thomas Concerts as soloist. His substitute as teacher at the Amsterdam Maatschappij was, meantime, Daniel de Lange.

Returned to Holland, Appy took up his residence in Haarlem, where he gave lessons on the Cello and Piano. Thence he again went to Amsterdam and opened there a prosperous music school, which he continues to superintend at the present time. His cello compositions consist of " Fantasias " on *Motifs* from the " Freischütz " and " Robert le Diable," as well as some smaller light pieces.

The above-mentioned DANIEL DE LANGE, born about 1840, at Rotterdam, was educated as a cellist by Simon Ganz and Servais, while Verhulst was his master in theory. On the completion of his studies he travelled with his brother, the pianist and organist, Samuel de Lange, through Austria and went to the music school at Lemberg, to which he belonged for three years. In 1863 he returned home and undertook the Cello instruction at the Rotterdam Music School, which his master Ganz had until then carried on. There is no further information regarding him.

JACQUES RENSBURG, born May 22, 1846, at Rotterdam, also began his cello studies under Ganz in his ninth year, and continued them under Giese, Daniel de Lange, and Emil Hegar.[1] Rensburg was destined for a commercial and not an artistic career, but his inclination for music so increased with time, that in 1867 he received permission from his father to devote himself to Art. He now went about the middle of the year named to Cologne, in order to pursue a course under the talented Violoncellist, Schmitt. The

---

[1] For the Cellists, Hegar and Giese, see pp. 130 and 152.

latter, however, was already, in consequence of a chest malady which, later, carried him off, so suffering that Rensburg's wish was not fulfilled of learning from him. Instead of becoming Schmitt's pupil he was his temporary assistant, as first Cellist in the orchestra of the Gürzenich Concerts, as well as teacher in the Rhenish School of Music at Cologne. Both offices were given over to him definitely on April 1, 1868, on account of his valuable services, for, in the meantime, Schmitt had died. Besides his official duty, Rensburg frequently performed with favourable success in the tours of the Rhenish Provinces, as well as in North Germany, and in 1872, also, in the Leipsic Gewandhaus as a soloist; but the ceaseless application with which he practised his profession brought on a nervous affection, which compelled him to retire into private life. In the autumn of 1874 he went to his native town, and since the spring of 1880 he has been living at Bonn, where he is partner in a mercantile undertaking. Of his compositions have appeared: "Recitative, Adagio, and Allegro, in the form of a Concerto."

An excellent Dutch Violoncellist is Louis Lübeck, born on February 14, 1838, at the Hague. His father, the "Hof-Kapellmeister," Johann Heinr. Lübeck, so highly esteemed by the Dutch musical world (died on February 7, 1865, at the Hague), gave him his first regular instruction, after he had up to his seventeenth year occupied himself with music as a dilettante. In order still further to perfect himself he studied from 1857-1859 under Léon Jacquard's direction in Paris. He then made successful journeys through France and Holland, took up his residence in Colmar, where he often joined in concerts with Clara Schumann and Jul. Stockhausen; in 1866 he was summoned to Leipsic as first cellist at the Gewandhaus Concerts and teacher at the Conservatoire. He fulfilled these duties until 1868, in which year he occupied a similar position in Frankfort-on-the-Maine, and he also undertook fresh concert journeys through Germany, Holland, and England. In the year 1871 Lübeck was a member of the Carlsruhe "Capelle." He did not, however, remain long in this position, but he next went, in 1873, to Berlin and St. Petersburg. From the latter place he went to Sondershausen, where he belonged to the Ducal Band as soloist, and afterwards to

North America. In the year 1881 he returned to Europe, and was engaged as successor to the Concertmaster, Jul. Stahlknecht, for the Berlin Royal Band, to which he still belongs as solo cellist. Besides a collection of small pieces, amongst which are some transcriptions, Lübeck has written two Concertos, of which, however, only one has until now been published.

Bouman and Maaré belong to the younger Dutch Violoncellists who have become prominent by their performances.

ANTOON BOUMAN, born in Amsterdam, in the year 1855, received his first instruction from one of his brothers, with whom he later for some time established regular Quartet Conversaziones. As a boy of twelve years he was able to appear before the King, William III., as well as at the public Concerts of his native city. In order to make further progress he attended the Rotterdam Conservatoire and enjoyed there the cello instruction of O. Eberle.[1] Returning home he again played before the King, who granted him the means of continuing his studies. He thus was able to work for some years in order to perfect himself, and had the advantage of the advice of Aug. Lindner, in Hanover; Fr. Grützmacher, in Dresden; Joseph Servais, in Brussels; and Léon Jacquard, in Paris. He then travelled in Southern France and England, where, during a residence of four years, he gave concerts with success. Since then he has acquired for himself a lucrative sphere of work in Utrecht as Director of the municipal concerts, as solo player and cello teacher. Besides several smaller compositions, Bouman has written two Concertos for his instrument.

From Eberle, who, as we have just seen, was for a time Bouman's master, TH. C. DE MAARÉ, born on January 14, 1863, also received his education as a Violoncellist. In his twenty-second year he received the appointment at the "Amsterdamsche Orkestvereenigung" of solo cellist, when the place of first solo player at the Royal "Fransche Opera" was also given to him, which position he still holds.

The two youngest cellists of Holland, of talent worth mentioning, are Snoer and Smith.

---

[1] See p. 131.

JOHAN SNOER was born on June 28, 1868, in Amsterdam, and received his first instruction from Alexander Pohle, a pupil of Fr. Grützmacher. After Pohle's death the younger Giese[1] was his master, and, when the latter went out to America, Henry Bosman undertook his training. Later on he learned the harp from Edm. Schuëcker, now teacher at the Leipsic Conservatoire. Snoer began his active career as a volunteer in the Amsterdam Park Orchestra. When he was dismissed from this he was appointed Violoncellist and Harpist at the newly-erected Park Theatre at Amsterdam. Since 1885 he has been first solo cellist and harpist at the Amsterdam Orchestra Union.

JOHANNES SMITH, born on January 27, 1869, at Arnheim, received his first Cello instruction from Heyn,[2] in Maestricht, where his father had been placed in the Dutch service. Later on the Smith family resided in Amsterdam and there Ernest Appy was the teacher of the artist boy, who went to Dresden in 1883 in order to complete his training on the Violoncello under Fr. Grützmacher and, in theory, under Felix Draeseke. Since then Smith has appeared with great success in Leipsic, Dresden, Berlin, and the Hague, as concert player.

VII.—ENGLAND AND SCANDINAVIA.

THE special attention which had been devoted to the Viola da Gamba in England during the seventeenth century[3] was not paid, in similar measure, to the Violoncello. This instrument, like the Gamba, was introduced into musical circles in London by Italians. Ariosti, Bononcini, Cervetto, and Caporale—all contributed to make it familiar in the English capital and other places. But it does not appear that Violoncello playing was taken up by English artists at first with the same alacrity as it was abroad—at all events, as a profession—and this left the field open chiefly to foreign Violoncellists, who came to England with the hope of a rich

---

[1] See p. 153.

[2] Alfred Heyn, a pupil of Fr. Grützmacher, was then solo cellist in the municipal orchestra at Aix and now lives at Darmstadt. Compare p. 138.

[3] See p. 15.

harvest, in which, says M. Wasielewski, they were too often disappointed. The number of professional English cellists is small as compared with those of other countries, though there are a few to be mentioned who, in talent and proficiency, will bear comparison with any of the great players of their time.

One of the first is

BARTHOL. JOHNSON, probably born in 1710, as he is said to have celebrated his hundredth birthday at Scarborough, October 3, 1810, when Lord Mulgrave and many distinguished persons were present in the Freemasons' Hall. During the evening the centenarian played the Bass of a Minuet on the cello, which he had composed sixty years before. (See Appendix.)

JOHN HEBDEN, who is supposed to have played the Violoncello, was probably born at the beginning of the eighteenth century, since his portrait was engraved by Faber in 1741. He is represented in this playing the Gamba. Gerber, at least, seems to have thought it worth while to mention him as a cellist, though Burney writes of a certain Hebden as playing the Bassoon at a concert in London where the best performers of the Italian opera were employed.

WILLIAM PAXTON also was a violoncellist, the composer of the well-known glee " Breathe soft, ye winds," besides other pieces. Burney praises his " full and sweet tone, as well as his judicious manner of accompanying the voice." He published amongst his other compositions also six Duos for two Violoncellos (Op. 1), eight Duos for Violin and Violoncello (Op. 2), six solos for Violin (Op. 3), four solos for Violin and two for the Violoncello (Op. 4), twelve easy lessons for Violoncello (Op. 6). and six solos for Violoncello (Op. 8). His brother Stephen also composed for the Cello.

JOHN CROSDILL, born in London in 1755,[1] whom Gerber mentions as an extraordinarily clever Violoncellist, and Fétis as distinguished, notwithstanding the presence of Mara in England, had a high reputation in his time. He was

---

[1] Grove's Dictionary gives the date of birth as 1751 Leslie Stephen, 1751 or 1755.—(Tr.)

educated in the choir of Westminster Abbey under Robinson and Cooke; on leaving the choir he studied the violoncello under his father, and is said to have had instruction from Jean Duport. He soon acquired a considerable proficiency, and in 1768 he was elected a member of the Royal Society of Musicians. In the following year he played at the Gloucester Festival, and was appointed first cellist, an appointment which he held until his retirement. In 1776 he was engaged as first Violoncellist at the Concerts of Ancient Music, and in 1778 as Violist of the Chapel Royal. He probably went to Paris 1778-9, and remained nine months, studying under the elder Janson. In 1782 he was appointed chamber musician to Queen Charlotte, and he also gave lessons to the Prince of Wales. About 1788 he married a lady of fortune, and retired from the practice of his profession, appearing publicly for one day only, in 1821, at the coronation of George IV. He died at Escrick, in Yorkshire, leaving a considerable fortune to his son, who, by his father's desire, presented a donation of £1,000 to the Society of Musicians.

Four other English Cellists of the second half of last century are—Hardy, Reinagle I. and II., and Gunn.

Little is known of HARDY, Henry (of Oxford), beyond the fact that about 1800 he published an instruction book with the title, " The Violoncello Preceptor, with a compleat set of Scales for fingering in the various keys," &c.

JOSEPH REINAGLE, born in 1762, at Portsmouth, was the son of a German music teacher who emigrated to England. He was originally intended for the navy, but gave it up after his first voyage. He was apprenticed then to a goldsmith in Edinburgh, but neither in this did he persevere, and his father resolved to let him be a musician. He at first chose the trumpet as his instrument, on which he acquired some skill, and entered the service of the king as trumpeter. He was obliged to give up the wind instrument on account of his health, and was then Violoncellist, Violinist, and finally Violoncellist again. For a while he was Concert Director in Edinburgh. In 1789 he went to Dublin, and in 1791 to London, where, besides obtaining a good position in the best orchestras, he was principal cello at Salomon's concerts. He finally settled at Oxford, where he died in 1836. He published, for the Violoncello, thirty Duos in four books, as Op. 2, 3, 4, and 5, as well as a School "Concise Introduction to the Art of playing the Violoncello," which went through four editions.

Reinagle's younger brother, named HUGH, born at Portsmouth in 1766, received his education from Crosdill, and was distinguished for his unwonted skill. He died while still young, at Lisbon, whither he had gone for the restoration of his failing health. Of his compositions appeared three works: two of them, Op. 1 and 2, consist of six Cello solos, and Op. 3 contains six Duets for two Violoncellos.

JOHN GUNN, said to have been born in Edinburgh about 1765, was not only a clever cellist, but also a remarkable writer on music. In the year 1790 he went to London as a cello teacher. He there published, in 1793, an instruction book for his instrument, under the title of "The Theory and practice of fingering the Violoncello, containing rules and progressive lessons for attaining the knowledge and command of the whole compass of the instrument." Fétis observes, with regard to the preface of this work, consisting of two parts, that it contains a remarkable account of the origin of the Violoncello, as well as of old and modern stringed instruments.

Gunn wrote another work, published in London in 1801, which has reference to the Violoncello. The title of it is, "Essay theoretical and practical on the application of Harmony, Thorough-bass, and Modulation to the Violoncello." Besides this he published, in 1794, a "School of the German flute," and in 1807 he brought out his most important work—viz., "An Historical Inquiry respecting the performance on the Harp in the Highlands of Scotland from the earliest times until it was discontinued about the year 1734."

In the year 1795 Gunn returned to Edinburgh to take up an advantageous post that was offered to him, and which he apparently held until his death.

The English possessed in ROBERT LINDLEY a Violoncellist of extraordinary capacity, who up to the present time has not been equalled, far less excelled, by his countrymen. He was born on March 4, 1775,[1] at Rotherham, and began his

---

[1] Grove gives 1776 as the date of his birth.– (Tr.)

musical studies when he was about five years of age, with his father, an amateur performer, who began by teaching him the violin, and, at nine years of age, the violoncello. At sixteen he had made considerable progress, and the younger Cervetto, hearing him play, undertook his gratuitous instruction, and brought him to the South of England. Even at this age he had commenced to compose for himself, and was sent for to take the place of the professor who was to have played the violoncello solo at one of the Brighton concerts, and who had been taken suddenly ill. Lindley's performance was rapturously applauded; he played Concertos at several subsequent concerts with the same result, and was then engaged for the Theatre, frequently playing before the Prince Regent.

In 1794 he succeeded Sperati at the Opera and was principal Violoncellist at all the concerts of any importance in London. In the following year began the intimacy with Dragonetti, the celebrated double-bass player, which lasted for fifty-two years. Forster quotes Chorley's remark that "Nothing could be compared with the intimacy of their mutual musical sympathy." They played together at the same desk at the Opera and every orchestral concert of any importance, and Lindley's performance of the accompaniment to Recitative from figured bass was most "elaborate and ingenious."

Concerning Lindley's playing, he was probably the greatest violoncellist of his time; he was distinguished for the beauty, richness, and extreme purity of his tone, and his great technical skill was remarkable, though probably in this and his manner of rendering he did not equal Romberg.

The story is well-known how, when Romberg, during his residence in England, heard him play, and was asked by Salomon what he thought of his performance, replied: "He is the devil." He retired in 1851, and died June 13, 1855.

His son, William, born in 1802, was also a violoncellist, and gave promise of future excellence, but nervousness and delicate health prevented his attaining to any great distinction, and he was compelled to withdraw from public appearances.

Lindley is less remarkable as a composer. He wrote four Concertos, Duets for Violin and Violoncello (Op. 5), Duos for two Violoncellos (Op. 6, 8, 10, and 27), Solos for Violoncello (Op. 9), and several Variations on Airs, as well as Potpourris.

Amongst Lindley's pupils, CHARLES LUCAS, born 1808, in Salisbury, was the most remarkable. He received his first musical instruction as chorister of the Cathedral, under Arthur Thomas Corfe, after which he attended the Royal Academy of Music in London. In 1830 he was named Composer and Violoncellist to Queen Adelaide, and performed the duties of Organist at St. George's Chapel. Two years later he was entrusted with the duties of Orchestra Conductor at the Royal Academy of Music, and succeeded Cipriani Potter as Principal in 1859. He had already taken the place of his master, Lindley, as first Violoncellist of the Italian Opera. He died on March 23, 1869, in London. His successor in the Opera was the cellist, Collins.

To Lindley's contemporaries must be added Cudmore, Crouch, and Powell.

RICHARD CUDMORE, born in 1787, at Chichester, in Sussex, practised not only as cellist, but also as a violin player and pianist. The organist, Forgett, of Chichester, was his first instructor, and from him he learned the violin, acquiring such proficiency that at nine years of age he played a solo at a concert in his native town. At ten years the elder Reinagle was his master for the Cello, and a year after he appeared again at a concert and played his own compositions. He then for two years pursued his studies under Salomon's guidance, in London, when he returned to his native town, and remained there for the next nine years. The desire of giving himself up anew to the study of the Piano drove him again to London, where he subsequently appeared frequently as a Pianist. He accomplished an artistic feat of a remarkable description in Liverpool by appearing there at a concert, which he himself organised, successively as Piano, Violin, and Violoncello performer. The solos which he executed were by Kalkbrenner, Rode, and Cervetto. He was also engaged as Director of the orchestra of the "Gentlemen's Concerts," in Manchester, for some years. His diversity of talent was naturally an impediment to his distinguishing himself specially in one department.

FREDERICK WILLIAM NICHOLLS CROUCH, best known as the author of the popular air "Kathleen Mavourneen," was born on July 31, 1808, at Devizes. He studied under Bochsa and

W. Hawes and at the Royal Academy, under Lindley. He played the cello at Her Majesty's Theatre, and was appointed principal cellist at Drury Lane, as well as member of Queen Adelaide's band. He went to America with Maretzek, the German composer, and has fallen into indigent circumstances "through all appearance by unavoidable misfortune." Besides numerous other compositions, " Songs of Erin," "Echoes of the Lakes," &c., he produced a " Complete Treatise on the Violoncello," Lond., 1827.

THOMAS POWELL, born in 1776, in London, early devoted himself to music, and studied, besides Violoncello playing, the piano and the harp. In 1805 he appeared with success in his native town as solo cellist, in a Concerto which he had composed. He then established himself in Dublin as a teacher of music He devoted his leisure to composition and earnest study of his instrument. His contemporaries considered him equal to Romberg, though this was probably going somewhat too far, as Powell's name was scarcely known out of England, while Romberg, by his performances, acquired a world-wide renown.

After several years' residence in Dublin, Powell took up his permanent abode in Edinburgh. His published compositions— amongst which is a "Grand Duo" for Violin and Violoncello— belong for the most part to the sphere of chamber music.

With regard to national English Violoncello playing, modern times have not been more productive than the past. Three names come before us for consideration—namely, Howell, Whitehouse, and Ould.

EDWARD HOWELL, born on February 5, 1846, in London, is a pupil of the Royal Academy, and specially a pupil of Piatti's. He belongs to the Italian Opera as cellist, and since 1872 to Covent Garden Theatre. Besides this he is Musician in Ordinary to the Queen, Member of the Royal Academy of Music, and of the Philharmonic Society. He works as a teacher at the Royal College of Music and at the Guildhall School. He is for the most part at all the musical Festivals in London and in the provinces, taking an active part.

WILLIAM EDWARD WHITEHOUSE was born on May 20, 1859, in London, and received instruction at eleven years of age on the violin from Adolphe Griesbach. At thirteen he showed a decided preference for the violoncello and was placed for four years under Walter Pettit. In 1877 he was received into the Royal Academy of Music and studied under Piatti and Pezze for the violoncello and Banister for harmony. He has on various occasions gained prizes and medals, and, in 1882, was appointed Assistant-Professor, and, in the following year, Professor of the Royal Academy of Music. In 1883 he was elected Associate of the same Institution and, in 1884, member of the Royal Society of Musicians. He is also Professor of Cambridge University, of the Royal College of Music, of King's College, London, and Manchester New College of Music under Sir Charles Hallé. During Piatti's absence Mr. Whitehouse has frequently taken his place at the Saturday and Monday Popular Concerts and has for some years been connected with Josef Ludwig's annual series of chamber concerts. The instrument on which Whitehouse plays is one of the finest specimens of Francisco Ruggierius.

CHARLES OULD, born at Romford, in Essex, came as quite a child to London, where he has remained ever since. Until he was sixteen years of age he practised flute playing and singing; but the wind instrument was abandoned for the Violoncello. He received his first instruction from a member of the orchestra of the Italian Opera in London. A few years later the Belgian cellist, Paque, was his master. Ould is Musician in Ordinary to Her Majesty, and also works as first Cellist at the Richter Concerts, as well as at all concerts of any importance.

SCANDINAVIA has, up to the present, only produced a very modest number of noteworthy Violoncellists, and these belong exclusively to modern times. It must, indeed, not be over-looked that the serious encouragement of instrumental music was taken up much later in the North than in Italy, Germany, and France. Denmark set a good example to her Northern neighbours, Sweden and Norway. The middle of the last century produced a noteworthy Violin player, who belonged to the Royal band in Copenhagen. About the same period there was no lack of able Cellists. But their names did not attain to any great publicity. This was the case with

CHRISTIAN KELLERMAN. He is a native of Randers, in Jutland, and was born on January 27, 1815,. It was his father's wish that he should devote himself to commerce, but in this he was disappointed. Young Kellerman had inclinations for Art and, in order to gratify them, he went, in his fifteenth year, to Merk, in Vienna, whose pupil he was from 1830-1835. After having finished his studies he was heard with success in Vienna and visited with good result the other large cities of Austria and Hungary. In the year 1837 he gave concerts at St. Petersburg. Further tours increased his reputation and, after his return, he was summoned to be first Violoncellist in the Royal Danish orchestra. During the year 1861 he made a journey which led him into Upper Italy and then to Germany, where he remained until 1864. In Mayence he was, unfortunately, stricken with paralysis. He was, indeed, able to return again in a helpless condition to Copenhagen, but he died there two years after, on December 3, 1866. Kellerman composed a few things for his instrument, but nothing of much importance. His successor was F. RAUCH, whose pupil, RÜDINGER, filled the place of first Violoncellist in the Copenhagen Band.

FRITZ ALBERT CHRISTIAN RÜDINGER was born in 1838 at Copenhagen. After he had gone through a preparatory course under Rauch, he received an appointment in the Royal Orchestra, but two years later he went to Dresden, to F. Grützmacher, whose pupil he was for some time. Having returned home, he again filled his former place as chamber musician, from which he was transferred, in 1874, to be first Cellist. He at the same time accepted the Professorship at the Copenhagen Conservatoire and he also takes part in the regular concerts and chamber music soirées of his birthplace.

Next to Rüdinger, SIEGFRIED NEBELONG must be mentioned as a Scandinavian artist. He went as a boy of five to Copenhagen, and later received his training as Cellist from Friedrich Grützmacher, in Dresden.

VIII.—THE SLAV STATES AND HUNGARY.

THE Violoncello was brought to Russia, as already pointed
out (p. 67), by means of the Duke of Holstein-Gottorp's private
band.   Joh. Adam Hiller's *Wöchenliche Nachrichten die͏Musik-
betreffend* of May 21, 1770, contains the following: "When the
Duke Carl Ulrich of Hollstein-Gottorp (Peter the Great's
future son-in-law) fled to the Russian Imperial Court, during
the distressed condition of his country, in the year 1720, he
conveyed with him the members of his small private band.
It consisted of about a dozen German well-trained musicians,
of whom the most famous were two brothers, Hübner—the
one was Kapellmeister and the other Concertmeister.   The
selection of music, until then unheard in Russia, consisted of
Sonatas, Solos, Trios, and Concertos, by Telemann, Keiser,
Heinichen, Schulz, Fuchs, and other famous Germans of the
time, as well as by Corelli, Tartini, Porpora, and various Italian
composers; but the instruments were a Piano, some Violins,
besides a Viol d'Amore, an Alto, a Violoncello or Bassetto, a
Contra-Basso, or great Bass Violin, a couple of Hautboys, a
couple of German Flutes, two French Horns, two Trumpets,
and Kettle Drums.   Peter the Great was not only very often
present at these ducal chamber concerts, but almost every
week had them to play once at his Court.   This music,
therefore, met with general approbation, as it appeared to
distinguished Russians more novel and more agreeable, when
compared with other music, than any they had hitherto heard.
. . . From that time many Russians offered themselves to be
taught by these German musicians, in order to study music
on various instruments.   The Emperor Peter II. also took
lessons on the Violoncello, from the clever master of that
instrument, Riedel, a Silesian, who was also a good fencing
master, and instructed the young Emperor likewise in that
knightly art."
During the life of the Empress Anna, the chamber
music once introduced into the Russian Court was retained
there, and in the absence of national artists was strengthened
by drawing into it foreign talent.   King August II. of Poland
also contributed to this by giving up " some Italian virtuosi

from his superfluity." Amongst these was the Violon-cellist, GASPARO. Later on GIUSEPPE DALL' OGLIO, from Padua, was attracted to the Russian Court. In the place of this artist —who, in 1763, after a twenty years' service took his leave in order to return home—came the Italian, CICIO POLLIARI. To this period belongs the first Russian Violoncellist, named CHORSCHEVSKY, who received a place in the Imperial band. Up to the present, however, in regard to the Violoncello, and especially with respect to orchestral instruments, Russia has remained mainly dependent for supply from abroad. Never-theless, since the middle of last century, the Cello has been cultivated with success by some Russian amateurs. Their names are—Prince TRUBETZKOI, Baron STROGANOW, and more recently Count MATTHEW WIELHORSKI. The latter, a pupil of Bernhard Romberg, specially distinguished himself by his performances. One of his nephews also, Count JOSEPH WIELHORSKI, who, with his talented brother MICHAEL, a pupil of Kieseweter and Romberg, lived in Moscow, played un-commonly well both the Violoncello and the Piano. Robert Schumann, who in 1844, during his residence in the Kremlin, had intercourse with both Counts, expressed himself most enthusiastically in a letter to Fr. Wieck concerning Michael Wielhorski, declaring he was the most highly gifted dilettante he had ever met with.[1] MICHAEL WIELHORSKI was born in Volhynia in 1787, and died in 1856. The Wielhorski family was of Polish descent, and took up their residence in Russia after the third division of Poland.

At the present time amongst Russian amateurs who play the Violoncello, Prince TENISCHEFF and the Senator MARKEWITSCH are distinguished; the Grand Duke CONSTANTINE NIKOLAJEWITSCH also, a pupil of J. Seifert already mentioned, is a zealous Violoncello player.

The first really remarkable cellist whom Russia can call her own is

KARL DAVIDOFF. He may be reckoned amongst the most famous representatives of his instrument at the present time. He was born on March 15, 1838, in the little Courland town, Goldingen, where he only spent, however, the two first years

---

[1] See Rob. Schumann's biography, by the author of this book (Auf. III., p. 195). Leipsic: Breitkopf and Härtel.

of his life, as his parents went to Moscow in 1840. He there began his studies with H. SCHMIDT, who was first Cellist at the Moscow Theatre. He carried on his further studies under H. Schuberth, in St. Petersburg. He received his theoretical training from Moritz Hauptmann, in Leipsic, where he appeared at the Gewandhaus Concert towards the end of 1859. This was such a brilliant *début* that, when Fried. Grützmacher was called away from Leipsic to Dresden in 1860, Davidoff was offered his place, which he accepted. He did not, however, long fill it, having conceived the desire of undertaking a tour, which led him into Holland. He then travelled through Russia, when he returned to St. Petersburg. Not long after he was appointed Imperial solo cellist, and somewhat later (1862) teacher at the Imperial Conservatoire. In 1874 he took part in the concerts of the Paris Conservatoire. Two years after he was named Director of the Russian Imperial Musical Society in St. Petersburg, as well as Director of the Conservatoire there. He gave up the latter about two years ago.

Davidoff's playing is especially distinguished for its perfect accuracy, as well as by a clever and easy mastery of the greatest difficulties. His Cello compositions consist of several Concertos and a collection of agreeable Drawing-room Pieces.

Amongst his pupils are ALBRECHT, KOUSNETZOFF, GLEEN, and WERGBILOWITSCH. The latter is famous for a fine, full tone. He played the Violoncello in the Auer String Quartet at St. Petersburg, and is also appreciated as a solo player.

To the most noteworthy cellists of St. Petersburg belongs also ARVED POORTEN, born at Riga in 1835. He was Kummer's pupil in Dresden, and attended the Brussels Conservatoire afterwards. When he had played during tours in Russia, Belgium, and Holland, he became a member of the Russian Imperial band and teacher at the St. Petersburg Conservatoire. Six "Morceaux caractéristiques" for his instrument appeared in print by him.

Amongst the younger Russian Cello players of importance must be mentioned : BRANDOUKOFF, DANIELSCHENKO, and SARADSCHEFF. These owe their training to William Fitzenhagen,[1] in Moscow.

---

[1] See p. 133.

ANATOLE BRANDOUKOFF, born in 1859 at Moscow, was Fitzenhagen's pupil in the Imperial Conservatoire of his birthplace, from September, 1870, to May, 1878, and received as an acknowledgment on his departure from the said institution for the distinction he had gained, a gold medal together with an honourable diploma. His first journey was to Switzerland, where he gave concerts in Berne and Geneva with success. He afterwards went to Paris in 1879, appeared there and in other French towns, and then proceeded to London. He everywhere experienced favourable receptions. He gave concerts with extraordinary success during the winter of 1887-1888 at Moscow and St. Petersburg. He chose Paris as his permanent residence, where he is greatly appreciated not only as a solo player, but also as a quartet player. Until now only a Concerto of his Cello compositions has appeared and a few small pieces.

PETER DANIELSCHENKO, born at Kiev in 1860, pursued his studies under Fitzenhagen, in the Moscow Conservatoire, from 1873-1880. He was dismissed from there with the small gold medal as well as an honourable diploma, and, besides, received a special prize for composition. For a year he was then teacher of Cello playing and theory at the Imperial Music School in Charkow. During that time he appeared at concerts successfully in South Russia, and had a brilliant success in 1881 at the Great Exhibition in Moscow. He now entered the Imperial Band and undertook the Cello instruction at the Institute of Music of the Philharmonic Society. He remained in that position until 1887. Since then he has travelled in Switzerland, France, and South Russia.

IVAN SARADSCHEFF, born at Tiflis, in the Caucasus, in 1863, received his training as cellist from Fitzenhagen at the Imperial Conservatoire in Moscow, during the years 1879-1886. Distinguished by the grant of the great silver medal together with a diploma, after his departure from the Conservatoire he undertook the direction of the Imperial Music School at Tambov, but soon exchanged this place, in 1887, for that offered to him of teacher to the Imperial Music School of his birthplace.

Amongst the Slavonian people, the Bohemians take the most prominent place, having ever distinguished themselves above others of their race in all that relates to music. The Bohemian Violoncellists of German extraction have already been noticed in the fifth section of this work. We shall now consider those of distinctly Slavonic descent.

The oldest Bohemian Cellist of whom we have any information, is

IGNAZ MARA, born about 1721 in Deutschbrod. He united to a fine intonation an execution full of expression. In 1742 he went to Berlin, was there married, and was received, apparently through the recommendation of his countryman, the Concertmaster, Franz Benda, into the Royal band, to which he belonged for more than thirty years. Mara died in Berlin in 1783. Of his Cello compositions, consisting of Concertos, several solo pieces and Duets, nothing has been printed.

His son, JOHANN BAPTIST, was more widely known. This was not due to his artistic endowments only, but to the dissipated wild life into which he fell from middle age in consequence of intemperate habits. Endowed with extraordinary musical talent, under the guidance of his father, he developed, during a proportionately short time, into such an excellent Cellist that Prince Henry of Prussia named him Chamber Musician. As he possessed a talent for mimicry, he had also to assist on the stage at the theatrical representations which took place in the Castle of Rheinsberg, inhabited by the Prince.

Mara was born on July 20, 1744. In the year 1773 he married the celebrated singer, Elizabeth Schmeling, who, at that time, belonged to the Berlin Opera. He made use of the large sums paid to his wife to gratify his passions, which led to many disasters and to matrimonial disturbances. Besides this he contracted debts. These irregularities increased to such an extent that his creditors were called together against him by the supreme court. As he had otherwise incurred the king's displeasure, he resolved, in agreement with his wife, to get away secretly by night, but the attempted flight of the married couple was stopped, and Mara condemned to imprisonment. After he had again been set at liberty by the intercession of his wife, he succeeded once more, in 1780, in escaping with her, to avoid the tyranny of the King. They took the road by Vienna and Paris to London, where they arrived in 1784. During the year 1788-1789, they travelled in Italy, returned to London in 1790, went from thence to Venice, and then lived in London until 1792, where Frau Mara, wearied with the restless, wandering life of her husband, finally separated from him in 1799. Mara now returned to Berlin, but fell into straitened circumstances from having become unaccustomed to work and having neglected his art. He appeared, however, at one concert and then went to Sondershausen, where Gerber heard him, the author of the well-known Musical Lexicon, who said of him that he so finely rendered his Adagio, no orchestra need be ashamed of his playing; "and if, so continues Gerber, any one of his tones was out of tune, it was not the fault of his handling, but the bad and unequal stringing of his instrument. Perhaps his show pieces deserved less credit, which, however, appeared to be entirely in accordance with the taste of forty years ago. In other ways he conducted himself, while he was there, as a serious, accomplished, and thoroughly educated man, and gave not the slightest sign of inclination to intemperance. But he was in needy circumstances, and although his noble-minded wife had been frightfully disgusted at what she had suffered from him, yet in spite of this he was, from time to time, supplied by her with considerable sums of money." Mara's end was a sad one. He went, as Gerber further says, to Holland, where "his unhappy inclination for drink so gained the upper hand, that after having lost all sense of honour, he used to play for dancing, day and night, in sailors' inns and miserable beer-houses, until at last, in the summer of 1808, at Schiedam, near Rotterdam, death set him free from this wretched life." The Violoncello compositions of Mara, which consist of two Concertos, twelve Solos with Bass accompaniment, a Duet with Violin, and a Sonata with Bass, remained unpublished.

The Bohemian, JOSEPH ZYKA,[1] was about twenty years

---

[1] Fétis says that Zyka was born about 1730. But his birth must have been earlier, for according to Fürstenau's account (History of Music and the Theatre at the Electoral Court of Saxony), he had been already. in 1743, appointed to the Dresden band, though Fétis erroneously makes him a member only in 1756.

older than Jos. Baptist Mara. He received his education as Violoncellist at Prague, and belonged, from 1743-1764, to the Electoral band in Dresden. He then went with his son FREIDERICH, who was likewise a good cellist, as chamber musician to Berlin, where, according to Fétis, in 1791, he died; but, according to Fürstenau, at the beginning of our century. He is said to have left behind him, in manuscript, several Concertos.

JOHANN HETTISCH is distinguished as a remarkable Violoncellist. Born in 1748, in the Bohemian town Liblin, he was educated at the Piaristi College at Schlan, and then went to Prague in order to train as a musician. There he still was in the year 1772. Later, and indeed in 1788, he was, as Gerber asserts, employed at Lemberg in the Imperial civil service, from which it appears that in the flower of his age he had abandoned the practice of Art as a vocation. His playing seems to have been distinguished especially for its rich tone. According to Fétis, he left several Concertos and Cello Solos in manuscript.

The Catholic priest, FRANZ MENSI, born on March 27, 1753, at Bistra, where his father was tutor to Count Hohenems, early occupied himself with music, and when his parents went to Prague he became Joseph Reicha's pupil for Violoncello playing while Cajetan Vogel instructed him in theory. Mensi also played the Violin. On both instruments he was considered clever, and not less so in composition. Some of his works, which consist of church music, Symphonies, and Quartets, are said to be preserved in the convent at Strahow. In the year 1808, Mensi was still living and working as curé at Pher. He also had some pupils, amongst these were JOH. BRODECZKY, WENZEL CZIZEK, and Count SPORK.

J. STIASTNY (Stiasny) should be mentioned as one of the most distinguished Bohemian Cellists. He was born in Bohemia (according to Fétis at Prague) in 1774. The information regarding his education and his life are very limited. He is said to have been in the Prague Orchestra in 1800. On the title-page of his Op. 3, consisting of a Divertimento for Violoncello, he describes himself as Violoncellist to the Grand Duke at Frankfort. As the brief existence of the

Grand Duchy of Frankfort, of which the Regent was Prince Primate of Dalberg, occurred within the years 1810-1814, there can scarcely be a doubt that Stiastny resided at Frankfort during that time. Later, about 1820, he bore the title of "Musical Director of Nuremberg," and in that year lived at Mannheim. He appears to have gone from there to Great Britain, for many of his later works—as, for example, the "Trois Duos Concertans" (Op. 8) and the "Six pièces faciles" (Op. 9)—are dedicated to Englishmen. Amongst these compositions the Concertino (Op. 7), dedicated to Robert Lindley, may be favourably distinguished from similar productions among the Cello compositions at that period. The remaining Cello pieces of J. Stiastny, which consist of Variations (Op. 10), Rondo and Variations (Op. 12), two Sonatas with Bass (Op. 2), twelve light pieces for two Cellos (Op. 4), six similar ones (Op. 5), three Concerted Duos (Op. 6), and Six Solos with Bass (Op. 11) are qualified to be placed amongst the best productions of the older Cello literature, as they contained effects which for that period were entirely novel.

Amongst Stiastny's pupils, Joseph Valentin Dont was remarkable for his performances as quartet and orchestra player. Born on April 15, 1776, at Nieder-Georgenthal, in Bohemia, he received instructions from Stiastny in Prague, where he attended the school. In the year 1804 he was enrolled into the opera orchestra of the Vienna Kärnthnerthor Theatre, from which he was transferred to the Burg Theatre orchestra in 1828. On December 14, 1833, he died. His son, named Jacob, is the Viennese violinist, who died on November 18, 1888, and who was well known by the publication of his excellent practical works for the Violin.

Stiastny's elder brother, Bernhard Wenceslaus, born at Prague, 1770, was also a Violoncellist, and was employed as first performer of his instrument in the orchestra of the Prague Theatre. Six Sonatas for two Violoncellos, and two instruction works were published by him. The first, entitled "Il maëstro e lo scolare, 8 imitazioni e 6 pezzi con fughe per due violoncelli"; the other is a cello school, entitled "Méthode de Violoncelle," in two parts. This school is carefully worked out, though somewhat too elaborately, and yet not exhaustively;

for the complicated technique of cello playing, especially as regards the thumb position, has not received adequate consideration.

Among the younger Bohemian cellists, WLADISLAW ALOIS is distinguished, who was born June 15, 1860, at Prague, and received his artistic education at the Conservatoire there. At the end of 1878 he went to Kiev, where he gave instruction in the Institute of Music of the Musical Society on the Violoncello and Piano. In this place he remained for seven years. Since September, 1887, he has been occupied as Solo Cellist at the Imperial Theatre, as well as at the Conservatoire in Warsaw.

The Poles have produced a longer list of violoncellists. They began with FRANZ XAVER WOCZITKA, a most distinguished artist in his department, who was born in Vienna about 1730. In 1756 he entered the service of the Court of Mecklenburg-Schwerin. He was subsequently member of the Electoral band at Munich, where he died. He left behind him in manuscript Concertos and Sonatas for Violoncello, which were highly prized in their time.

NICOL ZYGMANTOWSKI, born in 1770, in Poland. Gerber asserts that already, as a child of six years and nine months, he attracted the admiration of all who were witnesses of his artistic proficiency; he died young. The Polish Count Oginski,[1] who was formerly much noted as a composer of Polonaises, says in his "Lettres sur la Musique," that he had heard Zygmantowski when he was twelve years old, and adds that he possessed a wonderful talent.

ANTON HEINRICH RADZIWILL, Count of Otyka and Nieswicz, born on June 13, 1775, in the Grand Duchy of Posen, had a great musical talent, and was not only an agreeable Violoncellist but also a Composer. In the latter capacity he was extensively known through his music to Goethe's "Faust."

---

[1] Michael Kleophas, Count Oginski, was born at Gurow, near Warsaw, on September 25, 1765, and died in Florence on October 31, 1833. He was High Treasurer of Lithuania.

For the Violoncello he published only one work, "Complainte de Marie Stuart," with Piano accompaniment. The remainder of his published compositions consist of vocal pieces, of which one is arranged with guitar and cello accompaniment. He was appointed by the King of Prussia, in 1815, Governor of the Grand Duchy of Posen, and died in this prominent position on April 7, 1833. He spent a part of the year generally at Berlin. His house there was the centre of artist celebrities.

KORCZMIET, properly KALTSCHMIDT, of German descent, an accomplished virtuoso player, lived and worked, from 1811 to 1817, at Wilna. He had in his possession a magnificent Stradivarius Cello, which had formerly belonged to Count Michael Wielhorsky. This instrument is now in the possession of Davidoff. There are no more particulars extant concerning Korczmiet.

ADAM HERMANN, born in 1800, at Warsaw, likewise of German descent, was member of the Imperial Opera orchestra, and teacher at the Conservatoire at Warsaw, where, about 1875, he died. During the years 1830-1875 he formed a great number of pupils, of whom, besides his son ADAM, only KOMOROWSKI, THALGRÜN, MONIUSZKO, and KONTSKI will be mentioned.

ADAM HERMANN, the son, who changed his name into the Polish form of HERMANOWSKI, was born at Warsaw in 1836, received the first Cello instruction from his father, and in 1852 attended the Brussels Conservatoire for further training as a pupil of Servais. Dismissed from there after two years with the first prize, he returned home and undertook successful tours in Poland and Russia. He is at present living in the most absolute retirement at Warsaw.

IGNAZ KOMOROWSKI, born on February 24, 1824, at Warsaw, belonged for many years to the theatre orchestra there, after which he benefited by the instruction of Adam Hermann, the father. As a composer he attained great popularity in his native land by his charming songs, full of poetical sentiment. He died on October 14, 1857.

STANISLAUS THALGRÜN, of German descent, was born on August 16, 1843, at Warsaw, and is member of the theatre orchestra in his own country.

BOLESLAW MONIUSZKO, born on October 25, 1845, son of the
well-known Polish composer Moniuszko, belongs at the
present time to the Warsaw Theatre orchestra.

Finally, SIGISMUND KONTSKI settled in St. Petersburg, after
having finished his training under Hermann.

In chronological order, after Hermann (senior), follows
SAMUEL KOSSOWSKI, born in Galicia in 1805.   He was almost
entirely self-taught and, notwithstanding, reached a high
degree as a virtuoso on the Violoncello.   During the years
1842-1852 he performed at concerts, with success, in Vienna,
Berlin, Warsaw, Kiev, &c.   He died in 1851 at Kobryn,
in the province of Grodno.

JOSEPH SZABLINSKI, born on June 18, 1809, at Warsaw, was
employed as first Cellist at the Imperial Theatre for more
than forty years.   He was distinguished for his fine tone and
pure musical rendering.   He was especially famous as a
quartet player.

STANISLAUS SZCZEPANOWSKI, born, 1814, at Cracow, was so
accomplished as a Violoncello and Guitar player that
during the year 1839 he was able to present himself as a
Concert-giver with unusual success on both instruments in
France and England.   He was also favourably heard in
Berlin.   He died in 1875.

MORITZ KARASOWSKI, born on September 22,[1] 1823, at
Warsaw, was a pupil of Valentin Kratzer, at that time
director of music there, for Violoncello and Piano playing, and
was, in 1852, member of the Warsaw Theatre orchestra.   In
the years 1858 and 1860 he travelled for the sake of study and
visited Berlin, Vienna, Dresden, Munich, Cologne, and Paris.
Since 1864 he has belonged to the Dresden band as Royal
Chamber Musician.   Besides some compositions for the voice
and Violoncello with piano accompaniment, of which "Rêverie
du soir," a Nocturne, and an Elegy are the most important,
he published several books in the Polish language—as, for
example: "A History of the Polish Opera" (1859), "Haydn's
and Mozart's Life" (1860 and 1868), "Chopin's Youth" (Part
I. in 1862, Part II. in 1869), and Biographical Sketches of
Robert Schumann, Franz Liszt, and Edmund Kretschmer.

---

[1] Not on September 2, as occasionally given

His most important work in musical literature is "Friedrich Chopin : his Life, his Works, and his Letters." A German translation of the latter appeared in 1877 which went through two revised and enlarged editions.

JOHANN KARLOWICZ, born on May 28, 1836, in Lithuania, received his training as Cellist from Julius Lyko in Wilna, Göbella in Moscow, Sebastian Lee, finally from Servais also in Brussels. For some years he assisted in the instruction at Warsaw Conservatoire. In his native land Karlowicz enjoys the reputation of a learned linguist.

JOSEPH ADAMOWSKI, born in 1862 in Warsaw, perfected his studies—after he had attended the music school in his native city for some time—under Fitzenhagen, at the Moscow Conservatoire, in the years 1877-1883. On his leaving he was distinguished by the presentation of a diploma and of the great silver medal. After he had made some Concert journeys in Poland and Galicia, he was appointed teacher at the Cracow Conservatoire, to which he belonged until 1887. Since then he has been without a post and is only engaged as a Concert player. Adamowski has the reputation of being a clever Violoncellist.

Of Hungarian Violoncellists, only Kletzer and Hegyesi have made themselves known beyond their own country.

FERY KLETZER, born in 1830 in Hungary, travelled during his sixteenth year giving concerts. His performances showed more than ordinary talent, but were wanting in the higher artistic training. He attained, however, to a certain reputation, as his name was at the time frequently mentioned in the newspapers. Since then he has disappeared from public life.

LOUIS HEGYESI holds a much higher position. He was born on November 3, 1853, at Arpas ; at eight years of age he went to Vienna, and there received his first instruction from the Violoncellist, Denis. Later on, he was received into the Vienna Conservatoire and thus became Schlesinger's pupil. In order still further to prosecute his training he went, in 1865, to Franchomme in Paris. The outbreak of the Franco-German war obliged him, in the summer of 1870, to return to Vienna, where he found a post in the orchestra of the Grand Opera. Five years later he took Hilpert's place in the Florentine Quartet, to which he belonged until it was dissolved. From that time Hegyesi has travelled as a soloist. In 1887 he responded to an invitation to Cologne as first Cellist of the Gürzenich Concerts and teacher at the Rhenish School of Music.

CONCLUSION.

IN taking a retrospective glance at the progressive development which Violoncello playing has displayed from the beginning of the present century, it is evident that this branch of Art has reached so great a degree of perfection that it seems scarcely possible it can rise much higher. This result is not only to be ascribed to the deserving work of the leading Violoncellists—and here must be called to mind, besides Romberg and Dotzauer, pre-eminently Friedrich Kummer, Aug. Franchomme, and François Servais—but also to those famous German composers who brought the Violoncello within the sphere of their productions.

Already had Haydn and Mozart appropriated to this noble instrument, in their String Quartets, passages which contributed to the furtherance of the technique and the possibility of expression. Beethoven went much farther even than this. Not only in his String and Pianoforte Trios, as well as in his Quartets, but also in his Sonatas (Op. 5,[1] 69, and 102) and in the so-called Triple Concerto (Op. 56), he increased the demands on the Violoncello to such an extent that in certain respects a real impulse was given to the artistic manipulation of the instrument. At the same time, the works referred to had a stimulating effect on the productive work of the future in the field of Cello compositions, which received a considerable accession in regard to Sonatas especially. We will note here only the names of the best known composers, who used their

---

[1] In all probability Beethoven's Cello Sonatas (Op. 5), composed at latest in 1796, were the first of their kind. The Sonatas for Piano and Violoncello, written by Bonifazio Asioli, of which F. Grützmacher has brought out a new edition, appeared, as may be concluded from the dates given by Fétis in his "Biographie Universelle," Vol. I, p. 155, first at the beginning of our century.

genius in this direction. They follow in alphabetical order : W. STERNDALE BENNETT, JOH. BRAHMS, FR. CHOPIN, FR. GERNSHEIM, EDV. GRIEG, FERD. HILLER, FRIEDRICH KIEL, FRANZ LACHNER, FELIX MENDELSSOHN-BARTHOLDY, IGNAZ MOSCHELES, GEORG ONSLOW, JOACHIM RAFF, KARL REINECKE, JOS. RHEINBERGER, ANT. RUBINSTEIN, CHARLES SAINT-SAËNS, XAVER SCHARWENKA, BERNHARD SCHOLZ, and W. TAUBERT.

The following have written Concertos for the Violoncello : ALBERT DIETRICH, E. ECKERT, BERNH. MOLIQUE, JOACH. RAFF, KARL REINECKE, ANTON RUBINSTEIN, SAINT-SAËNS, ROBERT SCHUMANN, W. TAUBERT, and ROB. VOLKMANN. The Concerto which has lately appeared by JOH. BRAHMS, for Violin and Violoncello, must also be mentioned.

Besides these there exist a number, by no means small, of greater and lesser Cello compositions, which deserve to be prominently brought forward—as, for example : MAX BRUCH's " Kol Nidrei," Op. 47 ; CHOPIN's Introduction and Polonaise Brilliant, Op. 3, and Duo Concertant on Themes from " Robert le Diable " (the Cello part is Franchomme's production) ; FR. GERNSHEIM's Hebrew song, "Elohenu"; FERD. HILLER's Concertstück, Op. 104; Duo for Pianoforte and Violoncello, Op. 22, and two Serenades, Op. 109; FR. LACHNER's Serenade for four Violoncellos, Op. 29, and Elegy for five Violoncellos, Op. 160 ; LIMMER's Trio for three Violoncellos and Quartet for four Violoncellos ; M. MARX's three Quartets for four Violoncellos ; MAURER's Nocturne for four Violoncellos ; FELIX MENDELSSOHN's Variations for Pianoforte and Violoncello, Op. 17 ; IGN. MOSCHELES's Duo Concertant, Op. 34 ; L. PAPE's six Serenades for four Violoncellos; F. E. REINECKE's "Three Pieces," Op. 146 ; FERD. RIES's " Air russe varié," as well as Introduction and Rondo " Sur une danse russe "; ROB. SCHUMANN's five " Stücke im Volkston," Op. 102 ; and likewise L. SPOHR's Potpourri for Violin and Violoncello on Themes from " Jessonda."[1]

If to these be added the numberless compositions which Violoncellists of our century have produced in Concertos,

---

[1] I have only mentioned above the most noteworthy portion of the newer and newest Violoncello compositions. For the remainder I refer to Philippe Roth's " Guide to Violoncello Literature " (Breitkopf and Härtel, Leipsic, 1888).

Concert pieces, Variations, Fantasias, and Duets for their instrument, it must be admitted that Violoncello literature in the course of time has increased very extensively.

The "Etudes" compositions for the Violoncello left much to be desired during the first decade of the present century. On this account the theorist Siegfried Wilhelm Dehn, of some consideration in his time, and who occupied himself in his younger years with Cello playing, may have been induced to arrange a portion—twenty-two in number—of the Kreutzer Violin studies for the Violoncello. This work, however, published by him in June, 1831, cannot be accounted a particularly successful accomplishment. The finger and bow technique of the Violoncello require an entirely different manner of treatment from that of the Violin. And as these Studies were written according to the capacities of the latter instrument it is evident they can only be made available in a limited degree for the Violoncello. It is not then to be wondered at that the Kreutzer "Etudes," transcribed by Dehn with the best intention, should have fallen into oblivion, since Violoncellists have more and more sought after a thoroughly suitable system of "Etudes" literature, which has now grown to be a very rich field. During the last ten years the solo manipulation of the Violoncello has, in certain respects, undergone a change to its advantage in a very remarkable manner. The higher and highest tones of the instrument are no longer unduly preferred, as in Romberg's time; but the tenor positions, more in accordance with its character, are chiefly used, without, however, neglecting altogether the lower and the higher parts. The execution of passages has greatly gained thereby. In this respect, it is true, the Violoncello cannot rival the Violin in brilliancy and agility. The strings of the former being so much longer and thicker, of which the two lower ones are made of correspondingly stout wire, form a natural impediment to the rapid emission of tones in quick runs and groups. In addition the somewhat muffled, though at the same time powerful and full tone of the deeper strings renders difficult a brilliant execution. This is felt more especially in Violoncello Concertos with full orchestral accompaniment. The Violoncello has, however, this advantage : that it lends itself far less to virtuoso exaggerations and confusions than does the easily portable violin, so favourably disposed for every variety of unworthy trifling. The masculine character of the Violoncello, better adapted for subjects of a serious nature, precludes this. But then this instrument does not offer the same wealth in means of execution which the Violin is capable of developing as a solo instrument. In harmonics and *pizzicato* indeed it is at least equal to it, but in the speed and flexibility of passages, as well as in double-stopped playing, its limits are defined. It follows that on account of the larger dimensions of the Violoncello, and the character of the instrument, double-stopped combinations are far less suitable for the deeper than for the higher strings, a circumstance of which there is no question at all on the Violin.

One of the strongest points which the Violoncello possesses in its favour is its suitability as a solo instrument in *Cantilena* playing, in which it is not surpassed by any other. If the Violin, with melting soprano and tenor-like voice, speaks to us now with maidenly tenderness, now in clear jubilant tones, the Violoncello, grandly moving for the most part in the tenor and bass positions, stirs the soul by its fascinating sonority and its imposing power of intonation, not less than by the pathos of its expression, which by virtue of its peculiar quality of tone more specially belongs to it than to the Violin.

There is no rivalry between the two instruments, but rather do they mutually enhance each other's power. Even so is it with the themes which devolve on each in the sphere of chamber and orchestral music. It is greatly to be desired that future generations may foster and maintain what has been done for the art of Violoncello playing in so meritorious a manner by unwearied, self-sacrificing labour; but it is to be hoped, at the same time, that the technique of the instrument, so carefully and finely formed, to the subject of which this book is dedicated, may be ever applied in the service of true and noble Art only.

SUPPLEMENTARY.

At p. 107, I said that only Johann Baptist Baumgärtner's tutor (p. 76) could give an explanation concerning the method practised in Germany, with regard to the fourth finger in the thumb position, during the second half of the last century. It was only after this was in the press that the title of a second German Violoncello School of that time became known to me. It is that of Kauer, who was formerly distinguished as an operetta composer in Vienna—" Concise explanation how to play the Violoncello "—which appeared in 1788. It may probably be seen from this work of instruction what the opinion was at that time regarding the fourth finger in the case referred to.

APPENDIX.

A.

In England, the best violoncello as well as violin bow-maker was John Dodd, who lived and died at Kew; indeed, his cello bows are considered superior to his violin bows. *See* Ed. Heron Allen " On Violin-making, &c."

B.

BARTHOLOMEW JOHNSON.

The *Gentleman's Magazine* of 1814 records his death thus in the Obituary, February 14 : " At Scarborough, in his 104th year, Mr. Barth. Johnson, a celebrated musical character. He possessed to the last a vigorous mind and strong retentive memory."

In the " History of Scarborough from the earliest date," by Joseph Brogden Baker, among the biographical notices, is the following :—

"JOHNSON, BARTHOLOMEW.

" Johnson, Barth., was born at Wykeham, near Scarborough, October 3rd, 1710. He resided at Scarborough from the time of his apprenticeship to the time of his death. He was for seventy years one of the ' town waits.' As a musician, and for the many excellent traits in his character, he universally preserved the esteem of a highly respectable circle of friends. His constitution naturally was vigorous, and he lived to a great age. In 1810 he completed his hundredth year, which was celebrated by a jubilee dinner and musical performance at the Freemasons' Lodge, Scarborough, and a medal was struck as a memorial of this event; about ten o'clock at night the good old man bore a part in a quartette, performing on the violoncello the bass to a Minuet which he himself had composed upwards of sixty years before. Lord Mulgrave, the Honourable Henry Phipps, the Bailiffs, and about seventy gentlemen, visitors and residents of Scarborough and the neighbourhood, honoured the meeting with their company. Congratulatory letters from the borough members were read, whilst several poetical compositions, suitable to the occasion, from the classic pens of Archdeacon Wrangham and Thomas Hinderwell, Esq., were recited and sung. Lord Mulgrave afterwards commissioned the late J. Jackson, R.A., to paint the portrait of the venerable old man, which was presented to the Corporation by his lordship and now adorns the council chamber of the Town Hall. In 1814 he departed this life in the 104th year of his age."

A similar account, from which, perhaps, the above facts were taken, is to be found in "The History and Antiquities of Scarborough," by Thomas Hinderwell, Esq.

C.
REINAGLE.

A whimsical circumstance, which I cannot forbear mentioning, happened to Reinagle :—

The celebrated Mr. Curran introduced himself to Reinagle and invited him to dine with some musical friends at his country house, five miles from Dublin. Reinagle, anxious to embrace the opportunity of enjoying that great man's society, most willingly assented, upon which Curran, being in great haste, would not permit our musician to seek for any conveyance, but requested him to ride double on his horse. In this ludicrous way, sitting behind Mr. Curran, they reached his house, to the amusement of many friends they met on the road.

METHODS AND SCHOOLS.

Viola da Gamba, &c.

GERLE, HANS.—Musica Teusch, auf die Instrument der grossen vnnd kleinen Geygen, auch Lautten, &c. Nürnbergk, 1532.

DANOVILLE, LE SIEUR.—L'Art de toucher le dessus et basse de Viole, &c. Paris, 1687.

GANASSI DEL FONTEGO, SILVESTRO.—Part I. Regola Rubertina che insegna sonar la Viola d'archo tastada. Venezia, 1542.

PLAYFORD, JOHN.—Breefe Introduction to the skill of Musick for song and Viol. London, 1654.

——Introduction to the playing on the Viol de Gambo (or Consort Viol). London, 1660.

ROBINSON, THOMAS.—The Schoole of Musicke wherein is taught the method of true fingering of the lute, pandora, orpharion, and viol de gamba. London, 1603.

ROUSSEAU, JEAN.—Traité de la viole. Paris, 1687.

SYMPSON, CHRISTOPHER.—The Division Violist, or the Introduction to th playing upon a ground ; divided in two parts : the first directing the hands, &c. London : John Playford, 1659.

——A brief Introduction to the Skill of Music, &c. The second book contains instructions for the Viol. London, 1660.

WODICZKA, T.—Méthode nouvelle et facile pour apprendre à joue du par dessus de Viole. Lyons, 1760.

Violoncello.

From the middle of the Eighteenth Century up to the present time.[1]

ALEXANDER, JOSEPH.—Anleitung zum Violoncellspiel. Leipzig, 1802.

AUBERT, PIERRE FRANÇOIS OLIVIER.—Méthode pour le Violoncelle. Texte français et espagnol. Paris, c. 1800.

AZAÏS, PIERRE HYACINTHE.—Méthode de Violoncelle. Paris, c. 1820 (?)

BAILLOT, LEVASSEUR, CATEL ET BAUDIOT.—Méthode de Violoncelle adoptée par le Conservatoire. Paris, 1805.

——Method for the Violoncello. Translated by A. Merrick. London, 1850.

BANGER, G.—Praktische Violoncellschule. 3 Hefte, Op. 35. Offenbach, 1877.

BAUDIOT, CHARLES NICOLAS.—Méthode de Violoncelle. Two parts, Op. 25. Berlin, 1830.

---

[1] This list is not chronological, but arranged alphabetically according to the initial letters of the authors.

BAUMGÄRTNER, JOSEPH BAPTIST.—Instruction de musique théorique et pratique à l'usage du Violoncelle. La Haye, 1774.

BENITO, COSME DE.—Nouvelle Méthode élémentaire de Violoncelle.

BERGER, JOSEPH.—Méthode de Violoncelle. Paris, 1800.

BIDEAU, DOMINIQUE.—Grande et nouvelle Méthode raisonnée pour le Violoncelle. Paris, 1802.

BRAGA, G.—Metodo per Violoncello intieramente riformato. Milan, 1878.

BRÉVAL, JEAN BAPTISTE.—Méthode raisonnéé de Violoncelle. Paris, 1804. (This Violoncello School appeared in 1810, in London, translated into English by J. Peile, under the title, " New instruction for the Violoncello, being a complete Key to the Knowledge of that Instrument.")

CHEVILLARD, PIERRE ALEXANDRE FRANÇOIS.—Méthode complète de Violoncelle, contenant la théorie de l'instrument, des gammes, leçons progressives, études, airs variés, et leçons pour chacune des positions. Paris, 1850 (?)

CORRETTE, MICHEL.—Méthode, théorique et pratique, pour apprendre en peu de temps le Violoncelle dans sa perfection. Ensemble des Principes de Musique avec des Leçons à I. et II. Violoncelles, la division de la Corde pour placer si l'on veut dans les commencements, des lignes traversalles sur le manche du Violoncelle, plus une petite Méthode particulière pour ceux qui jouent de la Viole, et qui veullent jouer du Violoncelle composée par Michel Corrette, XXIVe Ouvrage. À Paris, MDCCXLI.

CROUCH, FRED. WILL. NICHOLLS.—Complete Treatise on the Violoncello. London, 1827.

CUPIS, JEAN BAPTISTE.—Méthode nouvelle et raisonnée pour apprendre à jouer du Violoncelle où l'on traite de son accord, de la manière de tenir cet instrument avec aisance, de la position de la main sur la touche, du tacte, de l'étendue du manche, de la manière de doigter dans tous les tons majeurs et mineurs, &c. Paris, before 1800.

DANCLA, ARNAUD.—Méthode de Violoncelle.

DEPAR, ERNEST.—Méthode Elémentaire pour Violoncelle à l'usage des collèges et pensions. Paris, 1850.

DESWERT, JULES.—The Violoncello. London.

DOTZAUER, JUSTUS JOHANN FRIEDRICH.—Violoncellschule. Op. 165. Mayence, 1832.

——Violoncellschule fur den ersten Unterricht. Op. 126. Vienna, 1836.

——Praktiche Schule des Violoncellspiels. 4 Hefte, Op. 155. Leipzig, 1870.

——Schule des Flageolettspiels. Op. 147. 1837.

DUPORT, JEAN LOUIS.—Essai sur le doigter du Violoncelle et sur la conduite de l'Archet avec une suite d'exercices, dédié aux Professeurs de Violoncelle. Paris, before 1819.

——English translation. Essay on the Fingering of the Violoncello, &c., by John Bishop. London, 1853.

ELEY, CH. F.—Improved Method of Instruction for the Violoncello. London, 1830.

FORBERG, FRIEDRICH.—Violoncellschule. Op. 31. Leipzig, 1882.

FROEHLICH, JOSEPH.—Violoncellschule. Cologne and Bonn, 1810 or 1811.

GROSS, JOHANN BENJAMIN.—Elemente des Violoncellspiels. Op. 36. Leipzig, 1840.

GUNN, JOHN.—The theory and practice of fingering the Violoncello, containing rules and progressive lessons for attaining the knowledge and command of the whole compass of the instrument. London, 1793.

——An Essay, theoretical and practical, on the application of Harmony, Thorough bass, and Modulation to the Violoncello. Edinburgh, 1801.

HAMILTON, J. A.—Complete Preceptor for the Violoncello with a selection of fávourite airs, &c. London, 1840.

HARDY, HENRY.—Violoncello Preceptor with a compleat set of scales for fingering in the various keys. Oxford, 1785.

HEBERLEIN, HERMANN.—Violoncellschule, neueste, praktische und leicht verständliche Methode für Schul- und Selbstunterricht. Leipzig, 1887.

HENNING, KARL.—Kleine Violoncellschule. Op. 37. Leipzig, 1864.

HUS-DEFORGES, PIERRE LOUIS.—Méthode pour le Violoncelle. Paris, 1805.

JACKSON, G.—New Instructor for the Violoncello. London, 1880.

JUNOD, L.—New and concise Method for the Violoncello. London, 1879.

KASTNER, G.—Elementarschule. Leipzig, 1846.

KAUER, FERDINAND.—Kurzgefazte Anweisung das Violoncell zu spielen. Speyer, 1788.

KUMMER, FRIEDRICH AUGUST.—Violoncellschule. Op. 60. Mayence, 1839.

LANZETTI, SALVATORE.—Principes du doigter pour le Violoncelle dans tous les tons. Amsterdam, before 1770.

LEBOUC, CHARLES JOSEPH.—Méthode complête et pratique de Violoncelle. Paris, 1850.

LEE, SEBASTIAN.—Ecole du Violoncelliste. Paris, 1845.

——Méthode pratique pour le Violoncelliste admise au nombre des ouvrages élémentaires servant à l'enseignement dans le Conservatoire de Musique, Mayence. Op. 30.

——An English translation, by J. Lidel. Mayence, 1875 or 1882.

——Méthode de Violoncelle et de Basse d'accompagnement rédigée par MM. Baillot, Levasseur, Catel et Baudiot. 1804.

——(Supplement to this School.—Exercices pour le Violoncelle dans toutes les positions du pouce.)

LINDLEY, ROBERT.—Hand-Book for the Violoncello, with numerous Gamuts, Scales, Exercises, and Examples. . . . Manner of holding the Violoncello and of holding the Bow, &c.

LUETGEN, H.—First lessons for the Violoncello. London, 1860.

MACDONALD, J. A.—Treatise Explanatory of the Principles constituting the Practice and Theory of the Violoncello. London, 1811.

MÜNTZBERGER, JOSEPH.—Nouvelle Méthode pour le violoncelle. Paris, before 1800 (?)

PHILLIPS, W. LOVELL.—New and complete instruction for the Violoncello. London, 1846.

PIATTI, ALFREDO.—Method for the Violoncello. London.

QUARENGHI.—Metodo di Violoncello. Milan, 1877.

RACHELLE, PIETRO.—Breve Metodo. Op. 14. Milan.

RAOUL, JEAN MARIE.—Méthode de violoncelle, contenant une nouvelle exposition des principes de cet instrument. Op. 4. Paris, before 1837.

REINAGLE, JOSEPH.—Concise introduction to the art of playing the Violoncello. London, 1835.

ROMBERG, BERNHARD.—Violoncellschule. Berlin, before 1841.

ROTH, PHILIPP.—Violoncellschule. Op. 14. Leipzig, 1887.

SCHETKY, JOHANN GEORG.—Practical and progressive lessons for the Violoncello, ded. to J. Crosdill, Esq. London.

SCHRÖDER, KARL.—Praktischer Lehrgang des Violoncellspiels. Brunswick, 1878.

——Neue, grosse, theoretisch-praktische Violoncellschule in 4 Abtheilungen. Leipzig, 1876-7.

——Schule der Tonleitern und Akkorde. Op. 29. Hamburg, 1877.

——Schule des Trillers und Staccatos. Op. 39. Leipzig, 1878.

SIEDENTOPF, C.—Violoncellschule. Op. 16. Magdeburg, 1881.

STIASTNY (Stiasny), BERNHARD W.—Méthode de Violoncelle. Mayence, 1832.

STRANSKY, JOSEPH.—Elementarschule des Violoncellspiels. Berlin, 1882.

SWERT, JULES DE.—see Deswert.

THOMPSON, C.—New Instruction for the Violoncello. London, 1780.

TIETZ, AUG. FERD.—Praktischer Lehrgang für den ersten Unterricht des Violoncellspiels. Brunswick.

TIETZ, HENRICH.—Praktischer Lehrgang für den ersten Unterricht im Violoncellspiel.

TILLIÈRE, JOSEPH BONAVENTURE.—Méthode pour le violoncelle, contenant tous les principes nécessaires pour bien jouer de cet instrument. Paris, 1764.

WAROT, ADOLPH.—Méthode progressive pour le Violoncelle. Brussels, 1873.

WERNER, JOSEPH.—Praktische Violoncellschule. Op. 12. Cologne, 1882.

ZIMMER, FRANZ.—Theoretisch-praktische Violoncellschule. Op. 20. Quedlinburg, 1879.

LIST OF NAMES AND INDEX.

(The Gamba-players mentioned in the Introduction are expressly so indicated in the following Index, in order to distinguish them from the Violoncellists.)

D90338   12.50

Wasielewski, Wilhelm Joseph von, 1822-1896.
    The violoncello and its history. Translated
[from the German] by Isabella S. E. Stigand,
with a new pref. by Robert C. Lawes, Jr.   New
York, Da Capo Press, 1968.
    225 p. illus., music, port. (Da Capo Press
music reprint series)

    "An unabridged republication of the first
English edition published in London and New
York in 1894."
    1. Violoncello—   History. 2. Violinists,
                                (OVER)
                             67-30401/MN

11/93 20